WHAT SHE ALWAYS WANTED

D1488011

Berkley titles by Camille Kimball

A SUDDEN SHOT
WHAT SHE ALWAYS WANTED

WHAT SHE ALWAYS WANTED

A TRUE STORY OF MARRIAGE, GREED, AND MURDER

CAMILLE KIMBALL

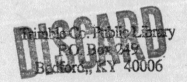
B

BERKLEY BOOKS, NEW YORK

THE BERKLEY PUBLISHING GROUP
Published by the Penguin Group
Penguin Group (USA) Inc.
375 Hudson Street, New York, New York 10014, USA
Penguin Group (Canada), 90 Eglinton Avenue East, Suite 700, Toronto, Ontario M4P 2Y3, Canada
(a division of Pearson Penguin Canada Inc.)
Penguin Books Ltd., 80 Strand, London WC2R 0RL, England
Penguin Group Ireland, 25 St. Stephen's Green, Dublin 2, Ireland (a division of Penguin Books Ltd.)
Penguin Group (Australia), 250 Camberwell Road, Camberwell, Victoria 3124, Australia
(a division of Pearson Australia Group Pty. Ltd.)
Penguin Books India Pvt. Ltd., 11 Community Centre, Panchsheel Park, New Delhi—110 017, India
Penguin Group (NZ), 67 Apollo Drive, Rosedale, North Shore 0632, New Zealand
(a division of Pearson New Zealand Ltd.)
Penguin Books (South Africa) (Pty.) Ltd., 24 Sturdee Avenue, Rosebank, Johannesburg 2196,
South Africa

Penguin Books Ltd., Registered Offices: 80 Strand, London WC2R 0RL, England

The publisher does not have any control over and does not assume any responsibility for author or
third-party websites or their content.

WHAT SHE ALWAYS WANTED

A Berkley Book / published by arrangement with the author

PRINTING HISTORY
Berkley mass-market edition / October 2010

Copyright © 2010 by Camille Kimball.
Cover photograph by Patrick Millikin.
Cover design by Rita Frangie.

ISBN: 978-0-425-23738-0

BERKLEY®
Berkley Books are published by The Berkley Publishing Group,
a division of Penguin Group (USA) Inc.,
375 Hudson Street, New York, New York 10014.
BERKLEY® is a registered trademark of Penguin Group (USA) Inc.
The "B" design is a trademark of Penguin Group (USA) Inc.

PRINTED IN THE UNITED STATES OF AMERICA

10 9 8 7 6 5 4 3 2

Most Berkley Books are available at special quantity discounts for bulk purchases for sales,
promotions, premiums, fund-raising, or educational use. Special books, or book excerpts, can
also be created to fit specific needs.

For details, write: Special Markets, The Berkley Publishing Group, 375 Hudson Street, New York,
New York 10014.

This is important. This is to take care of my family.

—JAY ORBIN TO GARY DODGE

Do I have to be completely honest about everything in the entire world?

—MARJORIE ORBIN TO POLICE

I said I will not lie to you. I might make a play on words, but I swear, I won't lie to you.

—BRYAN TODD CHRISTY TO POLICE

CONTENTS

CHAPTER ONE

Blue Tub in a Green Desert

Saguaro cactus, tall with funny arms raised as if for a stickup in a Road Runner cartoon, dotted the scene Robert Aime casually strolled through on a Saturday afternoon. It had rained two days earlier; the desert was now sunny and cool, with shallow puddles scattered across the sandy soil in a patch of scrub at the northern edge of Phoenix, Arizona.

Neither cared for by mankind nor protected from it, scrub desert retained some of its natural wildness, jackrabbits dashing across and bright orange mallow blooming in spring, but rather than being valued for its stark beauty, scrub desert was throwaway land. It was where off-road vehicles forged illicit trackways, beating down the desert under their ruthless tires. Or city dwellers quietly—and illegally—dumped unwanted old couches. Or snickering teenagers gathered for contraband beer parties, leaving their bottles, stogies and condoms behind.

Aime was traipsing across this scrub to the trailer where he was living temporarily. The patch of under-nourished desert formed the southeast corner of an otherwise commercial intersection, with a Superpumper gas station, a drugstore, a tile vendor and many other businesses at the other three corners. But in 2004 the intersection, Tatum and Dynamite, though still in the Phoenix city limits, was so far to the north that just beyond it the land gave way to real desert, where the puma roamed, javelina trotted and the saguaros grew truly giant, unmolested for a hundred years or more. The border to ritzy Scottsdale was a few hundred feet away, but not discernible to the naked eye. To locals, this northeast area of Phoenix was altogether more often identified as simply "Scottsdale," where the inhabitants were expected to be economically comfortable, socially competitive and commercially conspicuous. Jewelry was expensive, homes were spacious, and cars made a statement in north Phoenix/Scottsdale. People paid extra for the desert vistas and uncongested conditions found in this area, but Aime was not one of the glitterati native to the zip code.

When police came later that day, he described himself as a construction worker who was living on-site of a project. On Friday, the day before, he had hiked across the scrub desert, with its hazards and challenges, from his trailer to the stores across the intersection. It had rained on Thursday, one of those dramatic desert outbursts where lightning tears across the wide sky and the cactus wrens huddle in their saguaro cubbies. On

Saturday, the storm had moved on, toward the Grand Canyon and Utah or possibly the other direction to New Mexico and Texas. It left cool temperatures but sunny skies, the rays playing in the shallow desert puddles. Robert went to the shops again and bought himself some beer at the Safeway and a package of meat to take to a barbecue he planned to attend later in the day.

He then jogged east across the black pavement of Tatum Boulevard and reentered the scrub desert. After a rain, the Sonoran desert gave off a wonderful peppery smell. It could be a terribly unforgiving place in full sunshine, but cooled off and damp, full of scents and twinkles, it could be mysterious and full of enchanted possibilities. When Aime spied a piece of dirty white carpet balanced across what appeared to be a rock about stool height, he decided to use it as bit of makeshift patio furniture and enjoy his surroundings.

Aime sat down on the carpet, opened a beer and surveyed the cholla, palo verde, ocotillo and mesquite sprawling around him and the hills in the distance. He was immersed in infinite shades of green, from the silver-dusted desert velvet to the hedgehog cactus with its halo of gold. The bits of trash also mixed in were customary to scrub desert—electrical cord, some broken glass, a futon—and not a bother on this lovely Saturday afternoon in October. It was a few minutes after one o'clock.

He rolled a cigarette and lit it.

After settling in and enjoying the vista, Robert Aime noticed that the carpet beneath him was not supported by quite the texture he'd expect from a rock. Perhaps it was actually a stump under there; it might be rotted and unstable. It might be home to desert creatures best given a wide berth. He stood up and lifted the carpet to check.

That was no rock underneath, but neither was it a stump.

It was a plastic tub, incongruously blue amid the greens and browns of the desert. It was large, the type used to store toys or a cache of Christmas decorations. Aime's mind twinkled like the puddles at his feet. Up in this neighborhood, people might easily throw away something worth having. There might be something in there he could sell.

It couldn't be in too bad condition yet—he had walked this same path just yesterday and he knew there had been no blue tub here then.

The tub had a closely fitting gray plastic top in place, secured with zealously wrapped packing tape. Aime cast his eye about and easily spotted some broken glass. He set his fresh meat for the barbecue down nearby, then wiped off a piece of the glass and started using it like a knife, cutting through the tape. He would have taken another chug of the beer—although cool out, it was still the sunniest part of the day and this was vigorous work. He finally got enough tape off that he could set aside his makeshift glass tool and use his bare hands to pry off the snapped tight lid.

With the cigarette dangling from his lip, Aime lifted up the gray plastic rectangle and tossed it aside.

In the interior of the tub a large object seemed to be hidden by sheets of plastic. He found or tore an edge of the plastic with his bare hands, gripping it with one hand and managing the object with his other as he unwound the packaging. This was even tougher work than liberating the lid had been: the object was quite heavy. He would have reached for the beer at least another time or two before the plastic revealed its bounty.

As he got deeper into the tub, and more of the plastic was released, he found it messier and messier; the object was apparently leaking, maybe antifreeze or toner? The fluid had reacted badly to the sealed environment; it was getting more and more pungent. Perhaps someone had dropped their lunch in there before rolling the object in plastic. As Aime got in deeper, the plastic wrapping he was unwinding billowed out around the tub.

It may have taken a moment or two for Aime's brain to catch up with his eye. It was not the luxury car component or old copier he'd been expecting. It was not something anyone ever expects to see.

When it fully registered with him what he had plunged his bare hands into and what fumes he had been sucking into his lungs, Aime ran full steam across the desert, the cigarette dropping from his lips as he ran, back across Tatum through startled traffic, and burst through the doors of the Superpumper.

When the 911 call came in, Phoenix PD officer John Harma, dispatched on an "emergency check welfare," was first on the scene. He found Robert Aime at the Superpumper and asked him what the trouble was. Aime told the officer he'd been walking through the desert, got curious about a blue tub he saw, cut away the packing—and found "what looked like a man's body, from the chest down." Harma, cool in the face of this outlandish news, asked why Aime thought the thing in the blue box was human? Aime had an unassailable answer:

"Because of the belly button."

Harma began looping bright yellow crime scene tape off the side of Tatum Boulevard. He noted a dirt track diagonally cutting the desert to form a triangle, the little road leading from Tatum to Dynamite, with the paved intersection as the third corner. With Aime's help, he could see the blue tub in the interior of the triangle, just off the dirt track. He angled his patrol car to cut off vehicle access from Tatum to the desert trail but did not approach the blue tub. Moments later Phoenix PD officer Jay Krook arrived. He walked into the desert on foot. The blue tub was about twenty yards southeast of the intersection. He could see the heaps of plastic emerging from the container and piled up to the side of it.

As he got closer, Krook snapped a city-issued latex glove onto his left hand. He noted the puddles in the desert, separated by mostly dry sandy patches. Scorpions and spiders skittered away as his thick black work boots crunched into the hard soil.

At the tub, Krook reached with his gloved left hand into the container. When he moved aside the plastic sheets, he, too, found what the unsuspecting Robert Aime had already seen. Krook's trained eye and latex-protected fingers discovered "the lower portion of a human body inside." He saw a shaggy male abdomen, still wearing a belt around its waist and blue jeans covering what came below. The tub, however, was only about a yard long. It wasn't necessary to poke further inside to deduce that what came below the waist was just as horribly missing as what came above it.

There was a man inside this tub—but not all of him. Soon there were countless black-and-white units

swarming the scene, a helicopter or two buzzing over-
head with crime scene photographers snapping aerial
shots, and a Homicide detective named Dave Barnes
taking control of it all. Under the large swells of plastic sheeting, they found the makeshift glass tool Aime
had used. Farther out, among the creosote and prickly
pear, they found the rolled cigarette he'd dropped on
his sprint to the Superpumper. And inside the blue tub
they found lengths of orange electrical cord and plastic
rope, both severely discolored. The amount of packing,
yards and yards of sheet plastic and layers and layers
of packing tape, was voluminous. The person or persons who had prepared the bundle had been energetic
in their efforts to keep the body concealed. However,
as the crime scene personnel analyzed the situation,
they could hardly fail to take in that the tub could not
have gone long in this location without being noticed.
Indeed, within the first few moments of the investigation
it was determined that the tub had *not* gone unnoticed
for even twenty-four hours. Robert Aime was positive
it had not been there the afternoon before. The investigators corroborated this with the rain. Everything in
the desert showed signs of dampness—a futon near the
tub was soaked, there were puddles everywhere, and
other debris was even showing mold—except the blue
tub. Not only was it bone-dry on the exterior, but the
lid was devoid of the dusty brown spots left by desert
rain on similar surfaces, such as the hoods and wind-
shields of so many of the cars whizzing down Tatum
while the police worked. The great effort to conceal
the tub's contents coupled with its ostentatious place-
ment at the intersection seemed contradictory. The blue

tub would be within sight of hundreds of cars lingering at the stoplight every day. And on the desert side, off-roaders clearly ventured in frequently enough to keep the diagonal dirt track in easy working order.

Detective Barnes wrote down everything, especially the condition of the plastic tomb, which had clearly not been exposed to the recent rain. He impounded everything he could see, from the futon to the broken glass to the dirty white piece of carpet. He took DNA samples from Robert Aime and carefully recorded everything the witness said he'd touched.

The contents of the blue tub they left undisturbed. Everyone who looked inside it, from Harma on down, had no doubt of its sad contents. They would let the experts sort out the details. It took two body bags to accommodate the lonely package, with its soulless shape, but all too human prize.

It would have taken about thirty minutes for the ride to the medical examiner's facility in downtown Phoenix. The desert vistas were left behind as the convoy entered a collection of concrete and asphalt, towering commercial structures, the copper-domed capitol building and a steady supply of flat government buildings. The most nondescript of them all was the place where the county's dead were taken to have their secrets coaxed out of them by doctors trained to solve the puzzles of death, not life.

Dr. Al Zhang of the Maricopa County Medical Examiner's Office was tasked with plunging both hands into the blue tub and cataloging every bit and scrap inside.

It would be one of the messiest and most distasteful projects ever to come through those doors.

Inside the pockets, Dr. Zhang found over-the-counter contact lens solution, four hundred dollars in cash and a set of keys. There was no wallet, driver's license or any other potentially identifying material, such as a credit card, fishing license or prescription bottle.

But at the bottom of the tub, knocking loosely about, he did find a seventeen-millimeter bullet, spent.

He did not find a bullet wound in the portion of the body present.

The body had the belly button, as Robert Aime had described. Below that, a belt secured the blue jeans, just as it would have when the man was alive. The pockets were intact, as was the underwear below. The blue jeans were found to be shorts. The man had partial knees, but the shins and feet below were absent. Back up at the belly button, the remains continued northward to about the breast line. There were no shoulders, no neck and no head. No face. And there were no internal organs. They had been scooped out.

On Saturday October 23, 2004, Homicide detective Dave Barnes did not know who he had. But as he contemplated the detailed labor that would have been required to put the man into the blue tub in this condition, one thing stood out.

Whoever had done it must have been as cold-blooded as an Arizona rattlesnake.

CHAPTER TWO

Baby Brother, Baby Sister

In 1961, in southern Florida, little Allison Kroh* was awed at what her parents had brought home for her. It was tiny and pink and squirmy. Allison was six years old and now she was a real big sister. The newborn would be called Marjorie.

Allison was a towheaded child, but as she grew older, she took on the coloring of her mother, Janelle, a redhead. Her father, William Kroh, was a telephone lineman in the Miami area. By the time Marjorie was three, however, William and Janelle had called it quits on their marriage. William, for most intents and purposes, disappeared from their lives, and by 1970, he was gone for good. "He was cleaning his gun and it went off

_____

* Denotes pseudonym.

and the stock hit him in the forehead. He had just gotten home [from hunting] and was cleaning his weapons, apparently," Allison later recalled. Marjorie would have been no more than eight years old when he died.

Janelle always worked, as the girls remembered it, and Marjorie recalled being at Mom's knee at her job as a kindergarten aide. All three women were tall—"We've got tall in our genes," according to Allison, with Marjorie almost five-eight, Allison half an inch taller and Janelle a good five-nine—but of the two daughters, it was Marjorie who took after their mother more. "As a matter of fact, [in] one of those pictures of my sister she looks so much like my mother that it's scary," Allison said. Marjorie agreed, saying she was startled to look in the mirror sometimes and see her mother's face looking back.

Janelle Kroh soon remarried, to Pete Garrett, an air-conditioning repairman. In swampy Florida, there'd always be a demand for someone with his skills. The family moved to Belleview. "We had a triple wide *nice* trailer. Yeah, it was a trailer. But it was a triple wide, almost modular home. We lived on five acres and everything was fine," Allison recalled. Along with dogs, cats and even rabbits, they kept three horses there. There was the pony, Golden, who was a palomino. First, he'd belonged to big sister Allison, and when she grew too big for him, he got stair-stepped down to Marjorie. As the girls got older, two more horses joined the family. Little Joe was a quarter horse and he became Allison's pet. Pal was half thoroughbred, half quarter horse and Marjorie thought of him as hers.

Both girls considered Pete Garrett the father they knew best. Marjorie remembered the relationship between the two adults as Janelle being the high-energy, more dominant partner, while Pete adopted a passive style, content to relax around the home.

Marjorie hardly remembered her actual father, although Allison did. But the sisters split on the role of William Kroh. "Allison has this thing where she thinks she's adopted. She's not adopted," Marjorie said, rolling her eyes. Allison emphatically disagreed. "Bill Kroh [was] my adopted father. He adopted me when I guess I was about three years old."

Public records show William Kroh and Janelle married when Allison was about three.

Marjorie later claimed her mother was Jewish, although the family was not observant as she was growing up. Allison, although very careful not to contradict her sister, remembered it differently. "I am not Jewish. That is all I will say. I have always believed Bill Kroh was Native American and we *know* we're Native American on my mother's side." Marjorie's claiming of the Jewish faith was familiar to Allison. "She's told me that and I respect her religion. I don't know anything further on that. I know we had Jewish relatives, but I am not Jewish. I am Native American. And I am a Christian."

Allison was the only sibling that Marjorie acknowledged, but there were also two younger half brothers, Janelle's sons with Pete Garrett. There was a pronounced emotional distance between the older daughters of William Kroh and the younger sons of Pete Garrett. "I had to *take care* of them and *watch* them," Allison said. By contrast, "My sister and I could do things. She was my little sister. I guess most girls want a sister and she was my little sister. We liked the same things, we had the same things in mind. Don't get me wrong, I loved my brothers, I did. But my brothers were my *responsibility*, okay? My sister was my friend."

Allison's personality tended to the outdoors and the physical. Marjorie could be just as handy as her big sister, but she tended toward the girly and the sophisticated. As adults, both women described it as "Allison was country and Marjorie was city."

Allison and Marjorie both quickly said "it was fine" when asked about their childhood. But a shared philosophy of a hostile world emerged as they described their relationship. Allison said the two sisters were close because "I had her back and she had mine. It was always her and me against the world."

Some of their interests went down different paths. As Allison was tackling the great outdoors, Marjorie found she had a natural talent for and interest in dance and music. By high school, Marjorie was in the band and said that by then she could play several instruments—clarinet, flute, piano, percussion, kettledrums. She thought pretty much anyone could, if they made the slightest bit of effort. Her yearbooks listed her in the percussion section.

Marjorie tended more toward blond as she grew, while Allison was dark, with red tones. Allison was stout, while Marjorie's metabolism burned faster. Her constant dancing must have helped.

Marjorie was a majorette in high school. The school team was the Patriots, and Marjorie's majorette costumes had blue spangles with red and white accents. But by this time, her beloved comrade, Allison, had slipped out of her reach. At the age of seventeen, both sisters recalled, Allison had gotten herself in trouble and there was an angry confrontation with Mom. Allison was soon married to the father of the baby. She said she attended Marjorie's performances as often as she could, but under the circumstances, it was much rarer than she would have liked. Marjorie would have been eleven years old when her closest ally moved out of the house. "I was a little bit estranged from my mom at that time," said Allison, "as most young people do [sic] when they go out on their own. No big major problem, just I was doing my own thing." Allison and her new husband moved up to Paris, Tennessee, and continued having babies. Allison had a total of five children with her husband. Both sisters described the marriage, although long lasting, as abusive.

Marjorie, eleven, was now the oldest child in Janelle's household.

In 1974, according to Allison, Pete Garrett and Janelle divorced. Marjorie would have been in eighth or ninth grade and Allison would have been up in Tennessee with her husband and her children. Janelle and her children were living in Altamonte Springs, a suburb of Orlando, Florida, as Marjorie went through her teens. The area was heavily influenced by the entertainment industry, mainly Disney World and a cluster of nightspots known as Church Street Station. The area also had wild Florida territory, including the state's famous alligators, and guns and hunting were common hobbies. Marjorie entered Lake Brantley High School, which was brand-new and had an experimental design, somewhat famous in the region. But the radical design turned out to be a disaster, and Marjorie attended classes with leaky ceilings and other problems. The school was torn down a few years after it had been built.

In high school, Marjorie had a boyfriend named Kirk Rogers.* Decades after last seeing him, Marjorie's face still softened with fondness at the memory of this boyfriend. She was sixteen when they met, and she characterized the two of them as "inseparable" for her high school years. He was funny and drove around in a maroon-colored Vega hatchback. She described him as tall with sandy brown hair, and he made her laugh. She remembered that his musical tastes ran to Bad Company, the seventies rock band. Rogers was a year ahead of Marjorie in school, and she recalled that the summer he graduated, he joined the military and the couple had to split up.

·Some thirty years later, Kirk Rogers also remembered Marjorie with great detail and fondness, but his feelings were more conflicted. He said he was a teenage firefighter at the time he met Marjorie. The department let him on the crew because his father had been on their team and had passed away. The men "adopted" Kirk and he went out on real calls. One day, Kirk saw a pretty young blonde he knew from school holding a tray of cold beverages for the firemen, who were battling a blaze across the street from her house. When he pulled off his fire helmet, "Our eyes locked. She recognized me from school, too. It was like 'Oh! You!' That fire was on a Thursday. She actually was seeing somebody else at the time, but by that weekend, she was with me."

By that time, Marjorie had a new stepfather. His name was Tom Laurel†. Florida records show that Tom

---

* Denotes pseudonym.
† Denotes pseudonym.

Laurel married Janelle in early 1976, when Marjorie would have been fifteen. Kirk Rogers remembered Laurel as a very tall and imposing character who struggled with mental stability. On one of his first dates with Marjorie, Rogers ran afoul of Laurel by bringing her home too late. He remembered being physically frightened of the angry stepfather, who was well over six feet tall. Rogers made a point of returning to the house to make peace with him, in order to insure that he could continue to date the girl he considered so pretty "I kept pinching myself, I couldn't believe she was with me."

The young sweethearts spent so much time together that Kirk Rogers was present for an inexplicable moment of violence. Rogers was behind the house, a short distance from his girlfriend, who was out of view around the corner. He heard a shot and he ran toward her. He found Marjorie white as a sheet and her stepfather calmly walking back into the house, a gun in his hand. Marjorie was upset and told Rogers that Laurel had fired toward her.

Kirk Rogers's own home was very close to Marjorie's. On another day, she called him, he recalled, frantic for him to come get her because Laurel had just shot at her again. He arrived at her home within three minutes of the call. He could see the bullet hole in the wall of Marjorie's bedroom, and because of the floor plan of the house, he knew the gun that fired it must have been in the master bedroom when it discharged. Again, Laurel was calm, but Marjorie told her boyfriend that her stepfather had shot at her in her bedroom while he was standing in the doorway of his own. Rogers never knew why Laurel or anyone else in the house would have wanted to fire guns at Marjorie, though he did remember her mother Janelle, who did not usually approve of Rogers, being eager to have him help remove Marjorie from the house that day.

Kirk Rogers was in love with Marjorie and thought she was in love with him, too. Even so, stories got back to him from other kids at Lake Brantley High that Marjorie was "with" someone else from time to time. These incidents especially occurred when she was off performing with the band at away games. Other kids on the trip, sometimes even the other boy in question, would approach Rogers to "tattle" on her. But Rogers said his reaction was always "I don't know anything about that but she's with me now."

According to Rogers, the only differences the teenage couple ever had were over music. He loved his Bad Company and Led Zeppelin hard rock, "but she was always listening to disco: it was because of the beat, for all her [majorette] routines and dances. We'd have to split up over the music and then get together at the end of the night for pizza or something, because I couldn't stand her music and she couldn't stand mine. But that performing was everything to her and she became a great actress. The band teachers would tell them, 'It may be thirteen degrees out, but you've got to smile and sell it—don't let it show!' Marjorie got very good at acting." He remembered performing as a very big part of his girlfriend's life.

Rogers's feelings for Marjorie ran deep. As his senior year approached, he began to plan a future for them. He went to Kay Jewelers and bought an engagement ring.

Marjorie accepted it happily. But the teen engagement acted as a red flag for Janelle, who Rogers said began to interfere. He thought Janelle disapproved of his low income and modest prospects. He believed her advice to Marjorie was to "use her assets" to "do better." On a night over the Christmas break of 1978–79, the situation all came to a head. Rogers was on the phone with Marjorie trying to make plans and he could hear Janelle in the background, snarling at Marjorie to "hang up on him." And Marjorie did.

His heart broken, the eighteen-year-old packed a duffel bag, dropped out of high school and began to hitchhike north that very night, intent on reaching relatives in New Jersey. The thumb-ride trip took twenty-four hours. The next time he talked to Marjorie, she was angry with him and told him she had a message from her mother: "If you come near the house again and throw any more rocks like you did last night, she's going to call the police."

Rogers was puzzled and told Marjorie that he was in New Jersey. She acted angry and seemed to continue to believe her mother, rather than him. It was at that point that he began to wonder, after hearing this fabrication about himself, if the interfering mother had actually done him a favor. The teen decided not to return to Florida. It was the middle of his senior year.

Before Rogers left town, though, and while Marjorie was wearing his diamond ring, he'd already heard of someone new in his would-be fiancée's life. During the entire time he'd known her, she had worked in small taco shops. This new guy "had come in to the Mexican restaurant where Marjorie was working and that's how they met. I knew he had a lot more money than me and that Janelle was urging her to go with him, not me."

So Rogers dropped out of high school because of his broken heart and took an early entrance program into the army. It wasn't until much later that he got his GED. Rogers recalled that a year later, Marjorie never finished her senior year of high school, either.

By the time of prom after Rogers had hitchhiked his way out of Marjorie's life, she had the new boyfriend her mother approved of. Mitch Marqui was in his mid-twenties, and he and Marjorie married on March 28, 1981.* Marjorie was nineteen. By now, Marjorie was upgrading her employment and easily found work in the hometown industry, entertainment. She went to work as a waitress at Church Street Station, in Phineas Fogg's Old Time Saloon, the type of establishment where a floor show entertained the diners. Soon young Marjorie was not only making good tips but training others and taking over the choreography of the floor show. In Church Street owner/manager Porter Freeman she found a lifelong fan. Many years later he was still in the entertainment industry, as a motivational speaker in the fields of fitness and overcoming addiction, and he would reappear briefly in Marjorie's life.

Marqui, Marjorie's new husband, was a young entrepreneur who owned a motorcycle shop called Cycle Ryders. Marjorie was proud that he was the boss and master of his own destiny, but said their young marriage died on the vine because the two grew apart. Marqui

---

* According to Florida State records.

was inclined to stay home, she said, while she, working in the restaurant and entertainment crowd, often was too hyped after her shift to settle in. She'd head out for drinks with the rest of her coworkers, usually into the wee hours, since they'd worked till ten or later. "He seemed old to me," she said.

Mitch Marqui remembered their split differently. "She wasn't faithful," he said simply, his voice betraying the pain from thirty years into his past, declining to give details.

By the time she was twenty-one, Marjorie had divorced Mitch Marqui and gotten remarried, to Larry Tweed. A little wiser after her first failed marriage, Marjorie thought this one would work out better because they were the same age and in the same line of work. She said he was a bartender who also worked at Church Street. She found Tweed to be terribly handsome and fun. But she was on her way up. She was in management now and often had morning meetings. The late night partying had to be curbed. That marriage also failed.

Kirk Rogers, who occasionally stayed in touch with Marjorie over the years on the basis of old friendship, remembered finding a "wake" wherever Marjorie had been. He dropped by the Church Street Station once where he thought Marjorie and her then-husband, Larry Tweed, both worked. When he asked for her, he got a hostile reaction and understood he had walked into a situation involving an angry or jealous husband or ex-husband. He recalled having to assure the person he was nothing but an old friend and wanted no trouble. He took note, however, that this "wake" he encountered when he checked up on her over the years was beginning to look like a pattern. He had gotten a similar reaction when he once dialed Mitch Marqui's number. Even though he had his own family by then with someone else and simply thought of Marjorie as a high school memory, he felt that Marqui, also no longer with her by then, acted as though he had reason to be fed up and suspicious.

By the time that her second marriage broke up, Marjorie had become quite swept up in the entertainment industry. As an adult, she often told a story about how, when she was eighteen, gynecologists told her she had a case of endometriosis that would prevent her from ever carrying a baby. Marjorie's black eyes usually took a sharp turn and fixated somewhere to the side and her voice climbed into high registers when she frequently stated that this announcement formed the basis of her philosophy of life. Since she could not have children— the one thing she said she really wanted—she would "live only for myself" for the rest of her life.

Because of this longing of Marjorie's, her sister Allison felt somewhat embarrassed and vexed by her own fecundity. She felt her brood was a slap in the face to her little sister. She even let this discomfort discourage her from visiting as often as she otherwise would have liked to. She felt guilty flaunting two or three youngsters at a time in her sister's face. "I think it all boils down to I loved her so much I did not want her to feel like 'Oh, well, my sister's got everything, she's got the children and I don't.' You know? I didn't want her to feel like that. Whether she did or not—she says never, she never did—but I didn't want her to be in that position, you know what I mean?" Allison said.

Marjorie also felt a growing distance between the

sisters during her early adulthood, but she attributed it to a different cause. She said their mother made it difficult for the sisters to stay in contact, sometimes withholding addresses and other family details of one girl from the other. Marjorie's memories of her mother's sometimes difficult personality were consistent with Kirk Rogers's.

In the 1980s, in her mid-twenties and two failed marriages the wiser, Marjorie felt the siren call of Las Vegas. She followed a love interest, Rick Woods, from Florida to Nevada. But the relationship was explosive and she soon wanted to go home. The aftermath of the breakup placed her on the path that would define her life, both professionally and personally.

She told the story of her crossing over from dancer to stripper:

"I was in Las Vegas and I was on my way home to Florida. I had this bad situation in Vegas with a guy named Rick Woods. I had arrived in Phoenix and my car broke down. I could have called home for help but I just didn't. I was staying in a motel on Thomas Road. Across the street was a strip club called Bourbon Street. I noticed they were holding an amateur night contest that night. If you won, you'd get paid $600. I had worked around strippers for a long time by then and I had danced in pasties. I told myself, 'What's the big deal? Time to grow up.' I won the contest and got not only the $600 but also lots of tips. It wasn't bad. Nobody touched me or made me feel bad. My mother always told me if ever you do anything, always be a lady and you'll be fine. Some of those girls would do these trashy moves and bumps and grinds."

Marjorie was contemptuous of them. "I never did that. I was always a lady in my routines. I started making a lot of money. I could have fixed my car and gone on to Florida but I just didn't. I was doing fine."

Allison didn't remember the specific moment that she learned her baby sister had become a stripper, but she said she didn't have a problem with Marjorie's choices. "If she chose to do that then that was her business. Okay? She wouldn't do anything disrespectful, and if she did, she was an adult. Okay? I was *never* ashamed of my sister no matter what she did. Not ever. Because whatever she did, she did good. . . . She worked very hard for what she had, *very* hard for what she had."

Marjorie was very comfortable with the attention onstage. Making, she said, $10,000 within a few months at the age of twenty-four, she found that stripping was easy to grow to like. She began to learn stripper "culture." That, apparently, included a cadre of regulars.

"One of the regulars was a guy named Jay. He really liked me. He was going to do this multi-club volleyball tournament at his house. . . . I knew how much he spent at the club and what he drove, so I had a good idea of what he made. I was still living in that motel. Jay liked to help the girls.

"Jay kept telling me I could stay with him. I figured he lived in a nice place so I finally said yes. He said I could have my own room. I was shocked when we drove up to his place. It was a scrubby little house. And he had a roommate, he didn't tell me that. The place was filthy. I cleaned for three days," she said. "I did sleep with Jay." She went on to describe this sexual encounter in great detail. In what would become an important theme later at trial, she expressed contempt for his abilities, comprehension and endowment.

After a few months, Marjorie said that while she felt Jay, twenty-six years old, was a nice guy, she was a "firefly" and needed to indulge her restlessness. "Once you take a firefly, one of those pretty little twinkly bugs, and put it in a jar—what happens? It just becomes a black bug." She left.

In Cannonsburg, Pennsylvania, just south of Pittsburgh, Joann and Jake Orbin became first-time parents on September 10, 1953. Their delight in their first child, a son, was such that they named him after his father. But by the time he was three or four years old, Jake Jr. was having trouble breathing: the little blue-eyed, towheaded cherub had asthma. Jake and Joann packed him up, left their rust belt home, and settled in Arizona, where the skyline was dotted with saguaros, not smokestacks. Jake Sr. went to work as a U.S. Postal Service mailman and Joann joined an assembly line at Honeywell and became a supervisor. As a two-income family, not so common in the 1950s, they were able to afford a nice house with a swimming pool.

In 1959, the family got a little bigger. Another blue-eyed boy was born on September 8, 1959.

They named him Jay.

Big brother Jake, six years old by then, remembered the newborn. "Oh, absolutely. I remember holding him. . . . He's always been my 'little brother.'"

With a six-year age difference, Jay fit perfectly into the role of tagalong. "He wanted to hang around with my friends all the time around the house. We used to pick on him, actually, like 'the little brother.' You know, you hold 'im down, you get on knees and you hit 'im with their faces and eh-eh-eh! 'Quit hitting yourself!' That kind of stuff. You know, he was at that right age where he was just the cute little kid. He looked up to me. He always wanted to hang out and do things together."

Jake Sr. and Joann were the kind of parents whose home collected the neighbor kids and who were involved with their children's activities. When Jake Jr. entered Little League, Jake Sr. coached the team and baby brother Jay tagged along to help. Jake Jr. was a teenager by the time Jay got to play. "And then," said Jake Jr., his voice suddenly breaking into tears, "I helped my dad coach Jay's Little League."

The U.S. Post Office would hold picnics for the workers. "Kids would play at South Mountain and climb all over the hills and stuff. Back in those days that was probably safe. And then from that, they all used to come over to our house and go swimming," Jake recalled. South Mountain Park was a desert preserve at the edge of Phoenix. Roads and improvements were built in it through the Civil Conservation Corps during the Great Depression. It was a spot of great pride for Phoenicians, and Jake Orbin's childhood memories were a great example of why.

The year Jay was born, Alfred Hitchcock was busy memorializing how the city appeared at that time. The famed director was shooting his great classic *Psycho*. Janet Leigh's bank embezzlement scenes took place in downtown Phoenix, and the Bates Motel was up just north of town.

As teenagers, Jake and Jay also felt the attraction of that northern territory past Phoenix proper. Now called Thunderbird Park, in the sixties and seventies this area did not yet have the improvements, roads, picnic tables and barbecues that South Mountain Park offered to families and office parties. "There were no houses out that way. We called it 'boondoggers' on Friday night, where everybody goes out, parks their cars, lit a bonfire and blaze. It was fun . . . all the high school kids," Jake recalled.

Jay had a cheerful and gregarious personality. He had friends and girlfriends as he progressed through Cortez High School on the west side of Phoenix. And an eye for opportunity.

When Jay was seventeen, Jake was twenty-three, and working in management at a local retail company. He hired his kid brother to work in the garden shop. "From there, that was probably his first entrepreneurship— going out and starting a landscaping company. His gift of gab got him involved with all the ladies that came in. You know, he'd be talking trees, and the next thing you know he's doing landscaping for them. He actually started that business by helping people out. And from there it just blossomed into doing landscaping."

The young kid ended up getting a large client, a major home builder. Jake shook his head with wonder, saying that within a short time, teenager Jay was making more in one day than his big brother was making in a forty-hour workweek. "And he came to me and asked if I could help him run this business, and it was one of the things that got me involved in landscaping." Jake, who turned out to have a passion for trees and horticulture, stayed with the line of work that his kid brother lured him into. He followed that star and it became his life's career.

Jay did quite well early on. He bought a house in north Phoenix, on Sweetwater. It had a half acre, with a swimming pool and its own volleyball courts. In his mid-twenties, he hosted a party for "all the clubs," as his brother Jake remembered it. Jake was at the party and remembers the volleyball games. He does not remember meeting a girl named Marjorie at the party. Nor was he ever aware of any woman living with Jay at the Sweetwater house. He remembered some of Jay's girlfriends during this time, but he had no recollection of Marjorie.

Jake moved to California, pursued higher education in horticulture and settled into a long relationship with the prestigious Balboa Park of San Diego. Meanwhile, little brother Jay's own entrepreneurial nature matured rapidly. Jay was looking for a way to make the cash come in faster than it did in the landscaping business. He discovered a novelty item called Spectral Kinetics.

"Back in the eighties they were building these globe spheres that had some time type of rayon gas or gas in there. They were like lightning balls that you touch them and the lightning would follow your fingers around. They'd have them in nightclubs and stuff," Jake said. Jay and a partner started building them. Their designs were four feet tall on pedestals. "Instead of just a ball in there," Jake said, "they were more creative: they'd have a little brass golfer or an eagle in there or something customized. I've still got one today. They were usually balls of twelve to eighteen inches."

But international economics had a hard lesson for the

young go-getter. "China picked up on them and started mass producing these little gas globes," Jake said. "They were obviously more proficient at it because Jay's were selling for a thousand to twelve hundred dollars and the Chinese ones were selling for a hundred. So, really, he was not going to be able to compete."

Jay developed a taste for nightspots, and another of his ventures was a comedy club called Chuckles, where he was part owner. It may have been fun, but the club did not last.

Jay's flair for getting along with people served him well in business, and although not every venture prospered, his relationships did. Business associations that he formed in his twenties lasted him a lifetime. His partners tended to want to continue doing business with him and to introduce him to others who would as well, even if the product changed. For a while there was a solar energy product that took him to swap meets, a veritable cauldron of sales, free market action and networking among others with the entrepreneurial bug. He met a guy named Marshall Roosin, who introduced him to Jim Rogers. Both men became business associates of Jay's for decades. These friendships never failed.

After various ventures, all three went into the wholesale jewelry business, their partnership triangle forming and re-forming in various configurations as each found the part of the business he was best at and each prospered.

Jay ended up forming the company Jayhawk International. He specialized in Southwestern motifs, both jewelry and novelty items. The jewelry was mostly silver and turquoise, in Indian designs. The novelty items were things such as replica kachina dolls, sets of bows and arrows, Navajo-style pottery and other items intended to give a home or office a taste of the Southwestern U.S. tribes. Although duplicating Navajo designs, the items were manufactured by any artisan who could turn them out.

Jay developed a route that took him from coast to coast, selling the silver necklaces and freestanding kachina dolls to small retailers, the kind that often called themselves "trading posts" and catered to tourists and travelers along the nation's highways. He would load up a white cargo van with the merchandise and head out across New Mexico, through the Gulf States, ending up in Florida then turning back, hitting different cities on the return trip. Or he might head north through Utah, Idaho, over to Washington, down to Oregon and loop around again to Arizona. Sometimes his route went across the Midwest and ended in New Jersey. Along the way his customers looked forward to his jovial visits. He developed a reputation for returning phone calls promptly.

Jay spent a lot of time on the road. His trips were usually anywhere from ten days to two weeks, and he made them about once a month. One of those trips took him to Vegas in the mid-nineties.

Marjorie left Phoenix and Vegas and went back to Florida, where she hooked up again with Rick Woods, a hairdresser. They married in May of 1986,* but she

---

* According to Florida State records.

described their marriage as a "disaster" and said that she knew it would be a disaster even while she was saying her vows in a beach ceremony, which, she said, her own mother did not attend because "she couldn't stand him." On the other hand, she was very fond of her new mother-in-law. "I loved his mother more than him," she said. "Standing there I was looking at her [over his shoulder], not him." Indeed, the marriage to Rick Woods ended thirty days later.

By October of that year, Marjorie was working in Florida for a wealthy impresario named Michael J. Peter and she was married to her fourth husband, a tile contractor named Joe Cannizzaro, who worked for Michael J. Peter, too. Cannizzaro was very handsome. "He looked like Don Johnson; *Miami Vice* was big at the time," she remembered. "And just the sweetest thing." She was proud he owned his own business: "Seems like most of the people I've been with own their own business." But the marriage to Joe Cannizzaro didn't last.

Marjorie's next big romance was with a man twenty years her senior, whom she lived with in the New York/New Jersey area. Bob Mottram, her fifth husband, was into construction in a large way. She said he taught her to operate heavy machinery and she enjoyed running the giant excavators. He had many exquisite vehicles. She rattled off his roster of expensive automobiles with great detail and relish: "A Ferrari Testarossa, a Ferrari Mondial, a Ferrari 308, a Jaguar XK120, which is like an old antique, the real curvy ones, the Jaguar XKE, British Racing Roadster and Jaguar XKFJ6 . . . anyways like thirteen. Couple million dollars' worth of cars." Marjorie was proud of the lifestyle that Mottram provided, dressing up in fancy gowns and attending formal events with him. At some point, he set up a business in her name. Whether it was a business for her, an attempt at mentoring and generosity, or a manipulative use of her name to gain business advantages such as minority grants or tax dodges later became a point of dispute between the pair, but the one thing they both agreed on was that the marriage went spectacularly bad. The end was ugly and swift.

Milan Radesits was the sixth man to take Marjorie before a justice of the peace. A Dutch citizen, Radesits was in the nightclub business back down in Florida. Marjorie claimed that he was gay, and the marriage of April 1992 was a favor she granted him so that he could get a green card. Radesits confirmed that Marjorie was his ex-wife, but declined to comment otherwise.

The way was now clear for Marjorie's grand romance.

CHAPTER THREE

Michael the Mogul

Orlando, Florida, was very familiar with the name "Michael J. Peter." The newspaper there called him the "King of the Night." When Walt Disney came to Orlando in the 1950s, he envisioned a vast empire of amusements for children. He built Disney World. When Michael J. Peter came to town twenty years later, he also found inspiration.

Peter drove past a topless bar and noted that the parking lot was full, even in the middle of the day. Clearly, it was a product that had a market. But when he walked inside, the club "offended his sense of proper business practices." The place was tawdry. It was dirty, and the women stripping were often haggard and coarse. He found the same thing at every strip club he visited.

Peter was an Ivy League–educated business student who decided that the stripping industry was the place to spend his prestigious education. It was a product, in his view, that was sorely underserving its market. Which left plenty of room for him, "and convinced him that his education and experience would be the keys to bringing sophistication to what was then a 'sleazy' business."*

Peter had a good pedigree. His father, George Peter, had been a trustee at Cornell University until he went on emeritus status. Peter was a graduate of the prestigious Cornell School of Hotel Administration.

He had very dark hair, and his facial features had a certain exaggerated style to them. He stood only five-foot-six, but it wasn't long before his shadow loomed very large across the nude industry.

Peter bought one of the clubs on Orange Blossom Trail, a deceptively Disney-esque name for a red light district, and gave it a drastic overhaul. He started with good carpeting, fresh paint and quality lighting. He threw out the beer and put $200 bottles of Dom Perignon on the menu instead. According to an interview he gave the *Sun Sentinel*, he fired strippers he considered "fat and ugly." He put the bouncers in tuxedoes and the women—those who met his standards—in charm school. He hired a staff makeup artist. He dressed the girls in formal gowns. He had them tutored in such things as how to properly light a man's cigar and other niceties of "fine manners."

When he was done, he called the place Thee Doll House. He would frequently use the word "doll" in his branding over the years, as well as the double e's.

---

* From the *Sun Sentinel*.

Peter's concept paid off. He was widely credited with "inventing" the concept of the "gentleman's club" as opposed to a strip joint. Peter's overhaul of the stripping industry included the introduction of the "lap dance." His growing success in 1970s Orlando, as he bought up bar after bar on Orange Blossom Trail, brought him into direct conflict with the biker gangs that had previously dominated the trade. It was in his confrontations with bikers that Peter's name first became linked to organized crime, when stories emerged that he had blustered back that his mafioso pals would avenge his death if the bikers carried out any threats.

Peter's business was growing, too. He began franchising and consulting, always keeping his clubs "upscale" with their refinements of furniture and lighting and especially the tutoring of the girls. He began selecting an "elite" troupe of dancers who would become the Platinum Dolls. As his business model evolved, the Platinum Dolls would fly around the world to make special guest appearances to open new clubs. All the women in this troupe wore their hair platinum blond.

Marjorie Kroh Marqui Tweed Wood Cannizzaro Mottram Radesits often remarked that she was seventeen when she first met Michael J. Peter. She said that he came into the restaurants where she worked. In her twenties, she joined the Platinum Dolls both as a featured dancer and as the choreographer. She traveled constantly and loved what she considered a desirable, glamorous life. Paid well and famous, at least within certain circles, Marjorie felt like a star.

In the Platinum Dolls, Marjorie, dressed in black leather, would snap a whip playfully while five or six other dancers responded with catlike dance steps. In another number, the girls imitated famous singers such as Cher and Whitney Houston. Marjorie played Tina Turner, using a voluminous dark wig as she recreated the rock star's famous dance moves. In some numbers the girls in the Platinum Dolls wore long glittering gowns that later ripped away to reveal bikini-style costumes. In others they appeared in the motif of little girls with lollipops or stern librarians with black-framed glasses. With their platinum blond hair and perfect figures, it was often difficult to tell one girl from another as they pranced around the stage performing to mostly male audiences. Marjorie was listed as the choreographer for the Platinum Dolls. At home, she taped the dance segments from the eighties TV show *Star Search* and studied them for moves and techniques she could incorporate in the Dolls shows.

Marjorie was not only a featured dancer in Peter's prize troupe, she became the leading lady of his heart. Michael J. Peter was about thirteen or fourteen years older than she was and an inch or two shorter, but they got along extremely well. Marjorie moved into one of his mansions and was by his side when the ultra-glitz TV show *Lifestyles of the Rich and Famous*, starring Robin Leach, came to call. It was 1991, the tenth anniversary edition of the show. The British star with the distinctive voice told viewers there was a renaissance in topless clubs, defying what was then an economic recession, and introduced Peter as the man who "got in first and led the pack." The show featured footage of Peter's signature geisha-like training for his strippers. A patron in a business suit was shown being hand-fed elegant food by a young beauty who soon put down the fork and stood up to drop her dress, while the voice-over explained that Peter's clubs offered "silken temptresses who grin and 'bare' it for a price." With her dazzling blond hair and sleek figure, Marjorie was just the kind of companion Michael J. Peter liked to be seen with on TV, but her appearance on the episode was limited to short clips. She could be seen twirling rapidly in a short rain slicker in the show open and in another shot where she whipped her hair around, wearing a sparkling black and silver costume.

By this time, Michael J. Peter was a true world impresario, with clubs in places from Lima to London. He was interviewed on CNN in the business news segment and appeared on *The Montel Williams Show. Entertainment Tonight* did a piece on the trend, with Peter's standing in the industry featured. Marjorie could be seen in some of the background footage. Even the *New York Times* took notice of the trend in "upscale" topless clubs. In an article headlined "Topless Bars for a Crowd in Pin Stripes," the *Times* noted Peter's Cornell degree and said he was "widely credited with applying modern marketing techniques (like selling trading cards featuring his topless dancers) to what had been considered a seedy, small-time business."* The hometown newspaper, the *Orlando Sentinel*, frequently reported on his flashy accoutrements, so happily displayed for Robin Leach's cameras, such as his cage-like iron bed covered in satin, the red Ferrari, black Rolls-Royce, private

---

* *New York Times*, April 15, 1992.

jet and eighty-two-foot yacht. With many battles over zoning and city ordinances as neighborhoods fought to keep the "Doll" strip clubs out, the *Sentinel* had frequent occasion to report on the "King of the Night."

By the late eighties, Peter's skin empire included movies, where Marjorie, her platinum hair gleaming on the dimly lit sets, won some on-screen roles. In company videos for Michael J. Peter Club Management, Inc., she could be seen riding topless on a white horse; fully clothed advising other girls; riding Jet Skis with Peter; scurrying off to a helicopter with him, dressed in an outfit that matched another woman's on his other side; or fully nude, frolicking in a party atmosphere with many other naked women while Peter held a microphone and addressed the crowd. In some of these videos, "Marjorie Marqui" was credited as "choreographer," and when a roster of naked girls was whisked off to Peter's private island in the Exumas for a Caribbean fantasy video shoot, she was listed as "talent coordinator."

When not married to someone else, Marjorie often used her first husband's name, Marqui. She said it was a good stage name and felt natural to her.

Thirty years later, Mitch Marqui was well aware she was using his name: he occasionally fielded calls from skip tracers looking for her. He did not, however, know she used it in the skin industry. "Had she gone into stripping yet by the time you knew her?" he was asked and an audible wince came over the phone line. "No," he said, "I didn't know." It was a painful topic to him.

But Peter was supremely comfortable with it. He figured he was selling fantasy, and he was his own best advertisement. His jet-setting lifestyle was constantly on display. Someone who began watching was the U.S. attorney in Fort Lauderdale, where Peter had moved the headquarters for his dynasty. The feds were convinced Michael J. Peter's success owed more to mob bosses than to Cornell University.

The flashy lifestyle could be hard on a girlfriend, too. If Michael J. Peter was surrounded by anything other than money, it was definitely naked girls. Eventually Peter and Marjorie split up as a couple but remained very fond of each other. Publicly, Peter sometimes made statements about how Marjorie had wanted a family, something just not in his life plan. Later, he privately told detectives that he "threw her out." She, on the other hand, talked often of the difficulty of being with someone who was constantly surrounded by "girls offering him everything."

Regardless, by 1994 Marjorie was back in Vegas plying her trade as both a dancer and a sort of stripper's Fagin, teaching other girls the tricks of makeup, dance and costuming she had learned through the Platinum Dolls, beefed up by her own natural talent and gift for creating with her hands. But back in Orlando, trouble was brewing for Michael J. Peter. He eventually pleaded guilty to some racketeering charges and entered a federal prison. So much for lifestyles of the rich and famous.

CHAPTER FOUR

Happy Birthday Boys

One day in 1995 Jay Orbin was driving into Las Vegas. As always, the highway was decorated with billboards for the many revelries available in the famed and flashy city. But this time as he scanned the highway, one hand on the wheel, the other tuning the radio dial in search of a Rush Limbaugh station, he undoubtedly lifted his foot from the accelerator. A certain billboard had caught his eye up ahead; he thought he recognized a face among the otherwise anonymous showgirls painted large along the highway. The hair was very blond, the eyes fierce— yes! As he zoomed past, he was sure it was her, the woman he knew as Marjorie Marqui.

As soon as he got a chance, Jay Orbin picked up the phone and called the club advertised on that billboard. He must have been delighted when he got through to the girl he remembered from ten years earlier.

Marjorie agreed to meet up with Jay, and soon he was squiring her about Vegas, calling her on the phone when he returned to Phoenix and traveling back up to see her.

According to Marjorie, one special night Jay took her out to the fanciest of dinners, gave her gifts and then broached the topic of marriage. It was not a romantic proposal, in her memory, but a moment when he asked what she thought about it. She said she recoiled, and laughed that she had been married way too many times already and it had never worked out. At age thirty-three, she was done with marriage. She would never try it again. She said Jay bought her a lot of presents to prove his love and coax her into the marriage. She told him the presents and the attention were sweet, but she couldn't picture herself leaving Vegas and coming "to sit in Phoenix and do what? I'd become a miserable bitch and then I'd make you miserable, I'm not gonna do that to you."

According to Marjorie, Jay said he understood her misgivings. But, from their close friendship and long conversations, he thought he had something up his sleeve. What if, he asked her, he was willing to "aggressively pursue" fertility treatments for her? Would she be willing to consider married life again if it included a child?

Now that, Marjorie later recalled, got her attention. She described thinking it over. She knew what the drawbacks would be. First, marriage had never turned out the way she'd hoped it would, and second, she had a poor opinion of Jay's sexual prowess.

But there was no getting around the fact that having a child was a highly desirable jackpot for this showgirl.

Marjorie said she'd often thought of that gynecologist's pronouncement when she was eighteen years old, that she'd never be a mother. It had been the ruling event of her life, the reason she'd lived the life she had, made the choices she had. It was the reason she "lived only for myself." No one had ever before offered to help her fight back against fate.

She thought Jay was a good guy, dependable. He would do anything for her. It wasn't the great romance of the century and she considered him unable to satisfy her sexually, but "I'd had enough sex by then for a hundred people. I decided it didn't matter to me, I was done with that." She decided the whole deal was a good bet. She'd achieved so many other things—the high living, the success in choreography, the prestige within her industry—yet the one thing she couldn't do by herself was become a mother, and here was Jay Orbin offering her what she always wanted.

She accepted. It was with the caveat, she recalled many years later, that if they hadn't become parents after two years of trying to conceive a child, she and Jay would walk away from each other with no hard feelings.

They married in Vegas on July 22, 1995.

The wedding photos showed Jay in a black tuxedo with a red rose boutonniere. Marjorie's stark white wedding gown had highly poufed satin shoulders, and the décolletage relentlessly displayed the results of the augmentation procedures she'd undergone over the years. She was very tan, with platinum bangs across her forehead and a back-combed lift immediately behind them, crowning her head. The rest of the hair fell in smooth curls well past her shoulders. The bride's smile was even brighter than the groom's. No one would've guessed it was her seventh wedding, but only his first.

Neither one had any family present. Usually close to his family, it wasn't until a day or two after the runaway nuptials that Jay called his big brother, Jake, and told him what he'd done. Jake remembered being surprised, but happy for Jay.

Marjorie packed up her Vegas showgirl lifestyle and headed across the desert with her groom, to become a Scottsdale housewife.

Jay Orbin spent an estimated hundred thousand dollars in fertility treatments for her. Jay wanted the child just as much as she did. Marjorie described the treatments as viciously painful and "absolute hell." She took various drugs and had to give herself daily shots, attempting to stimulate the production of ova. A lifelong fitness fanatic, Marjorie also suffered the weight gain powerful hormones can bring. Jay sympathized with her and supported her. He was not required to go through any treatments himself.

At last, through the in vitro process, a successful pregnancy was achieved. Allison said the happiest her sister Marjorie ever was was when she was pregnant. Marjorie's belief in her infertility had always affected the sisters' relationship, but the successful pregnancy that Jay had paid for with money and Marjorie with physical suffering lifted a cloud from over the Kroh sisters. "I mean I felt when she finally was pregnant with Noah and had Noah, all the 'un-comfort' was gone. . . . I could talk to her about anything and everything. I did not feel uncomfortable around her because my sister finally had what she wanted, always wanted."

On August 28, 1996, a healthy baby boy entered this world. They named him Noah.

Allison remembered the birth announcement her sister sent her for this highly desired child. "It's a picture of Noah in the hospital laying on his little belly. And on it she wrote 'I finally met the man of my dreams.'"

On the other side of the family, the infant in the photo was the first grandchild born. "My parents were ecstatic," recalled Jake Jr.

And so was Jay, the proud papa. Everyone who had ever met Jay since 1996 talked about his adoration for his son. Some even said he "worshipped" the child. As did Marjorie. Whatever mild bonds held Jay and Marjorie together, they were redirected to the child they shared, achieved through a battle they had fought together. For both of them, their emotions toward the child dramatically intensified whatever feelings they had had for each other.

For the Orbins, the grandchild was a great gift to everyone. But for the Kroh sisters, he was even something a little more.

"After she had Noah, it was great," Allison said. "I can be myself with her. We can discuss kids and everything because she has a child. She had what she always wanted."

By all accounts, Marjorie enthusiastically threw herself into the role of mother. On her son's birthdays, she'd throw lavish parties with carefully selected themes. She monitored the child's entire life. Her friends began to think she was even overdoing it. Noah never had a babysitter, because Marjorie would trust no one with her child. Her friends also began to feel she was intensely strict with him. He was active and rambunctious; by the time he was four, he was on ADHD medications.

Where Marjorie was strict, Jay was lush in his affection. Photos show the child in the arms of a beaming man tickling a giggling preschooler, or balancing a T-ball, or playing a board game. In one particularly touching shot, Jay telegraphed fatherly pride and joy into the camera with one arm protectively around a little blond toddler. But Noah was not looking at the camera. The baby was captivated by his father's face. He reached up one tender little arm as if to catch the daddy smile that was so bright it was nearly tangible.

Every Sunday when Jay was in town, he'd bring Marjorie and Noah over to Grandma and Grandpa Orbin's for a family afternoon. The grandparents also doted on the little boy. Sometimes there were barbecues or backyard games, taking advantage of the beautiful Arizona winter weather. Jay and his mother might get into a zesty discussion of politics, with Joann Orbin deliberately using her Democratic Party views to tease her rabidly Republican son.

Marjorie never seemed quite comfortable at these otherwise idyllic gatherings. She'd typically leave early, while Jay and Noah would stay the whole day. If Jay was on the road on a Sunday, Marjorie *might* swing by with Noah. She'd stay a short time then leave the child to visit his grandparents without her, but as often as not, she wouldn't come by at all if Jay weren't in town. For the doting grandparents, time with Noah was precious. "My parents, they enjoyed it as much as they could get out of it," Jake Jr. recalled. "Marjorie . . . just wasn't an open person or friendly and did not want to spend time at my parents' house. Some people come over and call 'em 'Mom' [and 'Dad'] and hang out; Marjorie was just never that way. So any time they did get with Noah was appreciated."

The Orbins never felt close to their daughter-in-law, but Jay seemed happy in his marriage. He never complained about his wife to them.

Jake was close to his baby brother. Although Jake now lived in California, the two men communicated by phone and e-mail often. There were visits to California and reciprocal visits to Arizona. Little Noah knew his uncle well and always received a perfect birthday present from him, Jay having guided his brother through the gift selection. The brothers did this through habitual late night e-mails and frequent phone calls.

In an attempt to stay closer to home and spend more time with his family, Jay took a lease on a commercial property near one of Phoenix's famous resorts and opened a retail store for his goods. The shop was filled with postcards, pens shaped like cacti, play sheriff badges, glass cactus knickknacks and replica Indian artifacts like spears, pipes, bows, talking sticks, dream catchers and imported replica Indian turquoise jewelry. But the retail experiment failed to catch the tourists staying at the resort and Jay closed it. He went back on the road, and with his business sense, energy and charm, Jayhawk International prospered as a wholesaler.

In 2003, Marjorie and Noah and Jay moved to a bigger and better house, on 55th Street just north of Bell Road. Although still within Phoenix city limits, the area was usually thought of by locals as a Scottsdale neighborhood. Marjorie immediately set to with a long list of home improvement projects. She kept the house beautiful and was constantly adding to it and upgrading it. It became something of a family joke, Marjorie's nonstop quest for the perfect house, and her DIY abilities seemed endless. Marjorie, who had devoted her life to dancing since she was a schoolgirl, had now been in the north Phoenix area for several years. When she'd arrived, she'd been slim and muscular, with the perfect physique required to prance across a Las Vegas stage in a scant handful of sequins and feathers. But since marrying Jay, she had first been on powerful fertility drugs, and then had been pregnant. She no longer looked like a dancer. She looked like a very blond mother who lived a comfortable and relaxed life. There were Christmases and toys and gumball machines. All Marjorie's living needs were met. Jay paid all the household bills, including mortgage, insurance and utilities. In addition, he gave her about a $30,000-a-year allowance, most of it paid in $500-a-week installments, for her to use on whatever she wanted, considering her daily needs were already met.

But Marjorie was never satisfied to be relaxed. The soft waistline she now had was a source of irritation to her. When Noah was around kindergarten age, she started taking him to karate lessons at Phoenix Leadership Academy. She had been told that learning martial arts was excellent therapy for hyperactive kids because it taught them focus and concentration at the same time as offering them physical release for their energy.

Marjorie, always competitive, began spending a lot of time at the karate school herself and got to know all the other children and their parents. She got to know the teenage son of the school's owners. She began helping out in the classes and became a spotter for the kids tumbling through their various moves across the mat.

Marjorie began working harder on her own figure, too. For the first time in years, she set her sights on getting her dancer's figure back, and by the spring of 2004, she had succeeded. Wherever she went, she turned heads. Her platinum hair was eye-catching on its own, but now her slim physique, often displayed to advantage in her typical daily outfit of tight spandex dancer's pants, along with her large silicone-enhanced bust, made her an object of envy and desire. Earlier that year, she'd kicked it up a notch and embarked on an intensive weight training regime. At the gym, she sometimes talked to fellow exercisers about going on a competitive circuit. She looked like it could be true. Her muscle development was remarkable. She spent many hours at the gym.

In April of 2004, she opened up a separate bank account in her own name only. She had the statements sent not to the 55th Street house or to the family business's warehouse downtown but to a PO box. Around this time she also had a falling out with one of her best friends from the karate school. Later, when police entered her home and discovered several security cameras in place, she would explain that the cameras were to catch her former friend in the act of vandalizing her home.

While Marjorie was getting into the best shape of her life, Jay was working very hard to provide the lifestyle that allowed her to pursue her fitness goals to her heart's content. He worked long hours at the warehouse and logged thousands of miles on the road, visiting customers coast to coast. His endearing personality kept his order book full. He warmed up to each client, often leaving behind a picture or two of Noah. There wasn't anyone on his route who didn't know exactly how old Noah was or what his latest achievement was, from cutting a tooth to losing one, from learning to read to earning a karate patch. Nobody heard much about the boy's mother. Occasionally, Jay would make a remark that his wife didn't have much of a head for business. Everyone could see that Jayhawk International was strictly a one-man band. From time to time, if Jay was on the road, a customer would reach Marjorie on the phone because the warehouse number would roll over to their house. But usually it was Jay who called back, always that day and typically within a couple of hours.

Jay spent hours upon hours driving the white cargo van as he hauled merchandise to Utah, Oregon, Texas, Alabama, New Jersey, Florida and points both beyond and in between. He enjoyed his settled family life, too. Jay's style was casual, as befitted his warm and open-armed personality. He was almost never spotted in long pants, his shorts and cotton shirts keeping him comfortable year-round both at business and at play. By spring of 2004, as Marjorie's looks were easily convincing people she was a competitive weightlifter, Jay was looking decidedly middle-aged. Always a bit of a beefy fellow, his sedentary work and drive-thru habits began to catch up with him. As his forty-fifth birthday approached, his pant size had grown to a 44.

As Marjorie's relationships were devolving into bitter accusations and estrangements strong enough for her to install security cameras, Jay's were seasoning into lifelong loyalties. Many of his customers remembered times when he advanced them product on a mere handshake. Especially after the horrible events of September 11, 2001, when the transportation industry across America abruptly shut down, Jay stepped up in behalf of his slice of the suddenly brittle American economy. Most of his customers were little shops that sold to tourists driving through. That business suffered a terrible blow when Americans stopped traveling after September 11 and the economy as a whole took a terrible hit. Jay left the kachina dolls and silver and turquoise jewelry behind at every stop, telling the distressed store owners to "pay me when you can." His genuine care for his customers and his big heart certainly contributed to keeping some of these people in business during those trying times.

Always concerned about providing for his family and building a nest egg for Noah to inherit, sometime in 2004 Jay hooked up with one of the dads at the karate school who was a real estate agent. The pair scouted foreclosure bargains together.

He even enlisted his manufacturer, Gary Dodge, who built many of Jay's catalog items at a factory in the Philippines. Their relationship went all the way back to their freshman year at Cortez High. Jay approached

Gary and gave him instructions on how to help provide for Marjorie and Noah if something happened to him. He wanted Dodge to take over his biggest accounts and then devote 10 percent of the proceeds to his wife and son. Dodge was uncomfortable. "He had sat me down and goes, 'Gary, you know, if I die—' and I go 'Get out of here! I don't want to talk about this!' He goes, 'This is serious, this is serious. This is really important. This is to take care of my family.'" Jay never stopped thinking of ways to safeguard the welfare of his family. He had a large network of trusted friends, colleagues and relatives that he recruited to be part of the safety net.

In May of 2004, Jay Orbin updated his will. Marjorie knew about it, but the rest of his family did not. The same month he did this, he also approached his brother and asked him if he would be willing to serve as guardian to Noah, should something happen to both him and Marjorie. "It was basically a plural thing at that time," Jake said, his little brother seeming to have a car or plane crash in mind. Jake also remembered not taking it too seriously. After all, both Marjorie and Jay were several years younger than he was. He certainly did not expect to outlive them before Noah turned eighteen. "You just give it one of those 'yeah, no problem,' one of those 'don't even talk like that, whatever, sure, I'll take care of him.'"

The will that Jay wrote that month specified that Marjorie got all his assets. There was no trust for Noah. There were some special collector's items, which Jay expected to increase in value, set aside for his son alone, but the boy's care and inheritance, as spelled out in that document, were vouchsafed to Marjorie's judgment and goodwill. Jake Orbin Jr. was named as the secondary guardian, only if something happened to Marjorie as well as to his baby brother.

Year 2004 was a presidential election year. In the summer, the two political parties held their conventions. In July, the Democrats met in Boston.

Jay kept a close eye as an unknown named Barack Obama of Illinois gave a speech that seemed to mesmerize the opposition gathered in Boston. He took a vigorous interest in Democratic Party nominee John Kerry, the senator from Massachusetts. There would be plenty to argue with Mom about this election season. He had to be prepared. He listened to Rush Limbaugh faithfully on his long, long drives. When he was near a computer, he surfed the Internet for campaign news. He made a financial contribution to the GOP ticket.

That week, while the Democrats were in Boston and Jay was listening in, violent storm clouds were gathering off the Atlantic coast of Africa. The winds were blowing west.

On August 26, 2004, Noah turned eight years old. Shortly before the birthday, Jay took his blond little son on a father-and-son fishing trip in northern Arizona.

Jay and Marjorie had been together for ten years by the time the child they had both worked so hard for became a second grader. In Phoenix, the school year started in early August, so there were plenty of school chums to invite to Noah's birthday party. The family and several little boys from Noah's social circle gathered at a bowling alley on Saturday, August 28, to celebrate.

The little boys frolicked in the glow of purple and blue bowling alley lighting. Jay carefully carried out to the kids a white sheet cake that seemed nearly as big as Noah, with flaming candles on top. The child bent over low to blow them all out.

Back at the house, Noah was showered with presents. Marjorie, for the first time ever, was in the background as the child opened up the gaily wrapped packages. Her attention seemed focused more on tasks behind the scenes than on the birthday boy and the gathered family.* In years past, she'd been front and center as her "perfect man" reached for his birthday gifts, tore off ribbon and reacted merrily to his new toys.

The next day, Jay set out on a sales run. He'd be heading south and east, along the Gulf Coast. On his way, he would listen to George W. Bush and Dick Cheney be nominated to run for a second term, from Madison Square Garden in New York. He was a big fan. He had photos of George and Laura Bush at home, signed and addressed specifically to him. All along the drive, he talked on the phone constantly to his customers and business associates, enjoying his usual social network.

As Jay was heading toward Florida, the disorganized squalls from Africa had collected into a massive and destructive force, Hurricane Frances. Frances battered the Bahamas, the Caribbean and Florida for days. Jay arrived in tiny Crestview, Florida, on September 1. But he couldn't go farther in the rain-soaked and wind-whipped terrain. He stayed in the Panhandle for three

---

* From testimony, interviews and family home videos.

days before turning back. His Florida customers were not only battened down for Frances, but they had just suffered through Hurricane Charley three weeks before, a storm big enough to ruin the state's citrus crop and to close down schools. For Jay's business, this Florida run was not a good one. He left Florida on September 3 and hit Lousiana on his way out. He took two days to cross the ample expanse of Texas. One more day had him stopping in New Mexico and reaching an outpost of southern Arizona.

On September 7, Jay booked a room at the La Quinta in Tucson. He ordered pizza. He made some calls.

On the morning of September 8, 2004, Jay was back on the highway early. He talked to Marjorie and let her know to expect him home, but she told him he'd better stay away because both she and Noah had strep throat. He took a call from his mother and one from his father. They both wished him a happy birthday. Today he was turning 45. They asked if Marjorie had some celebration planned for him. Jay told them no, because she had strep throat and so did Noah. He planned to go straight to the warehouse and finish up a normal workday before going home and getting exposed to the germs. While he talked to his parents, around 9 A.M., his phone bounced off a cell tower in Tempe. He was on I-10 heading north, about to dogleg left into Phoenix. He would arrive at his warehouse in the downtown industrial district of Phoenix in less than half an hour.

Jay arrived at the warehouse and took more phone calls. He loaded merchandise, organized his inventory, gassed up his van. In the late afternoon, he also gassed up the family Bronco, green with brown trim, an Eddie

Bauer edition. He drove the Bronco home and that evening planted himself in front of the computer and opened some e-mails from brother Jake, who was asking for suggestions and making plans for a gift for his nephew. Jay rapidly caught up on the presidential election news, surfing from George Bush sites to John Kerry sites and back. He also wanted to know more about the affliction that was keeping his little boy locked away in his bedroom. He searched for "strep throat" and visited the boy's pediatrician's Web site. The Web surfing filled the evening till approximately 9:30 P.M.

At 11 P.M., his longtime friend and business colleague Marshall Roosin called to wish him a happy birthday, but had to leave his felicitations on voice mail.

Jay did not pick up the phone.

CHAPTER FIVE

Shell Game

On Thursday, September 9, 2004, Noah Orbin did not attend school. In the late afternoon, Marjorie went to Target and bought a Shark portable steam cleaning machine, several mops, seven scrub brushes, two buckets and a garden hose. She bought four bottles of Tilex, two bottles of Clorox bleach and a bottle of Liquid-Plumr. She bought a Game Boy, some cosmetics and other miscellaneous items. From the clearance aisle she bought men's boxers, briefs and long pants in size 32/36. The bill, most of it cleaning products, came to $482.31.

On Friday, September 10, Noah attended half a day of school. In the morning, Marjorie went to a Lowe's home improvement store and bought two blue Rubbermaid fifty-gallon tubs with gray lids, a box of Ruffies fifty-five-gallon trash bags and a pail. She bought a

Swiffer WetJet and the associated pads and fluids for it. She bought bottles of Pine-Sol. She bought a roll of plastic. She bought several other strong cleaning supplies such as acetone. This time the bill for cleaning products was $175.46.

That same Friday, Jake Orbin Jr. was in San Diego and cheerfully expecting his baby brother's return birthday call from Arizona. It was a long-standing tradition between the pair. First Jake would call Jay on September 8 for birthday wishes, then two days later Jay would reciprocate on September 10. It had been awfully convenient to have a birthday that neither sibling could possibly ever forget.

The call did not come first thing in the morning. It did not come after lunch. Jake thought surely it would come by bedtime. It did not. It was the first time the tradition had been broken.

Also on that Friday, Debbie Macy, a business associate of Jay's from northern Arizona, called the business line and Marjorie answered. The call had rolled over to the Orbins' home line. Marjorie said Jay was not expected home until Monday or possibly as late as Wednesday, the 15th.

This struck Debbie as a little unusual because her husband, Robert Macy, a supplier who made peace pipes and arrow sets, had spoken directly to Jay on the 8th and Jay had said he was already "home." Everyone knew Jay's trips lasted two weeks. He was a highly predictable and reliable man. A short run from the 10th to the 13th didn't make sense to the business associates who knew him well. Furthermore, Marjorie's statement and tone made it sound as if Jay had never returned from his original trip. The craftsman and his wife weren't sure how to reconcile Marjorie's statement on Friday with Jay's two days earlier.

By Monday the 13th, Noah was back in school and Marjorie was shopping again. At Home Depot she bought several garage floor surface kits in the color tan and semigloss paint in swiss coffee. She bought other garage resurfacing supplies. And she bought more acetone. The bill at Home Depot came to $318.94.

Tuesday the 14th, Marjorie went to WalMart. She bought another wet/dry vac. She bought Clorox bleach, Windex, Shower Power, two trash cans, several bath towels and a Clorox bleach pen. She also bought more acetone, sanding blocks and a sand sponge, Kwik Seal, etching solution, paintbrushes, paint tray kits, a caulking gun and lots of lavender scent. The bill came to $293.68. She then went to Green Goddess Nursery and spent twelve hundred dollars on plants and garden items.

On Wednesday the 15th, Marjorie went back to Lowe's and bought granite, laminate and Formica. She bought chip fix repair kits. The bill was $254.90. She also returned to WalMart and picked up yet more acetone, drywall tools, another caulking gun and lots of caulk. She also bought three car-related items: a jump-starter, a sunshade and a tri-fold ramp. The jump-starter was designed to juice up a dead battery without the use of another vehicle, such as would be the procedure with plain jumper cables. The sunshade was a must in

Phoenix, where UV rays from the sun could destroy the vinyl of a dashboard in a short amount of time. Parked cars were particularly vulnerable to cracked vinyl dashes. The ramp was typically used for loading an item with wheels, such as a motorbike or dolly, into a truck.

Apparently Lowe's didn't have everything Marjorie needed. She also went back to Home Depot, where she spent another $292.65 on grout sealer and related items. She bought an orange cord. She bought a hacksaw.

Jay's old friend and business associate Marshall Roosin expected some paperwork from Jay on that Wednesday. Like everything else in his life, Jay was almost compulsively punctual about this paperwork. It was a good policy for both of them because by turning in the monthly paperwork as soon as possible, both Roosin and Jay could cash out accounts and keep the revenue flowing smoothly. It was unusual for the fifteenth to pass without the envelope from Jay turning up in the mail or even a phone call to explain, but if anyone had earned the right to a few days' credit, it was big-hearted and overly punctual Jay. Roosin wasn't upset. But he did notice, because it was out of character.

On Thursday the 16th, Debbie Macy's husband Robert called again. He had to ask if Marjorie and Jay were fighting. He couldn't think of any other reason, short of a death in the family, why Jay would neglect to return phone calls. Marjorie did not respond to that question. Instead, she told the pipe maker that Jay was "missing."

Also on the 16th, Jan Beeso, the mother of one of Noah's schoolmates, was enlisted by Marjorie to watch him overnight. Beeso was surprised and reluctant because it was a school night. She also thought it was odd because she didn't feel she knew Marjorie very well. But Marjorie said she really needed the night off; she needed Noah out of the house. So Beeso took in the little boy. She noted it was odd that Marjorie and Noah made no attempt to call each other over the next twelve hours. In the morning, Beeso drove the two boys to school, though she had to drop by Marjorie's first because Noah had forgotten an item for school. Beeso thought Marjorie seemed overwrought, as if she had been up all night, when she came out to the car. She talked about "fighting" with Noah's father. Beeso still thought the interaction between mother and child was odd, considering they had not seen each other for twelve hours.

Over the next few days, Marjorie continued to shop, spending thousands on home improvement items, from a glazier knife to granite countertops. She bought even more acetone and Pine-Sol. She also bought groceries, including plenty of Cuervo Gold beer, Stoli vodka and Beringer champagne. She bought a car battery. She was also making daily cash withdrawals and transfers.

Jay's voice mail was collecting messages from business associates. No one was getting a return call. He had built up so much goodwill, though, that none of the messages turned ill-tempered. In San Diego, Jake wondered what had kept Jay so busy he couldn't find time for a birthday message.

On Monday, September 20, Joann Orbin left a message for her son over the lunch hour. She was calm and to the point. "It's your mother. Give me a call."

That day at least three of Jay's associates received calls from Jay's cell phone in quick succession. None of them heard Jay's voice, but the Rush Limbaugh radio show, a great favorite of Jay's, could be clearly heard in the background. Some of the friends called him back and left messages asking him to return their calls when he got a better connection, because they couldn't hear anything that he might have said, just the radio.

At 5:25 P.M., Marjorie called Jay's cell phone. She had a crying little boy at her side. A later police report transcribed the message as: "(Noah) Hi dad (crying). (Marjorie) Hello? Hello? Noah's trying to talk to you and your mother's been calling."

Joann called Jay's cell phone five minutes later. Now she was distressed. "Call me," she said into the voice mail, "I am really worried."

The next morning, the 21st of September, at 7:21 A.M., as he was getting ready to go to school, Noah left a message on Jay's voice mail, "Hi daddy. I just want to know when are you coming home? OK, daddy. Bye."

More business calls came in. Then Jake called his brother. "Hey, Jay, I was thinking about you last night when I saw the Monday night football, that Hank Williams Jr. intro talked about political stuff if mom forwarded the false CBS report on Bush to you like she mailed me—from September 8, *Arizona Republic*."

At 3 P.M., Joann's anxiety peaked. "Jay Michael," she said, using her son's full name in the way of stern mothers everywhere, "I am really worried, Jay. I haven't heard from you in days or weeks. I need to talk, please pick up your messages."

A few minutes later the voice mail recorded an open line where Noah can be heard in the background—but no message was directed to the phone.

Another of Jay's business associates, Mario Olivarez, was beginning to feel anxious, too. He was one of the people who had received a strange message from Jay's phone on Monday the 20th. Olivarez hadn't been able to connect with him otherwise. Some of the business associates were beginning to talk to one another and compare notes. Jay not returning phone calls was so out of the ordinary that they wondered if he was in some kind of trouble. At 3:53 P.M. Olivarez left a message saying, "Jay, when you get the message, dude, let me know so I can make sure everything is okay."

On Wednesday morning, the 22nd, Olivarez called again at 8:21 A.M. "Jay, give someone a call. Make sure everything is okay. Talk later, bye." Nine minutes later, he gave it another try. "Hey Jay, it's Mario. Give someone a call. We are all worried. Hope all is okay."

More associates called and left messages. Some seemed worried, some seemed unaware that Jay had been out of contact.

Marjorie fielded calls from several of them. To some she said that Jay had been delayed in Florida, due to Hurricane Frances. Some hung up with the impression that Jay had doubled back to revisit customers he could not reach during the storm. Others were told his phone wasn't working properly. Still others were told he should have been home by Monday the 20th.

The pressure from Jay's loved ones, which included

so many of his daily business associates, increased. Jake Orbin Jr. called Marjorie on Wednesday the 22nd. His parents had told him Jay was due home Monday; could he talk to her and offer some suggestions about how to handle this distressing situation? She was upset and irritated. She said that she didn't want more suggestions, she was sick of suggestions*. She told Jake that she had already explained things to her son. "Noah knows that his dad is missing and might not come home anymore. That there are terrible people out there and his dad would want him to be good and strong."† Jake wondered why she'd ever say something like that to a little boy at so early a stage.

At 1 P.M. on September 22, Marjorie called the Phoenix Police Department and officially reported Jay as a missing person. She told them he had been out of state and due home on the 20th, and was now two days late. She reported that he was driving a large white U-Haul type truck and carrying a large amount of cash.

On Thursday, more associates left messages on Jay's cell phone. One called repeatedly in succession as Jay was late for an appointment, while others called with pleas to get orders filled and out.

In the late afternoon, Jay's associate Mario Olivarez tried to flush out anyone who might've been holding or threatening Jay and controlling his phone. "I got this gold jewelry order that came in, about $50,000 worth,"

---

* Marjorie's own words repeated frequently in court transcripts, police records and author interviews.
† Police interview with Jake Orbin.

he said to the voice mail. "Call me." He hoped it might lure out some evildoer who could then be forced to reveal Jay's fate.

On Friday, September 24, Jay's longtime friend Gary Dodge called the ominously unresponsive cell phone. "Hey, Jay. A lot of people are looking for you. You need to call home. Call your wife. Do something. Or give me a call."

Jake Sr. called Jake Jr. and told him his mother was crying all the time and he really needed his elder son's help. Jake Jr. immediately notified his work, packed up his girlfriend and his dog and began the eight-hour drive from San Diego to Phoenix. En route, Jake Jr. tried to arrange with his sister-in-law to meet up with her. Jay had been missing four days now, if he had been expected home on the 20th. Marjorie told her husband's brother that she was very busy and Noah would probably have an after-school friend over and she needed to feed them and it was very inconvenient for her to meet with Jake that day. But he persisted, and she finally agreed that he could come over at six in the evening.

Before his appointment with her, Jake Jr. met up with his distraught parents, who could only tell him that they hadn't spoken to Jay since September 8. Jake, mindful of the birthday call he himself never received on the 10th, was all too aware that the 8th was the last time he'd heard his brother's voice, also. Jake headed to the public library for Internet access, where he looked up various resources, including the FBI.

He also took the step of hiring a private investigator. He told the PI to start working immediately on his brother's missing person case. The PI, with Jake's permission, hired a psychic that he trusted. But the news wasn't good; the psychic felt that "two men have been watching the warehouse for quite some time" and that it was the scene of "the crime."* The psychic reported that Jay's body would be found near his cargo van in a wooded area between Phoenix and Flagstaff. With that information, Jake then spent part of the afternoon on the phone to Flagstaff Police.

At the stroke of 6:00, Jake was in his brother's driveway. He brought his girlfriend Shelly with him, with the careful plan of keeping Noah entertained and cared for while Jake talked to the boy's mother. The first thing he noticed upon his arrival was a white plaster patch covering damage to the garage door, but Marjorie told him dismissively that she'd hit the door with her white GMC Envoy. Jake noticed, however, that not only was the Envoy undamaged, but when his eyes swiveled from the tailgate to the plaster patch, they didn't match. The tailgate wasn't high enough.

As he spoke with his sister-in-law, Jake realized that Noah was alone; there was no school chum after all. By seven-thirty, they were all hungry—including Noah—and it also registered with Jake that there had been no supper prepared for children at the house.

He ordered Chinese food and took his little nephew with him to go pick it up. As the SUV filled up with the smells of egg rolls, fried rice and General Tsao's chicken from Jasmine Palace, Jake took a call from Flagstaff PD. When the call was finished, Noah started to talk. Jake's

---

* Phoenix Police report.

nephew was trying to understand his dad being missing. He told his uncle Jake that his dad had called him, but it was "really weird." Jake didn't let the boy see his tension as Noah described his father asking how he was, pausing, then proceeding oddly to say, "Good, then, well you take care." Some of Jay's words or phrases had been repeated oddly, and then his father had hung up.

Noah felt, he told his uncle, that it was a recording, not a live conversation.

Back at the house, Jake's girlfriend Shelly was alone with Marjorie, who handed her a piece of paper and asked her to read it. Shelly started to do so, but as the first words hit her, she started to cry. The paper began, "Marjorie, if you are reading this, something has probably happened to me. I love you for giving me our son Noah . . ."

When he and Noah got back to the house, Jake was also shown the letter. Marjorie wanted her brother-in-law to see that it held instructions and information about insurance policies and other assets. But Jake could not read past the first line, just as his girlfriend had not been able to. He broke up.

Jake spent the rest of the evening amid the Chinese food boxes, going through his brother's computers looking for clues and getting details from Marjorie.

Saturday morning, September 25, Jake called his sister-in-law and said he'd like to come back over and go through more of Jay's computer information, maybe figure out when Jay last logged on to it and so forth.

Marjorie said she was very busy and she'd get back to him with a time he could come over.

So Jake and his dad drove over to Jay's warehouse instead, trying to investigate on their own. They thought the place looked secure, with a barbed wire perimeter, and could find no signs of forced entry. Joann Orbin called to say that Jay's associate Mario Olivarez had called her to let her know he'd already been by the warehouse to do the same thing. He wanted to join the Orbin men there now. The three men compared notes when Mario Olivarez arrived. There was no call from Marjorie yet, so when they parted from Olivarez, Jake Sr. and Jake Jr. headed for the public library. The younger man used the Internet services again, checking for messages from the FBI, Flagstaff Police, and every other resource he could think of.

As the weekend drew to a close, Marjorie never found time to allow Jake back into his brother's house.

CHAPTER SIX

"Unnecessary Emotion"

On Friday, September 24, 2004, Missing Persons detective Jan Butcher came into work and was handed a brand-new case. A north Phoenix housewife said her husband was overdue home from a business trip. The standard forty-eight hours since she first reported him had passed.

The first thing that Detective Butcher, a tall and lean woman with green eyes, did when she received the file on Jay Orbin was to start checking databases. She discovered that Jay had never been reported missing before and that public records on him indicated nothing but a calm and stable life, free of any hint of criminal involvement: no arrests, no warrants, nothing. By nine-thirty in the morning she was ready to call the reporting party, Marjorie Orbin.

Marjorie told the detective she had last spoken to her

husband on Friday, September 17, and he'd told her he would be home on Monday the 20th. Butcher would not learn until later that Marjorie had told pipe maker Robert Macy that Jay was already missing as early as the 16th.

In trying to rule out the typical explanations for the disappearance of a middle-aged man, Butcher asked Marjorie if it was possible that her husband was seeing someone else. The response was swift and confident: no. The detective listened carefully as Marjorie offered up details Butcher hadn't asked for. Jay had "no sex drive"; even she, his wife, was not involved with him "intimately." Odder still, Marjorie expressed a wish that Jay *would* find someone to show him "affection and tenderness."

Marjorie Orbin went on to paint an ominous picture of her husband's business activities. He carried a lot of cash, she told the detective, and his work was "high risk." He might have had as much as $30,000 on him, plus $700,000 worth of jewelry and other merchandise in the truck. He didn't tell anyone his route, even her, because of the security risks involved.

The detective had looked Jay Orbin up in the database for the Department of Motor Vehicles and found four vehicles registered to him. She read off a license plate to Marjorie and asked her if this was the vehicle she believed him to be driving when she stopped hearing from him. "I have no idea what the license plate number was," Marjorie answered. But she confirmed it was a big cargo-style truck, white in color.

"It's very important to have the correct license plate number of the vehicle he was driving," Detective Butcher urged, "so it can be entered into a nationwide database."

Marjorie promised to look for the plate number and get back to the detective. Stressing further how important the plate number was, Detective Butcher gave her alternate phone numbers to call and other detectives who would take the information and process it as soon as Marjorie found it, in case she could not reach Detective Butcher herself directly later.

Detective Butcher rang off with Marjorie and immediately dialed Jay's cell phone. It rolled over to voice mail, time stamped at 10:20 A.M. Her voice was soft and slow but professional: "Phoenix Police, Friday 10:20 A.M. This is Detective Butcher, Jay. I am following up on a Missing Persons report on you." She left her number. "I just need to make sure you are okay."

Butcher then began the process of subpoenaing Jay's cell phone records and bringing in more resources to check more databases.

By Monday, September 27, Detective Butcher still had not received any messages from Marjorie with the license plate of the van her husband was believed to be driving. She had not received any messages from Marjorie at all.

In all of Butcher's years as a Missing Persons detective, this lack of contact stood out as atypical behavior. At eight o'clock that morning, she herself initiated a phone conversation with Marjorie Orbin. She found Marjorie irritated about a business associate of Jay's named Mario Olivarez, who had been calling all over the country checking hospitals for John Does. Marjorie complained that Olivarez had been calling her six to eight times a day to check for new information on Jay's case. Olivarez wasn't even a good friend of Jay's, Marjorie said to the detective, they were barely business associates. In fact, she groused, he owed Jay $30,000.

Marjorie also complained about another of Jay's friends, Jim Rogers. This man, she unloaded, was not as successful as Jay and was thoroughly jealous of him. The two were in the same business and now Jim had started calling Jay's clients cross-country and telling them that he was missing. Marjorie thought it was odd that he would interfere like that.

On the other hand, Marjorie had a small piece of good news. Of the several people who had received phone calls from Jay the previous Monday, Marjorie had located one who had spoken to him directly. But she did not specify who.

The detective wanted to know about the state of the Orbins' financial affairs. Marjorie said everything was fine. In fact, Jay paid all their bills, utilities and so forth six months to a year in advance. He did this, she said, so the family would be in good shape if he ever had a bad month at the business.

After the two hung up, Detective Jan Butcher's phone rang. The male voice on the other end introduced himself as Jay Orbin's brother, Jake Orbin Jr. He had learned from his parents that Jay was missing, and he assured the detective it was very unusual behavior for his brother not to return home or to call anyone. Jake was phoning from San Diego, he said, but was returning to Phoenix right away. At Jake's request, the detective made arrangements to meet the next day. Jake also said, cautiously, that while he and his parents were frantic, his sister-in-law Marjorie did not seem very concerned.

Detective Jan Butcher next spoke directly to Mario Olivarez. In contrast to what Marjorie had said, Olivarez described himself as a twenty-five-year friend and colleague of Jay's. Olivarez wanted the detective to know that Jay was very organized and his business was "his love."* He assured her that Jay was not involved in drugs. Olivarez was concerned that he and several of his and Jay's mutual associates had received attempted phone calls from Jay in quick succession on the previous Monday, but no one had actually spoken to the missing man. Olivarez thought this had to mean that Jay was in trouble. He wondered if his friend had driven off the road, perhaps was now in a ditch, unable to speak but somehow able to hit speed dial. He was very worried. Disappearing was the last thing Jay Orbin would ever do: he fairly worshipped his little boy. On top of that, Jay was very social, always in contact with everyone and highly predictable and regular in his habits.

At one that afternoon, Detective Butcher, joined by Detective Mary Roberts, drove out to Jay Orbin's warehouse in the industrial district of south Phoenix. The warehouse for Jayhawk International was a good twenty-mile drive from the Orbins' home on 55th Street. As Detective Butcher let herself into the warehouse through the unlocked front door, the first thing she saw was a tall, blond-haired female approaching. She was very slim, and she was wearing black exercise

* Mario Olivarez's words, per Phoenix Police report.

pants. Her platinum ponytail poked through a baseball cap and tumbled past her shoulders. She introduced herself as Marjorie Orbin.

Marjorie told the detectives that she was at the warehouse picking up things needed to keep the business running. But she didn't have time to stay here and talk further to them about Jay's case. She had to run back up north to pick up her son Noah from school. Soon she was striding out the door, her ponytail swishing away.

The warehouse stored racks of kachina dolls, Indian pottery, bow-and-arrow sets, baskets, necklaces, Indian artifacts and similarly themed items. But what caught Detective Jan Butcher's eye the most was located at the far end of the warehouse: a large white cargo truck. "As soon as I saw the white truck at the warehouse," Detective Jan Butcher would later say, "I knew something was up. I was concerned."

She called into the office and switched her database search from the white cargo van to the green Eddie Bauer edition Ford Bronco.

She started getting hits.

Also present at the warehouse that morning were an elderly couple who introduced themselves as Jake and Joann Orbin, Jay's parents. Another officer, Detective Amy Dillon, arrived to help interview the pair. Jake Sr. told Detective Dillon that he couldn't believe his son would have any kind of "second life" with another woman; he just didn't have time. He said his son got along with everyone, had no enemies or medical or psychological problems. He himself was staying positive about Jay's location, but his wife was crying all the time and "thinking the worst."

Detective Butcher took Joann Orbin into an office area of the business.

The two women talked about Jay and what his mother described as his generous nature and big heart. She said that her grandson Noah and his father "idolized" each other. She mentioned Mario Olivarez and Jim Rogers as two of Jay's good friends and seemed unaware of the alleged animosity Marjorie had mentioned in regards to these two men.

Joann said she had called Jay on his business line on Saturday the 13th. The call had rolled over to the home line and Marjorie had answered, mentioning to her mother-in-law that she was in the middle of epoxy coating the garage floor.

Detective Butcher wanted to know if that was unusual.

No, Joann Orbin responded, her daughter-in-law was very handy and frequently attended do-it-yourself classes at Home Depot. She then put her skills to use at home, laying tile, painting and even repositioning the kitchen island.

Detective Butcher asked the missing man's mother a delicate question. Was it possible her son had a girlfriend? No, Joann told her, Jay did not have time for a girlfriend. In fact, she told the detective, her son was "married to his work."

Back in mid-September, on 58th Street just above Bell Road, Andy MacGregor had been out walking his dog when he noticed an SUV parked curbside. He saw it there for the next several days.

Sometime around the 16th of September Gordon Bourn also noticed the same Bronco sitting across the street from his house for days. From his backyard one day he heard some noise, so he went out front and saw a woman with a long blond ponytail and black exercise pants tinkering with the car. He thought she was "pretty skinny." He approached her and asked if she needed help. She seemed to be having trouble getting the car to start. The woman was not eager to be helped. She told him that the car belonged to her "flaky little sister" and she needed to jump-start it for her. Bourn offered, but again she declined to be helped.

Bourn stood by as the engine made futile clicking noises and refused to turn over. Bourn noticed the sunshade across the dash. In the September sunshine, that car would need it.

He saw the blond woman there another time, but again she refused help.

By September 19, Gordon Bourn was ready to stop being so nice about it. He called the police and reported the Bronco as abandoned.

Several other people who lived nearby also started reporting the Bronco at the curb.

One day an official orange sticker of some kind appeared on the vehicle. The next day there was a white SUV parked back-to-back with the Bronco and a tall white woman with a long ponytail and black pants fussing with the car.

Andy MacGregor saw the orange tag and the woman with the blond ponytail, too. He noticed her because she was scratching the orange tag off the Bronco. She caught his attention because she seemed to be looking around nervously as she scraped.

On the database search directed at the Bronco's license plate number, Detective Jan Butcher found a citation for abandonment. But there was no location for the abandoned SUV listed in this file. Butcher called the meter maid listed on the citation. The meter maid remembered the Bronco, but struggled to recall the location off the top of her head. But she called back later with the address; she had tagged the vehicle, she said, but when she'd returned to tow it, it was gone.

The address the meter maid gave was less than six blocks from Jay Orbin's home.

Butcher and a partner left the warehouse and headed north. They started knocking on doors at the address the meter maid had given to Butcher. The two detectives found Gordon Bourn and many others who remembered the truck.

Butcher found the story of the "skinny blonde" in black athletic pants, which many of the neighbors reported, highly interesting. She had met a woman who exactly matched that description, down to the black pants and ponytail, just hours earlier in Jay Orbin's warehouse.

Detective Jan Butcher called Marjorie. The detective did not mention that the Bronco had been spotted six blocks from Marjorie and Jay's house, but she did tell her that the K-9 team had not been available today and she would need to return to the warehouse in the

morning so the dogs could search it. She offered that
Marjorie could meet them there, but Marjorie preferred
to just give the detective the access code for the security
system; she did not feel the need to be present while
they searched the building for her husband. The detective then informed Marjorie that she needed to come
by the house now to look through Jay's things. There
might be clues in his pockets or drawers or desk files as
to what his plans were or who might wish to harm him.

But Marjorie said no, the detectives could not come by
the house that evening. She had to go to Noah's school to
help out with something. She was simply not available.

Butcher now had the missing man's relatives and
longtime friends and associates acting one way, and
the man's wife acting another. She was tracking financial activity and saw the man's wife spending large
amounts, making large cash transfers and withdrawals. She'd heard about a garage floor resurfacing with
epoxy, done by hand. She had several witnesses, including a meter maid, who had sighted the green Bronco
in an abandoned condition days *before* Jay Orbin had
been reported missing. And the vehicle had been within
walking distance of the missing man's home. And now
the detective had a wife who was not keen on having
law enforcement inside that home.

Then there was the white cargo van at the warehouse.
The missing man's wife, actually on the premises when
the detective had arrived, could not have failed to know
that this truck was *not* missing.

On Tuesday, September 28, the day after the visit
to the Jayhawk International premises, Detective Jan
Butcher assembled a SWAT team.

At six-thirty that morning, after working past nine the evening before in the neighborhood where the Bronco had been sighted, Butcher was at the warehouse to meet the K-9 unit. The dogs did not detect Jay there. By 8 A.M., Butcher was phoning Noah's school to see if Marjorie Orbin had had any involvement in his class.

And she started calling Marjorie herself. She got voice mail and left a message. She continued leaving messages throughout the day.

Marjorie did not return the detective's calls, but she withdrew $5,000 cash from one of Jay's accounts.

Detective Butcher was watching. She was faxing back and forth to Jay's bankers and following the activity, including on his credit cards.

Jake Orbin Jr., Jake Orbin Sr. and Joann Orbin arrived at Detective Jan Butcher's office that afternoon. The family filled in the detective on Jay's financial generosity, especially toward Marjorie. They talked about a damaged spot in the garage door of Marjorie's home. Butcher, who had seen a briefcase at the warehouse, wanted to know if Jay carried a briefcase when he traveled. His family all agreed that he did: he simply would not travel without it. They also were unanimous that it would be very unusual for Jay to take the Bronco on a road trip. It was a reliable vehicle, they said, but it was not equipped to handle the cargo that Jay transported.

Joann Orbin passed along photos that Marjorie had given her just the day before, on Monday. The photos were of items that Marjorie told her mother-in-law she was taking from the warehouse to her home. The detective accepted the photos and impounded them into evidence.

All three members of Jay's family had spoken to him

on his birthday, September 8, twenty days earlier. Not one of them had spoken to him since.

Jake Jr. then dropped an ominous bit of information. On the day he arrived in Phoenix, his young nephew, Noah, had mentioned to him that he had spoken to his father on the phone after he had left on the road trip. However, the child was puzzled because the conversation was so "weird." His father, Noah had explained, had paused at odd moments, as if trying to have an interactive conversation, but not really matching Noah's own responses. Jake Jr. had asked the second grader if he knew why he, his uncle, was in town that day. Yes, the boy said, it was because his daddy probably wasn't coming home. Jake Jr. had winced. He told the detective it was an odd thing for the child to say.

Detective Butcher had to agree.

After the family left, Butcher continued monitoring Marjorie's activities. By 4:40 that afternoon she was asking WalMart for surveillance video.

At 6 P.M., after having left several messages during the day, Butcher finally received a call back from Marjorie. In her calm and quiet way, Butcher explained to the housewife that she felt she was not making herself available to help with the investigation. Marjorie responded, "You think that, huh? I'm surprised that you would say that."* She had still never provided the plate number for the cargo van. Detective Butcher informed her that Jay's Bronco had been sighted very close to her home; she asked Marjorie what she had to say about

---

* From Phoenix Police transcripts of the call.

that. Marjorie said that first of all, she'd have to know who claimed to have seen it and whether or not they had a plate number. In any case, she thought it was "weird" but did not know what to make of it.

She did, however, have an opinion about her in-laws. They were "running around like chickens with their heads cut off, running in circles, stirring up unnecessary emotion and effort that's not being productive." She did not like that they were calling Jay's customers all over the country. Getting the news out that Jay was missing, Marjorie complained, would just cause her problems: customers would stop paying on their accounts, she believed, if it got out Jay was AWOL.

Detective Butcher decided it was time to turn up the pressure. She said that she had called Noah's school, and Marjorie had *not* been there the night before. Now Marjorie got angry. She said she *was* at the school but a lot of other places as well. She was *very* busy and she did not know she had to report every single thing to the detective.

Detective Butcher now asked Marjorie if she'd be willing to take a polygraph test right away. In an angry voice Marjorie reported this to someone in the background. A truculent male voice responded, "You tell her to go fuck herself!"

Butcher calmly asked Marjorie whose voice she'd just heard. In an echo of the unseen male, Marjorie answered, "None of your fucking business. A friend of mine."

Marjorie then changed her tone. She wanted to explain, she said. About her relationship with Jay, it just wasn't the kind of "entanglement that begets that kind of emotion." Having another man around, she implied, would not be a reason for "trouble." After all, she and Jay were not "intimate." She did have a "great deal of love and respect for the man," but she had something to reveal: she and Jay were no longer even married.

The detective was not happy to be getting such an important piece of information this late in the game. She confronted Marjorie about not mentioning it earlier.

Marjorie's ire returned. How was she supposed to know what the detective was going to want? Did she have to report the color of her toenail polish, as well?* The detective asked her to simply be honest. Was she supposed to be "completely honest about everything in the entire world?" Marjorie retorted.

She then continued to urge that jealousy not be an issue the detective should be exploring, because she and Jay were good friends. They originally divorced, she said, to protect Jay from an IRS debt that Marjorie had carried over from a previous marriage. They represented themselves as husband and wife but privately lived rather separate lives. Jay was even planning on buying a separate house nearby so he could live on his own but still be near Noah. So far, she had promised Jay that she would not reveal their divorced status, so as to "avoid humiliating the man." Marjorie then editorialized that all Jay's family and friends "think he has been living a normal perfect little life with a pretty wife and a beautiful child and everything is happy and rosy and it has all been a farce—well, not a farce but a facade."

The detective asked Marjorie about Jay's bank accounts.

---

* From the transcript of the recording of the call.

Marjorie admitted she had been making withdrawals and moving money around. She also admitted she was not a signer on any of the accounts. But she was only doing what Jay had asked her to do, she insisted. She volunteered to the detective that she had both Jay's will and his power of attorney and that in the will, she "gets everything, no one else gets a penny."

Butcher returned to the subject of Jay's personal life, asking about the possibility of Jay having a girlfriend. Marjorie's first response was "I hope he did, I hope he did." But she went on to say she didn't think it could be true and that it was physically unlikely. When pressed a bit, she again spelled out what she had already told Butcher in their very first conversation, that Jay was sexually impotent.

At last, Detective Jan Butcher confronted Marjorie with the information that she had several witnesses who had seen a blond Caucasian female in a white SUV near the Bronco. Marjorie interrupted and let her know she was not impressed. There were probably fifty white SUVs nearby, she pointed out. But the detective explained the witnesses had seen *her* getting into and out of the Bronco. Marjorie's answer was vague: "I wouldn't know anything about that."

But she began to stammer, "How do they—suppose I've—taken care of—this situation. And what—is the crime?"

Detective Butcher simply said it was a Missing Persons investigation. But she wanted to know what Marjorie's own gut instinct was telling her: was Jay dead or alive? Marjorie said she had no way of telling, but she didn't feel fearful because she didn't think he was dead.* She said she couldn't get all emotional because she was "more of a logic-based person."

At last, the detective turned her attention to the missing man's only child. What had Noah Orbin been told about the situation? Marjorie said she had informed him that his dad was missing and the possibilities included that his truck might have broken down, or he might have been in an accident, or "he could be dead." She had told him that "some bad guy could have robbed him and killed him and that would be terrible but you know what he'd want us to do: be brave and take care of each other."

Marjorie then volunteered to the detective that she now had male friends spending time with Noah in order to "give him the contact he needs" and that she had been "enlisting people to do it intentionally." She'd arranged a sleepover for the boy, and the little friend's father had spent some extra time with Noah.

Detective Jan Butcher had heard enough.

---

* Moments earlier Marjorie had emphasized to the detective that she had the right to move money around in Jay's accounts because she was the executor of his will. If she believed him to be alive, as these optimistic statements claim, she could hardly have been acting as executor.

CHAPTER SEVEN

Action

At sunset on September 28, SWAT team member Victor Roman was dispatched to do surveillance on the Orbin residence in preparation for an evening raid. He parked his car a little bit down the road and watched, working on a hand-drawn diagram to help the team later on. After five to ten minutes a well-muscled man emerged from the residence. "He looked up and down the street and eventually saw me. He walked toward me with a purpose. I made a U-turn and drove away. He broke out into a run, chased my vehicle, pointing his finger at me and yelling at me. It was very unusual. I had never had that happen before."

Well after nightfall, a full SWAT team in protective gear approached the front door of the 55th Street residence. They loudly proclaimed their intention to serve a lawful search warrant and demanded entrance. From inside, they could hear adult voices, both male and female, but there was no response to the SWAT team. The commands were repeated, but the people inside again gave no response.

This time, instead of to the private citizens, an order was directed to the team: ram the door.

The battering ram punched through the front door, and Victor Roman was the first one to charge through. "Ten to twelve feet back a male was standing. A female was behind him. I yelled 'Get down! get down!' He refused. He clenched his fists and raised them to his waistline in a hostile manner. He was the same guy who had chased me. I kept walking toward him—he was not complying. I hit him aside with my open palm, pushed him to make my entry. I did not see what happened next."

Everybody else, including Marjorie Orbin, did see.

Two tiny points flew forward, trailing long wires, and landed on the man's flesh. From the handheld Taser, 300 kV traveled down the wires and forced the man to do what the officers wanted—drop to the floor.

The man's big muscles didn't matter anymore. His fists went limp, his arms twitched, and his legs went slack. The cold ceramic tile hit his face full-force, and the unidentified man lay tasting his own blood.*

An open phone line crackled nearby. Marjorie had been talking to her brother-in-law when the SWAT team arrived. She had been standing behind the now bleeding man when the officers came crashing through. Marjorie

---

* In a dispute with police over what happened that night, he claimed he was also kicked and punched.

dropped to the floor of her own accord when she saw what had happened to her erstwhile protector. She started screaming that there was a child in the house. SWAT team members were already heading down the hall.

In the bathroom, they found a white blond eight-year-old boy, wide-eyed.

Marjorie then screamed toward the phone, "Jake, if you are still listening, please come watch Noah!"

Detective Jan Butcher entered the house. In Noah's bedroom, the detective with the gentle green eyes spoke carefully with the child. He had last seen his father around his own eighth birthday in August, he said, somewhat matter-of-factly. Then he pointed to a picture of a stream on his wall. It was given to him recently by his mother, he wanted to tell his visitor. The tall lady in the bulky vest agreed with him that that was a pretty cool picture. He showed her his new night-light. Butcher took note of the child's demeanor in this frightening situation, for any clues it might contain about his father's fate or his mother's actions, then deftly handed him over to another member of the team who carried him out of the house.

In the well-kept home, the team found one room devoted to a tanning bed. They confiscated some blond hair extensions lying on the floor there, and some from the trash as well. In the hallway, quite a few picture frames on the wall were empty. The rest were filled with family photos—but none of them featured Jay.

In the master bedroom Marjorie's clothes filled her closet and drawers, but men's clothing was scarce. As everywhere in the house, the drawers were neat and organized. There were a few items such as men's briefs in the drawers—bikini style—and some shirts and pants hanging in the closet. None of them looked as if they could fit a 260-pound man. The men's underwear was in bright colors and appeared straight from the package new.

Several of the dresser drawers were completely empty. A further check revealed a jumbled heap of men's clothing, this time in Jay's size, in a bin as if for discard.

Also in the master bedroom were a brand-new Pioneer stereo system, DVD player and home theater loudspeaker system. They were so new they were still in boxes, unopened, around the bed.

Upon entering the home, Detective Butcher had seen a large piano, a baby grand, on full display in the living room. It was a very expensive piece, equipped with a "player" mechanism so that it could move its keys automatically. A family could enjoy actual piano music without anyone having to know how to play. The price tag on this item was close to $12,000. Receipts from the Piano Gallery on Scottsdale Road, dated just days earlier, were found in the master bedroom. In a black purse tucked away in a drawer was over $3,000 in cash.

Detective Butcher was ready to have another conversation with Marjorie. She hoped it would be more productive than the one she'd had on the phone with her a few hours earlier.

Marjorie was in cuffs now and her attitude much chastened. She had been cooperative with the SWAT team ever since the man at her side had been Tasered.

Her hair was several inches shorter than it had been the day before at the warehouse. Detective Butcher read

Marjorie her Miranda rights. When that was taken care of, the first thing the detective wanted to know was what was the name of that man, the one they'd had to Taser. He was Larry Weisberg, Marjorie said; she had known him two or three months. They'd met at LA Fitness, a gym on the north side, and, yes, Marjorie conceded, they were intimately involved. Noah, she said, had known his mother's boyfriend for about a month.

In an aside, Marjorie complained that the child's social life was going to be ruined in the neighborhood because of the police raid.

Until this moment, Marjorie had been prickly and uncooperative in all her dealings with the police, which had been mostly over the phone. In her SWAT vest and regalia, Detective Butcher brought the full force and power of her position to ask Marjorie Orbin the main question: did she know where Jay was?

"No," she responded, "I wish I did."

"When did you last speak with Jay?"

"It was Friday [September 17]."

"Do you know what time?"

"It was after Noah came home from school." Marjorie was eager to add that "Noah also talked with Jay during this time."

"Is Jay involved in anything illegal?"

"No. Jay's a Boy Scout."

"Is anybody mad at Jay?"

"His brother. Jake is jealous of Jay. And Jim Rogers, Jay's ex-partner, is jealous of Jay."

"Did Jay know about Larry?"

"Jay knew that I knew Larry and we worked out together, but Jay did not know we were involved. But

Jay and I had started to talk about living separate lives. Jay is not a sexual person and cannot 'do' anything."

In another part of the house, Detective Amy Dillon was facing off with Larry Weisberg, a man who *could* apparently "do" something, but who, in a display of courtliness, was not admitting to anything that might besmirch the lady in question's name.

Even with his forehead and nose trickling blood, cut and smashed from his impact with the floor's ceramic tiles and then some restraining actions, Weisberg had not lost his machismo. He wanted the detective to know he lived across the street from the mayor of the city of Phoenix, and if the SWAT team wanted to go to Weisberg's house and break his door down, he had nothing to hide. If they did so, he added, he'd just "walk across the street," presumably to pull strings through his neighbor the mayor. He said he was Marjorie's friend and had met her at the gym about three months ago. He exhibited a protective attitude toward her, telling the detectives they were "barking up the wrong tree" and that what they expected to find in her home was "beyond my imagination." He pointed toward Marjorie down the hall. "She does not know one thing. She is worried sick because of that little guy [Noah] in there."

He said Jay Orbin was Marjorie's ex-husband and had been planning to move out soon. He had no idea if Jay had a girlfriend. When pressed further about the nature of his own relationship with Marjorie, Weisberg said it wasn't his place to disclose anything further. As far as he knew, the Orbins had "an arrangement" where

Jay provided so Marjorie could take care of Noah and all was fine and that's all he'd say.

He himself had "never met the man" and wouldn't know him if he bumped into him in a store or on the sidewalk.

His animosity toward Detective Jan Butcher came out frequently as he dismissively referred to Detective Dillon's "partner in there." He said he and Marjorie had been trying to get answers from Butcher, without success. This statement was in direct contradiction to the official record, which showed that Marjorie almost never called Butcher, had rebuffed her at the warehouse the day before, and had ignored several phone calls from her that very day. Weisberg affirmed, "We're totally innocent." When asked details of Jay's whereabouts and his recent trip, he said that Jay had been in town after September 8, although he himself hadn't known at the time, but "your partner in there knows it." He was unclear when Jay had last been seen and seemed to be somewhat detached. But he seemed to have a favorable opinion of the missing man, to the extent of his knowledge of him. He didn't know much about the man's recent movements, but he was certain that Jay "idolized Noah and vice versa" and that he seemed like a decent enough man who never missed calling his young son. He understood Jay to be having some kind of trouble with his cell phone. He said Jay drove around in a truck with a lot of jewelry, but other than that he knew nothing about Jay's business and did not care to know. Police noted that Weisberg referred to Jay in the present tense, as one would when discussing someone presumed alive. The use of tense is something police pay attention to when dealing with persons of interest in a serious crime investigation. It is a clue into that person's mind-set and what that person knows in contrast to what police still consider an unknown.

Larry Weisberg denied that he was living in Marjorie's house. He did pretty well for himself, he asserted; after all, his own house was across the street from the city's mayor. He was a production manager at a successful marketing concern. Ultimately, he admitted that he thought Marjorie and Jay's relationship was a little strange, but it was none of his business. Marjorie, he said, was a good woman and highly intelligent.

He refused to go into any further detail about his relationship with her or the feelings he might have for her. But he wasn't surprised the detective would want to know. "I can understand where you're coming from. You know, am I gonna knock off this guy?" He laughed then and said, "I don't even know what he looks like."

Weisberg was taken downtown. His bloody face was photographed, his prints were taken. But he was soon released.

Noah did not attend school the day after the raid. He did not return to school for a full week.

Multiple files had been removed from the 55th Street home during the raid. Over the next several days, Detective Jan Butcher waded into them and made a lot of phone calls to banks and merchants. She called Larry Little, Jay's insurance agent, who told her the same thing that all of Jay's friends and associates had been telling her since the investigation began: Jay was a highly responsible man, a creature of habit, well loved and not at all able to walk out of his son's life voluntarily. He had insurance policies on his vehicles, his buildings and his life. In fact, he had two separate policies on his life, but the policies were not both made out in favor of Marjorie. One was for the benefit of someone named Marshall Roosin.

Butcher had already talked to Roosin, Jay's longtime friend and business associate. He had called her the day after the raid at Marjorie's. He had been on a cruise, he told her, and had only recently heard that Jay had gone missing. He told her he was putting his own business resources on the case. He owned a car lot and had set his "repo" man to checking "the system" for Jay's missing Bronco. He also had jewelry contacts searching high and low for cheap silver jewelry coming onto the market, in case Jay had been robbed for his inventory. He was worried that Jay could have fallen victim to something awful on the road.

Marshall Roosin told the detective that he'd been friends with Jay for twenty years, and he also "factored" Jay's receivables. This meant Jay went on the road to sell his jewelry wholesale to shops, and gave these retail customers thirty, sixty, or ninety days to pay. But Jay himself needed cash to keep his inventory up. So every month Jay sold Roosin his new receivables and paid for his old receivables. Roosin volunteered that he required Jay to keep an insurance policy in his favor because Jay's business was dependent on sales that could fluctuate wildly. The insurance policy was to protect him in case Jay was unable to make good on the accounts.

Roosin also knew about the paperwork with instructions for Marjorie in case something happened to Jay.

He said that Jay had a deep fear of getting in an accident because he spent so much time on the road. He knew Jay wanted to be prepared, as he was for everything, and that he, Roosin, was the one whom Marjorie was supposed to turn to if anything bad happened, per Jay's instructions.

Marshall Roosin also told Butcher about how the paperwork had not showed up on the 15th of September. It was now the 30th, and he still hadn't seen it. It was all very unlike Jay, he assured her. Jay wrote lists and followed schedules "to the nth degree." He told her Jay would never leave town without his checkbook. Roosin did not believe that Jay would carry a lot of cash with him on his person. If he had a couple thousand, he told Butcher, that would be an unusually high amount.

Over the course of their twenty-year friendship, Roosin said he would not describe Jay as a drinker, nor had he ever known him to be involved with drugs.

He believed that Jay considered Marjorie the love of his life. Like so many others, Roosin couldn't conceive of Jay having a girlfriend on the side, even if he was wrong about Jay's feelings for Marjorie, because his friend simply didn't have time.

He was less positive about Marjorie's fidelity, though if she had someone on the side, he didn't know about it. He did know that she went to the gym an awful lot. Roosin repeated what Marjorie's mother-in-law had already mentioned to the detective, that Marjorie was very handy around the house. She could lay tile, build room additions and was even good at automotive body repair work.

Marshall Roosin told the detective he believed Jay

had never come home from his Hurricane Frances trip. He based this on the missing paperwork, his inability to reach him, and on the things Marjorie had said. He himself had called Jay at 11 P.M. on September 8 to wish him a happy birthday. He'd gotten voice mail. Jay had not called him back. He left another birthday message for him the next day. That call was not returned, either.

Detective Butcher then dangled a bit of information out in the open air: Jay's white truck was at the Phoenix warehouse right now.

Roosin had been a friend of Jay's for twenty years, and he was the person Jay expected the mother of his child to turn to. Upon hearing that the white truck was at the Phoenix warehouse, the detective wrote in her report, Marshall Roosin "freaked out."

Detective Butcher talked to a cavalcade of Jay's friends, including Mario Olivarez, who told her all the people in Jay's business life were "good people." Indeed, all sounded deeply concerned about Jay, far more concerned than his wife, Marjorie, did. Marjorie had told the detective that Jay did business with a bunch of "con men." Butcher kept looking for evidence of criminal activity, but she found none. She had many conversations with Jay's frantic friends and family, very few with Marjorie. She talked to neighbors on 55th Street who told her about a muscled blond man who was often at the Orbins' house and who played basketball in the driveway with Noah. She kept an eye on Jay's accounts and watched Marjorie spend and spend.

Detective Jan Butcher was also looking hard at the

calendar. She called United Parcel Service, where Jay had a regular account. She found the last date anyone had shipped anything out of the warehouse: September 8.

She also heard more from the Orbins' neighbors. Marjorie, she found, had made a deep impression on people. One neighbor described her as "the most unfriendly person I have ever met" and claimed that at Noah's school Marjorie was referred to as "Barbie" behind her back. Neighbor Stuart Cramer had the kindest things to say about Marjorie, calling her "an intense lady and hardworking." More neighbors detectives interviewed continued to describe Marjorie as "unfriendly."

Neighbor Carl Brown told the investigative team that he saw Thunderbird Painting at Marjorie's house the week Jay had been reported missing. He watched a crew paint on the exterior of her house, and Marjorie herself painting the garage door. Later the same day he also noticed a patch on the garage door where she had just painted.

Neighbor Lou Dziedzic had also seen the Thunderbird Painting crew working on the exterior of Marjorie's house. He had not seen the green Bronco recently. Neighbor Arlen Wong had noticed the older man with the impressive build playing basketball in the driveway with Noah. Wong was a substitute teacher at Copper Canyon, the school Noah attended. He said that to his knowledge, Marjorie was not involved in the activities there.

Detectives Alan Pfohl and Jan Butcher next drove over to Larry Weisberg's street and started canvassing his neighbors. No one there had ever seen the green Bronco.

Butcher followed paper trails of both Marjorie's

activities and Jay's. The purchases each had made often led the detective to surveillance tapes from Kohl's, WalMart, Exxon and more. She continued to check on Jay's last-known activities in Tucson, but found little evidence there of anything other than a tired and hungry salesman settling in for the evening.

She followed up on Marjorie's assertion that Jay was planning to buy himself a separate home nearby. Marjorie had not come forth with contact information for any real estate agents, so Butcher contacted the state real estate department and started from scratch. She narrowed it down and made cold calls until she found the correct agent, a man named Tom Ellis, who knew the Orbins from Noah's karate school. Sure, Ellis told her, Jay *had* been looking at a house nearby. It was in foreclosure and looked like a good investment, but Ellis seemed surprised and puzzled when the detective asked if Jay intended to occupy the house himself. Not at all, Ellis said. It was just an investment. Furthermore the deal had already fallen through well before the time Jay went missing, so Ellis didn't understand how it could figure into Jay's disappearance. He said it was "totally out of character" for Jay to be missing; he just wasn't the type of person to walk away.

Detective Jan Butcher had had the SWAT team briefed on September 28 that the case was a Missing Persons investigation that was a possible homicide. Marjorie's behavior was sending up a flurry of red flags: she was uncooperative, was liquidating the missing man's assets quickly, was being coached by a hostile and unknown male, and was giving details about the subject's last known movements that did not always add up. Many of Jay's friends had told the detective that Jay traveled with a gun at all times in order to be able to protect himself if necessary. The detectives were very interested in that gun. Marjorie had not volunteered whether she knew its current whereabouts.

By mid-October, Butcher was still trying to determine when Jay Orbin was last known to be alive. Marjorie claimed both she and Noah had spoken to him as late as September 17, but others had been complaining of his unresponsiveness much earlier. Besides Marjorie, no one else could verify they had spoken to Jay himself any later than September 8. Marshall Roosin had even begun to "miss" connections with Jay as early as 11 P.M. on September 8 itself. So when during the course of her voluminous phone calls and follow-ups over the next few weeks, the detective found a supplier who was certain she had spoken to Jay Orbin on September 9, Butcher was highly interested. Marjorie had already begun to use Jay's travel credit card for large purchases by September 9. If he was alive and well and doing business on September 9, his wife's use of the credit card was likely authorized by him. That might cast all of Marjorie's subsequent purchasing behavior in a new light. Was it possible that Jay was even now alive and in collusion with his wife, perhaps in regards to insurance fraud or debt evasion?

The supplier with the September 9 date was Kachina House of Sedona. Firmly planted in Indian country, Sedona, Arizona, was a center of commerce for Indian artisans. The Kachina House produced and brokered items largely from the Southwest tribes such as Navajo and Hopi but also from tribes as far away as Alaska. With its five-thousand-square-foot warehouse, it had room to be inclusive. Kachina House proprietor Patty Topel told the detective she was absolutely certain that she had spoken to Jay on September 9, and he had placed an order. She had the paperwork to prove it. Detective Butcher very much wanted to see that paperwork. Topel said she'd put it in the mail. She was sorry about Jay being missing, everyone liked him. It was very unlike him to do such a thing on purpose.

On October 20, 2004, Detective Butcher received a piece of mail postmarked Sedona, Arizona. With great interest, she opened it up. It held an invoice #006805 from Kachina House. The customer was Jayhawk. The name Jay Orbin was written on it, with the notation "to be delivered in 2 weeks." There was a Post-it note attached to the invoice. On the Post-it was written "ordered 9/9 2:40 pm." The invoice itself was also dated 9/9/04.

The date on this invoice would baffle and intrigue investigators for many more months. Finally, in June of 2005, the team called Topel back. They were studying the phone records and had found two phone calls between the Kachina House and Jay, one around eleven-thirty in the morning and the other around two in the afternoon of September 8, 2004. They could find no calls between the two after that. Topel told them the phone records must be correct. She said she had written out the invoice directly after speaking to Jay the last time. She said that she often made mistakes with dates, and she must have made one this time.

Once again, it seemed no one other than Marjorie claimed to have any evidence Jay was alive after September 8, 2004.

Also in mid-October, insurance agent Larry Little received a phone call from Marjorie Orbin. She knew her husband had insurance policies, she told him, and she had this sheet of instructions from Jay. She wanted to know when the insurance would pay out. There would be no payout, Little explained, for quite some time. Jay was a missing person, he told her, not a dead one. It would take years, not weeks, of no sign of him before Jay could be legally declared dead. Only then, Little said, could the policies pay out. Marjorie Orbin said she hadn't known that. The conversation ended and she hung up.

Since that first Friday, September 24, 2004, when Jake Jr. had arrived in town and ended up driving with Noah to pick up Chinese food, none of the Orbins had been invited back to Marjorie's home, with the exception of the night that the house was raided and Marjorie had screamed into the dropped phone for Jake to come and pick up Noah. But even then, though Noah spent some time with his Uncle Jake and Child Services, Marjorie hadn't spent the night in jail and Noah came home that same evening. The family was anxious to talk to Marjorie and piece together as many details as they could to help determine exactly what Jay's movements might have been, but she was always busy. She felt persecuted by now. She was suspicious of how the police had interpreted what they saw in her home, and how they'd asked about things they'd found—or hadn't found, such as photos of Jay—there. She did not want anyone else coming in and judging her and reading into things in a way that wasn't necessary.

"She said she was upset by the fact that I talked to police about that hole in the garage door and how she patched it and painted the whole door a day from the trip that I came in on Friday [September 24]," recalled Jake Orbin Jr. "Meanwhile, the concerns were that 'my brother's missing, everybody's looking for him but you, and here you were working on your house as if there's not a care in the world!' There's red flags popping up everywhere. 'Now, why weren't you doing anything?' And she would say that she was trying to run a business but . . . she wasn't doing any business work. She was shopping at every store every day for three weeks straight, four days in a row."

At last, Jake Jr. offered a compromise. They did not need to come to the house, if it upset her that much. But they very much wanted to see her and talk with her. Jake offered to have them all meet at a park. Marjorie agreed to do so and picked the park. The meeting would be October 16, a Saturday, at Road Runner Park. Part of the urgency of meeting in the park was the elder Orbins' longing to see their grandson. "My parents still hadn't seen Noah," said Jake Jr., "since probably [his birthday] party."

Waiting at the park for Marjorie, the family was eager for the reunion but became upset when she arrived. As she came into view, they could see an unknown man with her. The implications were galling to them. The attractive and highly muscled man, who had two little boys with him, kept his distance. Marjorie explained she had brought the man and the children so that Noah would have someone to play with while she talked to the Orbins. The family did not know who he was or that the park had been chosen because it was across the street from the man's daughter's house and the two boys were his grandsons.

The Orbins did not feel the meeting was very productive. They expressed their anxiety to her that Jay at least be found. Don't worry, she tossed off, he'll be found soon.

With that, she strode off with the family's only grandchild at her side.

CHAPTER EIGHT

A Set of Keys

On Saturday, October 23, 2004, Robert Aime had left his trailer to get beer and barbecue meat. On his trek back across the desert, he sat down on a blue Rubbermaid tub for a cigarette and a sip. He got curious. He made the discovery of his life, ran back across the desert and asked store clerks to call 911.

Detective Dave Barnes was called out that day. A tall man with a long face and blue eyes, he had been promoted to Homicide just a few months earlier. On Saturday, October 23, 2004, the weather was the kind that made Phoenix famous, a perfect seventy-two degrees with clear skies. Twenty-four hours after rain, the desert was redolent with herbal breezes and spangled with sunlight reflecting in puddles.

Detective Barnes had never heard of Jay Orbin or

the Missing Persons investigation that Detective Jan Butcher was conducting.

The grisly discovery in the blue tub made the news. For the city of Phoenix news audience, it was a horrible case of déjà vu: a man's torso had also been retrieved just four years earlier. The new discovery was a big story. On Monday the 25th, first thing in the morning, Jake Orbin Jr. was on the phone from San Diego to Detective Butcher. His parents had seen news accounts of a body discovered in the desert over the weekend. Could it be Jay?

Butcher promised to look into it. She called the Homicide Bureau. They told her that Dave Barnes was the lead detective on the case. She called him. He said only the torso had been recovered. There was no head. He'd be attending the autopsy later that day. He'd call her back after that.

Butcher had barely hung up the phone with Barnes when her phone rang again. It was the meter maid. She was that very minute standing next to the missing green Bronco. It was on 58th Street, a scant mile from the location where it had originally been sighted by Gordon Bourn and others. It was a little farther from the Orbin home now, but not by much.

Detective Butcher told her to stay with the vehicle at all costs, she'd be there right away. As she gathered her own car keys, Butcher dialed various departments for a photographer, a tow truck and so forth.

Within moments she had slid in behind the wheel of her vehicle, navigated out of the police HQ parking lot and headed north.

*   *   *

The Maricopa County Medical Examiner's Office was a few blocks to the west of police headquarters. Detective Barnes pulled into the highly anonymous yellow block building and descended to the basement. The proceedings, with medical examiner Dr. Al Zhang at the helm, began. The torso was dressed in jean shorts with a belt. There was no shirt. The body had been severed at approximately the breast line. There were no shoulders and no head. The legs disappeared in the mid to lower knees, slightly different from one leg to the next. While Barnes looked on, Dr. Zhang looked for signs of what might have happened to this man other than the obvious. When was this done to him? And how had he died?

At 58th Street, Detective Butcher was pacing around the Bronco, peering in the windows and grilling the meter maid. The officer remembered putting a red tag on this vehicle, after a citizen called it in abandoned, but the tag was now gone. They could both see a can of Glade air freshener inside the car. Butcher found a piece of paper under the driver's side windshield wiper. It was signed "Ted" and read "If you would like to sell this truck, please call me." On the driver's side window a yellow sticker issued by Arabian Trails was pasted: "Warning: Your car is in violation of our community policies." The tag was dated October 22—the day before the blue tub was found.

Detective Butcher approached a man walking his dog on the apartment grounds nearby. He certainly had noticed the vehicle for some time, he responded to her questions. He thought it had been there for three weeks.

He remembered the red tag placed by the city. It had been on the passenger side window. He also had another detail for the detective: he had seen a white SUV pull up and park, then a white female with long blond hair had exited the white car and pulled the red tag off the green Bronco. She had then returned to her white SUV and driven away.

Other neighbors began to approach the growing number of officials surrounding the green Bronco. Apartment leasing agents told the detective that people had been complaining about the SUV for weeks. They'd written notes and the notes had disappeared.

At twenty minutes to noon, the tow truck arrived. The green Bronco was loaded up. Detective Butcher followed the tow truck back to police HQ. At 12:20 P.M., she and a couple of others, including a Detective Tom Kulesa, pushed the Bronco from the tow truck into a forensic examination bay. Detective Butcher drove out to the Property Bureau to retrieve other items that had been impounded. Detective Kulesa went to the "drying room." This was another property impound facility, where evidence in a wet condition is taken to air out. After having helped Butcher push her seized Bronco, Kulesa was returning to the chores of his own caseload.

In downtown Phoenix, the autopsy was wrapping up. Detective Barnes now needed to transport some items from the blue tub to the drying room. He took with him a set of keys found in the pocket of the shorts worn by the partial corpse.

In the drying room, Barnes encountered Kulesa. They

exchanged greetings and Detective Barnes mentioned he'd just been at an autopsy. He showed him the keys they'd found in the pocket of the shorts the victim had been wearing. On the ring was a key to a Ford Bronco. Detective Kulesa responded that he knew Detective Butcher was working on a case with a Bronco. They had just now brought the vehicle in. Kulesa himself had helped roll it into the forensic bay only moments earlier. He suggested it would be easy to go back down and see if the key in Barnes's hand fit the Bronco in the bay.

Together the two men walked back down to the evidence bay where the Bronco was waiting for full processing. Detective Barnes slid the key into the door. The metallic clinking sounded, the detective pulled on the handle, the door opened. He slid into the driver's seat and tried the ignition with the same key. The engine easily turned over.

Jay Orbin, it seemed, had been found.

CHAPTER NINE

Revelations

Detective Jan Butcher had feared, as early as the first Monday after the file had landed on her desk, that the missing person's case for Jay Orbin would be a homicide investigation. Now she was right.*

Detective Dave Barnes met with Butcher and started wading into the file with her. There were more trips to stores, this time to photograph the items that Marjorie had purchased on September 9—the mops, buckets, acetone and bleach. The receipt for Thunderbird Painting, for exterior house painting, had been found. It was dated September 22, the very day the Missing Persons report had

---

* They were waiting on DNA for confirmation, but the keys that had been found in the pocket of the jeans shorts were definitely Jay's and everything else in the tub pointed to the fact that the partial corpse was Jay.

first been filed. Several different power of attorney documents were found on Marjorie's computers, giving custody of Noah to Michael J. Peter, Larry Weisberg, Susan Dermott or Bryan Todd Christy. The detectives did not yet know who most of these people were. They found no attempt by Marjorie to turn the child over to his paternal relatives in case of emergency, but they did find a pamphlet advising how to legally fight against "grandparents rights." Other paperwork they found showed that the loose bullet found in the blue tub would have been a good fit for Jay's missing gun, but without the gun itself, forensic testing was limited. Jay's checkbook, credit cards, inventory and truck had made it home, but what had become of his phone and his weapon was still unknown.

There were more phone calls to be made, more of Jay's friends to be interviewed.

Jay Orbin, it was obvious, was a very social man. Some of his closest associates were scattered far, however, and their awareness of the news was scant. They were shocked and horrified when one or the other of the detectives informed them that Jay had been found.

As word spread, more of Jay's business associates contacted police. Jennifer Destefano sold kachina dolls, and Jay was her supplier. She had met with him at the warehouse on August 27. He'd told her he was leaving on one of his regular runs and it would be a short one. By the time September 11 rolled around, she had not heard from him and she felt this was unusual. She called the Jayhawk business line, but Marjorie picked up and told her that Jay was "off to Florida" because sales hadn't been good. She also told Destefano that something was up with Jay's cell phone and it wasn't working properly.

Destefano had called Jayhawk again around the 16th of September but ended up with Marjorie again. Destefano felt it was very unlike Jay to leave messages unreturned this long, and she really needed product, her customers were complaining. Marjorie reassured her that she had recently spoken to Jay and he was on his way home to Phoenix. Destefano pleaded with Marjorie to meet her at the warehouse and let her retrieve the dolls she needed. Marjorie rejected this idea. Destefano called several more times and began to feel she was being screened. She'd call from her own line and get voice mail. She'd then immediately call again from some other phone line and easily get through. She thought Marjorie sounded upset when she answered and realized it was Destefano after all.

The last time Jennifer Destefano had called was September 22, 2004. This time Marjorie informed her she had notified police and considered Jay a missing person.

Destefano told Detective Barnes that she had always found the relationship between Marjorie and Jay Orbin to be a little different. She had noticed there were always multiple pictures of Noah at the warehouse but only one or two of Marjorie. In all the years she had done business with Jay, she had never met his wife and had never even spoken to her until Marjorie started answering the business line in September. Jay never spoke ill of his wife, but he had mentioned to Destefano that he considered her not very business savvy and he didn't trust her to run his business. Destefano described Jay as very "happy-go-lucky, always happy to see everyone." She remembered with fondness that he was a Rush Limbaugh "fanatic."

Jennifer Destefano's own business had taken a terrible hit due to Jay's absence. She had had to take her Web site down while she looked for another supplier. Yes, she'd found one now, she told the detective. It was Jim Rogers, Jay's former business partner.

The detective was interested in that development, but Destefano told Barnes that Jay had never expressed any dissatisfaction in his relationship with Rogers, and Rogers hadn't done so, either.

On Thursday, October 28, 2004, Marjorie Orbin was brought downtown in the early evening. Although the secret divorce had been confirmed by now, she was still being treated as Jay's widow. Dave Barnes intended to interview her and serve her with a search warrant for DNA swabs, hair samples, photographs and fingerprints. This time Marjorie refused to speak unless she had a lawyer present. About 6:15 P.M., Detective Barnes entered the room where Marjorie was waiting. Her attorney arrived at the same moment. They could talk now.

Barnes told her that Jay Orbin's remains had been found. His opinion of the grieving widow was not favorable. He felt she showed no emotion at all and even "acted as if she was faking a cry."* He then informed her that "parts" of Jay were missing. Her response was that "he doesn't have anyone that would do this to him." Detective Barnes got more specific with her. He told her Jay's legs were missing, his arms and shoulders . . . and

---

* From Dave Barnes's written statements in official police documents.

his head. Detective Barnes watched Marjorie closely. Her behavior, he felt, gave him a great deal of information. He wrote that she "again acted as if she was crying and upset but there were no tears in her eyes at all." Finally, he told her where the remains had been found. At this, the detective noted, "she did not seem surprised at all Jay was found in Phoenix or so close to her home."

Now she wanted to ask something. Had Jay's truck been found?

Yes, Barnes told her, the truck had been located and the keys in the pocket of the corpse's jean shorts had opened it. Upon hearing this news, "Marjorie shook her head as if upset with this."

Detective Barnes moved on to what might be considered more routine business. Bank of America had been notified, he told her, and they had frozen all of the murdered man's accounts. Now the detective felt he had hit a nerve with the blond woman sitting in front of him: "Marjorie got upset at this and now had some tears in her eyes, saying her [sic] and Noah will be kicked out of her house."

Eight-year-old Noah Orbin was at that moment being interviewed himself at a different location. After having her photos and fingerprints taken, Marjorie's attorney drove her away from the police station Marjorie hated to pick up her son from ChildHelp. He advised her to get a hotel for the night.

Search warrants were served again that night on both Marjorie Orbin's and Larry Weisberg's homes. At Marjorie's, the police found meth and coke and razor blades in a wooden box in the master bedroom closet. Also on display in the master bedroom was a framed photo of Marjorie and Noah in front of the white SUV. From Larry's house they confiscated love letters and cards and photos from Marjorie.

By the end of the week, Detective Dave Barnes was at the home of Jay Orbin's parents. They told the detective everything they could think of that might help. They also had the tragic duty of letting a technician swab their mouths for DNA samples in order to match with the horribly mutilated remains found in the desert, the remains believed to be their own son.

CHAPTER TEN

Love at the Gym

Larry Weisberg and Marjorie Orbin had vastly different recollections about how they'd met and fallen in love.* Although some bits of their stories were corroborated by third parties, such as Larry's daughter and Marjorie's neighbors, it was impossible, as with most love affairs, for anyone to know the truth of what happened between them. On several points, the two agreed easily—they met at the gym, he usually did not stay over on weeknights, they had a fight on the night of Larry's birthday party. But the details of how and why were radically different. Only the two of them know which account is more accurate.

---

* Larry Weisberg's recollection was compiled from his interviews with police and his testimony under oath. His daughter Jodi's comes from police transcripts and court testimony. Marjorie Orbin's was taken from letters written to and interviews with the author.

LARRY'S VERSION

A disciplined weight lifter, Larry Weisberg often made the drive from his Central Phoenix home up to LA Fitness gym in the north Phoenix/Scottsdale area. He kept his blond hair short and feathered, and his stunning physique turned heads and often had him mistaken for up to ten years younger than his real age of sixty. At LA Fitness he began to notice someone else with blond hair, a tall woman in excellent shape who could out-bench-press many men. She was often at the gym at the same times he was. One day in July 2004, she walked up to him and handed him a slip of paper. It had her phone number on it. He looked at her left hand and was confronted by the sight of a large diamond ring. She was terribly attractive, with her slim waist, long legs, bulging breasts and striking hair. But he did not consider himself a "side dish."

"You're married," he said.

"No, I'm not," she protested.

"That indicates to me that you are," he said, pointing to the diamond ring.

"Oh that," she said. "I just wear that to keep the men from hitting on me. I'm actually divorced."

With that, the bodybuilder felt the possibilities were agreeable. He used the phone number a couple of days later, and that Saturday night they went out for dinner. She showed up with her divorce papers in hand; she wanted him to know she was truly a single woman. After dinner they came back to his charming but sparsely furnished (in a bachelor kind of way) home, across the street from the mayor. Following a little bit of after-dinner repartee, Marjorie took Larry Weisberg by the hand and led him down the hall. He went, he said, "like a lamb."

As the pair spent more time together, Weisberg learned that although Jay Orbin and Marjorie were divorced, Jay still lived in the house with her and their little boy Noah. He traveled a lot, though, and even when he was in town he often bivouacked at his warehouse, where he kept a few domestic items for just such a purpose. Weisberg asked Marjorie about the sleeping arrangements when her ex-husband stayed at her house, and she assured him that Jay usually slept on the couch. But sometimes she ceded the bed to him in deference to his bad back. At such times, she would traipse down the hall with a blanket and pillow and sleep on the couch herself. Recently, Marjorie told him, she and Jay had talked about making their lives more completely separate. He was in the process of buying another house in the neighborhood so he could stay near Noah. The house the family currently lived in would be hers. Jay paid her child support of $500 a week, she said, adding that she also applied hair extensions to other women for extra money. Plus, she also made sure her new boyfriend knew that she helped out an awful lot with Jay's business. He could not run that business without her, Marjorie swore.

That was enough for Larry Weisberg. He did not want to know anything else about this man in his girlfriend's background. He was satisfied that they were divorced and that the man was doing right by his little boy. The ex-husband seemed decent enough. Marjorie had no complaints about him, such as domestic violence or stinginess, though Weisberg was taken aback during one of their early dates when, while telling him about how much time Jay Orbin spent on the road, Marjorie expressed wonderment that he had not "driven off a cliff" at some point. His truck was old and "statistically," she thought "it ought to have happened by now," with that old car and the many thousands of miles he put on it every month. These statements are taken from police and court transcripts.

If these comments were a bit odd, Weisberg was even more startled to hear her say she wished Jay Orbin was dead.* But Marjorie's figure was dazzling, and as a bodybuilder, he could really appreciate that. She was into fitness as much as he was, and they had other things in common. Her interest in sex was quite compatible to his, too. She asked him to stay over sometimes on weeknights, but Larry was a working man. No, he said, he could not stay over during the week. He had to get up for work and keep his focus. But the couple did begin to talk about the future. He was not averse to cohabiting with her. He understood it would have to be up in north Phoenix, because of Noah. He understood Marjorie would not uproot her child from his school and neighborhood playmates. His downtown home did not hold him; he could picture himself buying a house with Marjorie and moving up north,

July 31, 2004, was Larry Weisberg's sixtieth birthday

---

* Marjorie's remarks as reported by Larry Weisberg in recorded and transcribed interviews with police.

and his thirty-one-year-old daughter, Jodi, was throwing him a party. Weisberg came to the house on 55th Street and picked up Marjorie and Noah. At the party, Noah played with Larry's grandsons, and Jodi asked her father about his plans with his new girlfriend. He was open with her and told her they were talking about moving in together. She wanted to know more. What did this woman do? she asked her father. Weisberg told her about the child support and the hair extensions. Jodi wasn't satisfied. She urged her father to explore the subject further with his ladylove.

Weisberg and Marjorie left the party together and returned to the Orbins' house on 55th Street. Noah stayed at Jodi's for a sleepover with her sons. That night, Weisberg broached the subject of their future shared finances. What did Marjorie plan to do in the future? he asked. Her answer did not satisfy him, so he was more specific, asking her what kind of job she saw herself having. She scoffed at the idea of work. She didn't work. She was a soccer mom, she took care of Noah. Well, Weisberg told her, if they lived together, she'd have to have a job. He would want her to contribute.

Now they flared into a full-on argument and it quickly got very unpleasant. Weisberg left. A short time later, his daughter called him, distressed that Marjorie had just shown up and retrieved Noah. The sleepover for the boys was ruined. Weisberg explained to her about the argument he and Marjorie had just had, including that it was about the very thing his daughter had recommended he bring up. Marjorie and Weisberg stayed away from each other for days.

But Marjorie eventually called him and the couple

managed to smooth things over. They talked every day and continued their romance through August. Sometime in early September, Weisberg got sick and told his girlfriend he couldn't see her while he was down. Soon she reported that she and Noah were sick, too. She also mentioned that Jay was in town and had decided to stay at the warehouse so he wouldn't pick up their bug.

Larry Weisberg was under the impression that Jay Orbin was on the road again pretty quickly. Marjorie began to mention to him that she found it odd Jay was missing his usual morning phone calls to his little boy. When he was traveling, Jay always called Noah as his son was getting ready for school, but he hadn't done so for the last few days. Weisberg thought that was a shame but paid little attention. The other man in his girlfriend's life was not his favorite topic.

Eventually, Larry Weisberg became aware that Jay Orbin was officially missing. He got all his information through Marjorie, and based on her reports, the police seemed to be very misguided and unpleasant. Marjorie could never find out anything from them about the investigation. He was protective of his girlfriend and felt sorry for the little boy. Marjorie asked him to go down to Jay's warehouse and help her move some things. One day it was boxes of stuff, another day it was a desk. They dismantled the desk and loaded it into the white cargo truck. First, though, they had to make room for it by unloading merchandise from the back of the truck. They drove the desk up to the house on 55th Street, unloaded it and reassembled it. Then they took the truck back to the warehouse. From there, Weisberg went on home.

This New Year's Eve photo is an Orbin family favorite because it captures Jay's personality so well: he is surrounded by friends and welcoming more.   *Courtesy of the Orbin family*

Noah completes this photo of three generations of Orbin men, a heritage of camaraderie, dependability and self-sacrifice. [Right to left:] Jake Orbin Sr., his two sons, Jay Orbin and Jake Orbin Jr., and his grandson Noah in front.

Courtesy of the Orbin family

Jay worked very hard to bring this child into his life. He showered him with affection and made the most of their time together. When Jay was on the road, Noah could expect a call from his father every morning. *Courtesy of the Orbin family*

Jay loved to play with Noah and care for him. He was working on ways to reduce his traveling, yet keep his business prospering, so he could have more moments like this. *Courtesy of the Orbin family*

Jay's happy temperament was easily shared with his little boy. He showed his love for his son in a myriad of practical ways, planning for his needs well into the future.

Courtesy of the Orbin family

Marjorie with her whole life ahead of her. As a teenager, she made an impression with her love of dancing and performing. From the Lake Brantley High yearbook. *Lifetouch National School Studios, Inc.*

Marjorie (center) as a high school majorette in Florida. All the kids are dressed in "Patriot" costumes. Her boyfriend, a teen firefighter, loved her, so he shut his ears to the rumors other kids in the band told him. *Lifetouch National School Studios, Inc.*

Marjorie's spectacular figure was something she worked hard at. It was an important asset to her career.
Taken from a billboard

TOPLESS DANCER WORLD CHAMPIONSHIP

1ST PLACE
$20,000
CASH

CASH & PRIZES AWARDED TO ALL FINALISTS

QUALIFYING ROUNDS HERE
CHECK WITH THE CLUB FOR TIME & DETAILS
Finals to be held at the Stardust Hotel & Casino
Las Vegas
November 14–19, 1993

Marjorie in her glory days as a choreographer and featured dancer at Pure Platinum.
Taken from a Pure Platinum brochure

Marjorie living the high life with her lover, mentor and lifelong friend, impresario Michael J. Peter.
Courtesy of friends Jim and Jodie

The blue tub was found in this patch of rough desert, surrounded by saguaros, cholla and barrel cactus. But just across the street were busy commercial developments, seen in the background, about a hundred yards from the crime scene. *Camille Kimball*

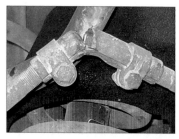

A view of the tie rod in the truck Jay drove from Arizona to Florida and back. Note the clean cut bifurcating what should be a straight rod. The amount of rust on the cut became an item of hot debate.
Courtesy of the Orbin family

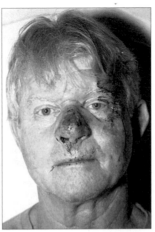

Larry Weisberg after he tangled with a SWAT team. He left his blood on Marjorie's floor. *Phoenix Police Department*

Valerie Pape on the day she was taken into custody. It was alarming when yet another blond Scottsdale housewife was accused of cutting up her husband, but Arizona's history of female murderers involved in dismemberments actually went back much further. *Mesa Police Department*

Marjorie's official mugshot on the day she was arrested. Her life as a comfortable Scottsdale housewife with a generous weekly allowance came to an abrupt end. *Phoenix Police Department*

Five years later, during an interview at the Maricopa County Jail, Marjorie had learned to cope with imprisonment and was eager to explain her relationship with Jay. *Patrick Millikin*

During the time that Jay was missing, one of Weisberg's grandsons had a birthday. His daughter Jodi was uncomfortable when Marjorie somehow managed to insert a pony into the party. No one had asked her to do it; she had simply hired the pony of her own accord. Jodi wasn't sure how to handle it and found the situation with her father's girlfriend distressing.

Larry Weisberg himself had been disconcerted one day when he was at the 55th Street house and Noah walked down the hallway toward him calling him "Dad." He was nonplussed enough about it to tell Jodi. Jodi was quite upset by the little son of a missing man calling her father "Dad."

MARJORIE'S VERSION

Marjorie had worked hard to lose the extra weight from the fertility drugs. She became very serious about her workout routine. At LA Fitness gym, she wore headphones in her ears plugged in to an iPod. It wasn't the music that was so important to her, it was the earphones. This was her way of telling everybody to stay away: she was not available for small talk or otherwise.

She was not there to socialize, but she did like to watch the other exercisers because she got ideas from them on new techniques to try. She noticed the bodybuilder with the blond hair and thought he seemed like a "showboat asshole."* He would "make a big production"

---

* In letters to and interviews with the author.

of loading weights on his equipment. "When he lifted weights he would posture and pose and check in the mirrors," she said, which she found laughable. "Then he would step away puffed all up and circle the weights looking at them like they were a rattlesnake ready to strike. Then he would do another set. He did this whole big dramatic Incredible Hulk routine." She thought it was "beyond stupid" and had him pegged for "a real bonehead loser." On the other hand, she did consider him very good-looking.

Sometimes Noah came to the gym with her and used the aerobics studio to practice his karate. One day she did not have her "leave me alone" headphones on yet. The blond man whom she considered a "bonehead loser" came up to her and told her that her little girl was very cute. Noah's hair was "longish" at the time. She responded that she hoped her *son* hadn't heard him say that. The two adults laughed and chatted.

This initial conversation, she said, had occurred in April 2004. The next time she came to the gym, Larry Weisberg "corrected" her position during one of her exercises and she immediately felt the difference. He stuck around to chat her up when she was done with her set. She began to feel pursued, and she enjoyed it. Feeling very cute and fit after her long fertility and pregnancy ordeal, Marjorie said she began to notice feelings she had thought were long dead.

The following week, Noah was once more with her at the gym. Weisberg joined her again to watch the little boy practice his karate and complimented the mother on her child's focus and concentration. This, Marjorie said, was her soft spot. She had taken Noah to karate in the first place to help him achieve those very qualities. The blond bodybuilder no longer seemed like such a bonehead. He helped her more often with her weight lifting technique and he always seemed to have the right touch. She found she could talk to him, and they shared interests that left Jay cold. She gave Weisberg her number by May, but she considered him only a good gym friend. She had talked to Weisberg about Jay and, as with everyone else in her life, had left him with the impression that she was married to him. Weisberg certainly knew that she lived with Noah's father.

She "rationalized" to herself that lunches with a friend were harmless, but she knew that when they worked out together the sexual tension was high. She loved Weisberg's touch. By the end of May they had kissed. But there were no real "dates" yet.

At the end of June, Jay took Noah to Sonoma, California, for a "boys' weekend." Weisberg swooped in. It was a Saturday and it would be their first real date. Weisberg made an excuse to get Marjorie to his house. Then they went to dinner. Afterward it was back to his house since her car was there. There was wine. And nature took its course, Marjorie said.

Later, she claimed, Weisberg admitted to her that he'd had the whole seduction planned. She was "hungry" for it, though, and enjoyed being up all night with him. Her allegedly sexless marriage to Jay had left her craving what Weisberg had to offer.

They began spending as much time together as they could. But Weisberg knew he could not spend the night on weeknights because Jay might call. If Jay was in town, Weisberg knew he couldn't call after 4 P.M.

When he did spend the night, he saw Jay's clothing and toiletries—he knew he was "in another man's bed." By July, Weisberg was asking Marjorie if she would leave Jay for him.

When it came time for Larry Weisberg's birthday party, he came to her sheepishly and confessed to her that he had lied about his age. She thought he was fifty, but at the party she would find out he was sixty. She forgave him and thought his embarrassed confession was "cute." But the day of the party he was in a foul mood as soon as he picked her up. At the party itself, she found him rude and surly, but his close friends and family assured her that he just sometimes "gets like this." Weisberg's grandsons and Noah got along so well the little hosts begged Noah to stay for a sleepover. When Marjorie was slow to agree, Weisberg taxed her with the accusation "What's the matter, don't you trust my daughter?" Marjorie, hard put by her boyfriend's crankiness, gave her permission.

When the couple returned to the 55th Street house, they talked about their future. She said she wasn't ready to present the situation to Jay. She had to be very sure of Weisberg before she could break up her family. The bodybuilder asked her what her job would be when they moved in together, then became incensed when she told him she would expect to continue to help Jay with his business even after she moved in with her new boyfriend. Jayhawk International was her son's legacy and she had built it up with his father—she could not abandon it. But Weisberg was upset at the prospect of his girlfriend maintaining such close contact with an ex, even if he was the father of her child. "Larry blew his stack. He said that Jay didn't appreciate me while he had me and that there would be no way he could stand that." Marjorie said that "he stormed out."

Now Marjorie was worried about Weisberg as much as she was vexed with him. She called Jodi and asked if she thought her father was okay, but his daughter told Marjorie that she wasn't surprised at all that her father had acted like "such an asshole." Jodi repeated what the other guests at the party had said, that "sometimes he just gets this way." Marjorie thought he must be mad at himself for lying about his age, and annoyed at being sixty and aging. She told Jodi the whole situation was making her uncomfortable and she would like to come get Noah.

Larry Weisberg and Marjorie did not speak for several days. When they did, it was he who called and apologized.

JODI WEISBERG'S VERSION

Thirty-one-year-old Jodi Weisberg enjoyed a strong relationship with her father, Larry Weisberg. She also had something many women would envy, a husband who was close to his father-in-law. Jodi and her husband, Brad Fritz, and their two young children had even moved in with her father for a time while the young family got on its feet. By the summer of 2004, Jodi and Brad and their kids were living on their own, and Brad was applying for certification as a peace officer through the Arizona Peace Officers and Standards Training Board, but they still spent a lot of time with

Grandpa. Jodi was well aware of when her father began dating the blond woman from the gym; it was mid-July of 2004.

Jodi understood her father's girlfriend to be living only with her young son, Noah. In conversations with Marjorie, she learned that Noah's father was on the road constantly. As early as July, she noticed Marjorie trying to get her little boy to call Larry "Dad." She even told Jodi that Noah already thought Weisberg was his father. Marjorie confided to Jodi that Noah was not actually even Jay Orbin's son biologically but that Jay's relatives did not know this. Marjorie wanted to sell her house. She wanted a committed relationship with Larry and to have them start living together.

Jodi babysat Noah one Saturday in early September so Marjorie and her father could go to a concert. Marjorie never mentioned to her that night anything about Jay Orbin being missing. She did remark that Jay had failed to call Noah on Friday, but she downplayed the significance. Jay, she claimed, would sometimes go a full week without calling. When he reappeared, he'd be "Disneyland Dad" to make it up to Noah.

On September 26—the weekend in which Jake Orbin Jr. was anxiously waiting for his sister-in-law to call him so he could come over and look for clues—Jodi's own little boy had a birthday party. He was turning six. To Jodi's surprise and discomfort, Marjorie hired a pony for the celebration. She seemed carefree and never mentioned anything amiss in her own family. Two days later a SWAT team battered in Marjorie's door and raided her home. After that, in Jodi's presence Noah began to "be vocal" about "how bad the police

were" and how they had "beat up" her father, Larry.*
She did not notice the child complaining about his own
father being missing.

Now that Jodi was aware of the disappearance of Jay
Orbin, she asked Marjorie if she had checked the man's
house. Marjorie told her Jay had no house. When he was
in town, he stayed at his warehouse.

Jodi believed that it was in September that her father
began staying overnight at Marjorie's for the first time.
Marjorie was fretting that people were following her.
She and Noah were afraid, and she wanted Weisberg to
stay with them at the house and protect them.

Later, Jodi said, she put two and two together. Marjorie had never admitted, as far as she knew, that Jay
lived in her house. So Jodi's father could not stay there
overnight until after the man went missing.

After the SWAT raid, Jodi saw her father begin to
act in a way she had never seen: emotional. He cried
almost every day. He had never even acted like this during his own divorce. He was frightened by the police
raids and wondered what was going to happen next. By
contrast, Marjorie never showed any emotion about the
missing man. Weisberg's daughter thought she put on
a "good show" about her fears at night, but the woman
had little credibility with Jodi. One day, after the police
had searched his own home, Jodi's father broke down
in front of the two women, and Marjorie said to him,
"I wish you would just get over it." Jodi defended her

---

* From police reports and transcripts of interviews with Jodi
Weisberg.

father, declaring to Marjorie that they were all involved in a very serious situation. Jay Orbin might even be dead. Marjorie's response was "What am I supposed to do?"* She preferred to "let it go and let things happen."

Jodi also took note of how efficiently Marjorie cleaned up Larry's blood from the spot where he had fallen during the SWAT raid at her house. She said she had seen all of the blood on Marjorie's floor after the raid but that the next day when she returned, there was not "a speck of blood." She further told police that Marjorie had then told her she knew how to clean up blood, "no problem." Jodi also absorbed Marjorie's comments that, while she was running low on cash right now, Jay had left her a lot of money and she would "be a millionaire" and Noah would be "set for life."

On October 28, 2004, the day Marjorie was officially informed that remains found in the desert were believed to be those of Jay Orbin, search warrants were served at her house and at Larry Weisberg's. From Weisberg's home, they confiscated a letter to him from Marjorie. The scene in the letter is set in Desert Ridge mall, an open-air center landscaped with tall palm trees and green-skinned palo verdes, surrounded by mountain vistas. Carved out of the raw desert past the northern edge of the Phoenix metroplex, it mixes community fireplaces and fountains with open skies, creating an atmosphere of beauty and privilege.

---

* From Phoenix police reports and transcripts of interviews with Jodi Weisberg.

She began by addressing him as "Dearest Larry." She described to him an evening she'd spent alone with her then seven-year-old son, a "magical and beautiful" evening under the desert sky. However, loneliness had overcome her, and she'd teared up. Her little boy noticed. "Before I realized what was happening, Noah was wrapping his arms around me saying I love you Mommy, I love you, as if he knew why my heart was broken." She wondered if her little boy had made a wish on her behalf, because the next day "you walked up to me and it was like a slow motion scene in a movie." She said she'd felt powerfully compelled to approach Weisberg, despite how she usually rebuffed eager men, because with Larry, it was different. She thought of him as a "giant, crumbling every wall I have."

Marjorie declared her love to Larry in the letter and told him he was just the kind of man she'd dreamt of, then wished him a happy sixtieth birthday and advised him to plan to make a wish himself for her birthday a few months later because it had the potential to turn out as wonderful as her wish had, in bringing him into her life.

Whether Larry made any wishes around Marjorie's autumn birthday can't be known, but in September, Marjorie opened this letter from Jay's desk:

Marjorie,

If you are reading this, then something has happened to me. I'm sorry, dear, just remember you were the love of my life and Noah you are the best thing I have ever done. I will love you both always and I thank you both for all you've given my life.

The letter then proceeded to list "info you may need" on everything from the mortgage on the 55th Street house to several insurance policies on property and on Jay's life. He estimated the amount of death benefits Social Security would pay to Noah. He then urged Marjorie, "Marshall [Roosin] will help with anything" and supplied his friend's phone number.

His last wish, expressed in the letter, was: "No open casket for me."

Given the condition of his remains, there would certainly be no argument with that.

CHAPTER ELEVEN

Martial Arts

Much of Noah Orbin's daily life and that of his mother's centered on Rueckert's Phoenix Leadership Academy, a karate and tae kwon do school. Marjorie Orbin thought her son was struggling with ADD, and she hoped studying martial arts would help him learn to focus and concentrate, and that the entire experience would give him confidence.

At the academy, Marjorie found the opportunity to help out the other parents. She had excellent sewing skills—she enjoyed altering fine garments she bought on sale off the rack in the wrong size, and back in her show-girl days, she'd often duplicate expensive costumes with cheaper materials. She turned these skills to her life as a housewife and said she often offered to help the other karate families sewing on the patches the kids earned.

The school was owned by David Rueckert and his wife Theresa. Their young son, Jessiah, was an outstanding martial arts student himself. Jessiah was fourteen when Marjorie started bringing her kindergarten-age son for karate classes. Marjorie had such excellent fitness skills, she also helped "spot" some of the kids, including Jessiah. She got to know Jessiah quite well.

Marjorie also picked up a new girlfriend among the parents at the academy. A woman there named Sharon Franco was trying hard to improve her life. She felt dowdy and unfocused. But Franco was adamant about leaving her husband, whom she considered a ne'er-do-well, and exploring the new possibilities of the world outside their dysfunctional family. Signing up her son for karate lessons was part of starting a new life. When she met Marjorie Orbin, Franco admired the blonde's fantastic figure, her sharp way of dressing and grooming and her many skills. Franco's daughter began learning to sew from Marjorie. With money virtually nonexistent at the Franco household, it was a rare chance for the teenager to increase her wardrobe. Her son also struck up a friendship with Jessiah Rueckert, who by then was seventeen.

Marjorie always loved having a protégée, and Sharon Franco paid close attention to the lessons Marjorie energetically applied. With Marjorie's great organizational skills, Franco's home life was in better shape than ever. She also began to lose weight. She developed some style. She gained confidence. For the first time in the sixteen years that she had been married, Sharon Franco began to feel attractive. Members of the opposite sex were beginning to pay attention.

With her newfound confidence, Franco found the teenage karate master who ran around with her son to be rather attractive.

Jessiah Rueckert had some heartache of his own. His parents had plunged into a bitter divorce. His mother, Theresa, at five-one and roughly 170 pounds, did not share the family obsession with fitness. His father David had found a new girlfriend, Jennifer Longdon, who did. The acrimony between the Rueckerts reached epic proportions. David and Jennifer both filed for orders of protection against Theresa. One day the karate school was rocked when a man came in brandishing firearms in front of the children and parents, saying he was Theresa's bodyguard and warning David and Jennifer they'd better watch themselves. The children were upset, and angry parents filed affidavits in support of David. Theresa had acted as bookkeeper for the family businesses, and David now asked the court for an injunction. He claimed that his ex was deliberately running all the businesses into the ground, failing to accept payment from clients and refusing to pay bills.

Teenager Jessiah Rueckert—so involved in the family business—was very much trapped in the cross fire of his parents' melodrama. The attentive mother of his teenage pal was an inviting place to escape. At some point, the forty-something Sharon Franco and the seventeen-year-old Jessiah entered into a romance. Marjorie Orbin kept a close watch on her protégée and the boy she had known since he was fourteen. At first the couple did not say anything outright, but Marjorie's experienced eye could see for itself.

As Phoenix PD investigated the suspicious disappearance of Jay Orbin, they found the ties to the karate school where Marjorie had made a big impression, and a lot of karate school gossip came their way. Sharon

Franco, in particular, had a lot to say. Now that Jay Orbin's remains had been located, the police were more intensely interested than ever in Marjorie's behavior and reputation.

On November 15, 2004, some three weeks after Jay's remains had been found, owner of the karate school David Rueckert and his girlfriend Jennifer Longdon were turning down an access road for a drive-thru dinner at Filiberto's when a red truck peeled out with a loud screech. The screech was so loud it masked the sound of the first few shots fired.

A total of five rounds were fired into Rueckert and Longdon's vehicle before the red truck sped away. Both of them had been shot.

Jennifer Longdon saw her boyfriend's bloody head as she felt the life draining from her own body. With her last strength, she dialed 911. "My boyfriend's been shot and he's dead," she told the dispatcher, "and I'm dead, too."

A bullet had entered David Rueckert's head and lodged behind his eye.

When paramedics arrived, Jennifer Longdon was "coding." Her injuries were just as bad as Rueckert's.

If it was a shock to everyone that the couple had been targeted like this by a gunman in broad daylight, it was even more of a shock when they were both still alive the next day.

On November 22, 2004, not a full week after this traumatizing incident and shortly after her own husband's remains had been found, Marjorie Orbin sent then nineteen-year-old Jessiah Rueckert a text: "Want to play?"

Jessiah told police that the message frightened him and disturbed him. He was already deeply upset about his father's tragedy. He wanted no part of Marjorie Orbin's flirtations and he did not respond to her message. He did, however, show it to police. He told them Mrs. Orbin was very flirtatious with him and was also very irritated over his romance with Mrs. Franco. He told police that Mrs. Orbin had once been close friends with Sharon Franco and that several months ago, long before Jay went missing, Franco had told him that Marjorie often said she wished Jay was dead.

Sharon Franco confirmed Jessiah's comment. Yes, her ex-friend Marjorie Orbin, someone she had once fairly "worshipped," had made several statements about wishing Jay was dead. As she had to Larry Weisberg, Marjorie had expressed frustration to Franco that statistically speaking Jay should have driven off a cliff by now or that his truck should have had a brake failure already.

Sometimes Marjorie would muse to Franco about how she would defend her territory as a mother if Jay ever tried to challenge her for custody. If Jay found her with another man, she said, she knew he'd leave and he'd try to take Noah. There was no way she'd let that happen, Marjorie insisted. What she would do instead, Franco claimed Marjorie said, was "shoot Jay in the head, chop him up, wrap him up in a blanket and then drop him in the desert."*

The police wanted to know why Sharon Franco and

---

* From police interviews and court testimony of Sharon Franco.

Marjorie had had a falling out in the springtime of '04. Marjorie had tried to break up Jessiah and Franco but had failed, the couple said. It was at that point, they said, that Marjorie "turned" on her former protégée. Franco now felt stalked and harassed by Marjorie. She was full-on afraid of her former friend.

Franco also realized she owed an apology to a third woman, Laura McMann,* whose child had been highly successful at the karate school. McMann had become so afraid of Marjorie, she had moved away and even changed jobs so Marjorie couldn't find her. The reason for the harassment? Laura McMann believed it was because her son was so talented at karate and Marjorie's son was not. McMann felt that her son, as well as other children, had even been sabotaged at karate tournaments by Marjorie Orbin. She said the pranks went as far as putting itching powder in the uniforms of the little competitors. Noah would be the only child left standing and would win events by default.

Laura McMann had told her children never to play in the yard for fear of Marjorie Orbin casing them, and if they ever saw her they were to run inside. She said she'd received multiple phone calls from Marjorie's phone number, with nothing but breathing.

Franco told police she had not believed McMann at the time and had remained staunchly loyal to her highly organized and sexy friend who was teaching her so much. But now, she told them, she was very sorry. All of Laura McMann's stories were true, she believed,

---

* Denotes pseudonym.

because now Marjorie was doing that kind of thing to her, too.

She was very afraid of Marjorie Orbin.

Marjorie was not having a very good November. On November 13, 2004, two days before David Rueckert and Jennifer Longdon were shot, Marjorie had been shopping at Circuit City with Noah. It was a Saturday. When she went to pay, there was a fuss at the cash register. Instead of loading up her purchases, Marjorie and Noah were escorted by the store security into a back office. The credit card she was using was not hers; the store was now going to conduct a fraud investigation. To Marjorie's horror, she and her child were taken to the downtown Phoenix Police headquarters, some twenty miles or more from their home neighborhood. Up at Desert Ridge, they were surrounded by open spaces and crests of mountain ranges with storied pasts of conquistadors and silver mines. The downtown police station was in an area of total concrete, urban hustle, carbon monoxide and street characters of vivid but dubious persona.

It was chilly and overcast as Marjorie and Noah were driven downtown.

Noah was taken into a different part of the building at the police headquarters while his mother was interviewed. She told the store she certainly was not committing fraud of any sort. She had frequently used this credit card. The trouble was, the store told her, the person who owned the card could not give his permission. But the person who owned the card was her husband, it was as good as hers! Marjorie insisted. No, the store told her, the person who owned the card was not only dead, he had been murdered. All his accounts were frozen. To try to use the frozen card was fraud.

But Phoenix Police sergeant Dave Lane, in an interview room down at police headquarters, told Marjorie that he really didn't think the card thing was that big of a deal. The important thing was to focus on little Noah and what was right for him.

Marjorie couldn't have agreed more. She clearly equated the September SWAT raid—which had nothing to do with the credit cards at Circuit City—as also an overreaction, even though that had been performed in pursuit of a potential homicide. "A SWAT team comes through my door and Tasers a 60 year old man . . . a friend of my husband's that was there . . . and throws me on the floor. Handcuffs me and I'm screaming— what the fuck? There's a little child in the house! . . . and you know, [Noah] was traumatized. He's in therapy. He's sittin' there traumatized. Whatever I can do to make him not be afraid is my main, main goal." To Marjorie, Jay's being missing was "no big deal," about the same as a small credit card mix-up.

Marjorie hoped to smooth over the credit card problem. "I did not know I was doing anything wrong. I was just trying to get a computer and spend tomorrow getting ready to try and get some orders out [for Jayhawk International] so that we could pay some bills, cuz I have no money."

Sergeant Lane took this in, but he wanted to guide the conversation elsewhere, although he found it difficult to say the words. "So . . . the thing about Jay. . . . and Jay's location and everything . . . what happened to Jay . . ."

"It's not him. It's not him."

"It's not who?"

"It's not Jay."

"It's not Jay? You mean that what they found was not Jay?"

"I don't think so."

"But the keys . . . there were the keys . . . they were the keys to his Bronco, weren't they?"

"That's what they said, so, but I don't know . . ."

Marjorie went on to insist that if keys were found in the pants pocket, the man in the blue tub could not be Jay because Jay only carried his personal items in his shirt pocket. Sergeant Lane forged ahead in the face of this denial. Marjorie suddenly admitted that the man Tasered at her house was not Jay's friend but hers. Lane already knew this, and he wanted to stick with this topic. Didn't she have something to say about her boyfriend? Exactly how long had she known this guy Larry Weisberg?

"Three or four months," Marjorie said.

"He's using you," said Lane.

"Using me for what?" she asked.

Lane said Weisberg was a big guy, a tough guy, he must be jealous of Jay. Marjorie said there wasn't really anything for him to be jealous of, there was no physical relationship between her and Jay. She amended that to say that "there were attempts, but they were humiliating."

Marjorie was very sorry to be at police headquarters, trapped in this interview room going through this frightening fuss. She said, "I have nobody. I have nobody. Nobody in the whole world knows I'm here tonight." She said she used to have three friends here in town but one moved back to Vegas, one got married . . . and then her voice trailed off without accounting for her third friend. She explained to her interrogator that she had been living in Jay's life, "I mean I'm just kinda like mooched into his life. . . ."

Sergeant Dave Lane then revealed he himself was part of that life. He had been friends with Jay's parents, Jake Sr. and Joann Orbin, for thirty years. He even remembered meeting Marjorie once at a party. He told her that he would like to help. He started talking about Larry Weisberg again, hinting at the boyfriend's jealousy, his desire to take Jay's place and his status as a mysterious character Marjorie barely knew. Marjorie vigorously defended her lover at every turn. The conversation went around in circles.

Finally, Lane broached the idea that before Marjorie got released from Circuit City charges, Phoenix PD detective Dave Barnes wanted to come down and talk to her. So far she'd displayed a type of calm, a certain confidence that she might be able to talk her way out of the credit card mix-up. But with that announcement, Marjorie became spooked. Did she have to talk to Barnes? Was it something they required before they'd let her go? Lane was conciliatory and fatherly. He didn't want her to worry too much about the fraud charges, but again urged her to focus more on the fate of Noah's father and the suspiciousness of Larry Weisberg. Marjorie defended Weisberg again and said that whoever did this terrible thing to Jay was "an animal" and she would never be involved with such a person, it couldn't be Larry Weisberg.

Marjorie was getting anxious to see Noah, though,

asking about him repeatedly. She had no one to look after him while she was detained. The child's grandparents were too old and frail and they were unable to drive.

At last the child was brought in to her. He seemed calm. Marjorie herself nibbled on a snack. Noah wanted to know if he could go home now with his grandparents. He wanted to stay overnight with "Gram." Marjorie was startled and unhappy to hear what the child was telling her: the Orbins were already here at police headquarters and had been helping keep the little boy entertained and comforted. "You don't go anywhere . . . they might . . . You do not leave this building with anybody, okay?"

"Okay."

"Not until you see me."

"Okay. Hey, Mom, they might tell you if I'm gonna go over there or not and if they—"

"Go over where?"

"Over their house."

"Oh, to Grandma and Grandpa's?"

"Mm-hm."

"I don't think so. I don't want you to. I want you to stay with me."

"Well, I know . . ."

"Why, do you want to?"

"I don't . . . I'm not . . ."

"Is that what you wanna do?"

Silence.

"Answer your question."

"Mom—"

"Hm?"

"You . . . it's cuz . . ."

"Cuz??"

"I wanna visit 'em."

"Oh, yeah, well we can go visit tomorrow."

Noah was reluctant to accept the deal. He told her he'd take her future visit but he wanted the visit tonight, too.

"Not tonight. Honey, cuz I'm upset and I really would like you to come home with me cuz I want . . ."

Noah interrupted and she made more promises about the future. But Noah was now ready to leave.

"We'll talk about it later," she said.

"Okay, see you, Mom."

"I love you," she said.

He walked out of the room.

Marjorie remained.

Detective Dave Barnes arrived in the little interview chamber with the plain table and folding chairs. Marjorie began to put him off, asking for a later appointment, a daytime one, when her attorney was present. She claimed to be "terrified" of something she said being taken out of context and her little boy losing his mother after he may already have lost his father. Detective Barnes dodged her worries and reverted to the credit card issue. He told her that the credit card was used by her at Target in September and they had checked the records and knew who was using it the day before that.

"So the question is this: how did this credit card come into your possession? Because Jay had it on September 8, and you have it on September 9."

"On the 9th?" she asked.

"I have surveillance photos of the store at Target," he told her, going on to detail the large amounts of cleaning supplies she'd bought—Tilex, Clorox—but she interrupted him to say her use of the card was not unusual. She failed to react to his ominous sounding list of cleaning supplies, so he doubled back to the original question she still hadn't answered.

"Well, it's unusual that you're using the credit card." Over the last three weeks the PD had determined that the card in question was Jay's business travel expense card. They had gone back over a year's worth of records on the card and found it was always used for gasoline, hotels and incidental expenses on the road. It was used in Phoenix for gassing up the trucks and virtually nothing else. It had never had a $500 charge on it for any reason.

Until Marjorie started using it and Jay had vanished.

"I . . . that I understand, that I understand." Marjorie's response was vague and quickly weaved off topic. She wanted to convince the detective that her putting large sums on credit cards, even hundreds of dollars' worth of cleaning supplies, was not unusual.

The detective wanted her to focus again on the issue of the card itself: "How'd you get Jay's credit card?"

"I don't know, I don't know."

"Did Larry [Weisberg] give you the credit card?"

"Larry's never given me a credit card."

Sergeant Dave Lane was still in the room as well and offered Marjorie a way out. "You have to understand, Marjorie, we think Larry is the one who manipulated your credit cards and—"

Marjorie insisted that she had no suspicions of Weisberg, and she wanted to erase the idea that her use of the card was unusual in any way. "I used . . . I used Jay's credit cards . . ."

Barnes snapped her back to solid fact: "But Jay used this card on September 8."

Marjorie was now flustered and frustrated, and ready to look again at the issue of Larry. "I mean, like you said—would I know if Larry had removed one from my purse? No! I wouldn't know if one were missing from my purse from this day to that day . . . to when Jay would tell me to use . . ."

The detectives and Marjorie wrestled through more circular conversation. Barnes pointed out she had bought some items of clothing for Weisberg. "Did Larry ask you to buy any of this, Marjorie?"

"No, no."

"But on September 9? You reported Jay missing on September 23.* Why are you using Jay's credit card? The one Jay used on September 8, on September 9?"

"I don't know, I don't know. . . . There is . . . there is, um, cards in my purse all the time . . ."

"There's only one of this credit card."

"I know! I know! I understand what you're saying. This is not an unusual, mmm . . ."

"I know, but, but it being on this credit card when Jay's supposedly out of town—"

"That is unusual, I understand."

"Which means you had to have seen Jay."

"No."

"Marjorie, there's no other way you could've got this credit card."

---

* This conversation was taken from an official transcript, and here the Homicide detective, who was not part of the case in September, made an error. Jay was reported missing on September 22, not 23.

Marjorie's voice dropped to a whisper. "I don't know . . ."

"Well, I think you do know,"

"Okay, I need my lawyer present in here, okay? Cuz you're scaring me . . ."

"You're scaring us, too."

"And I would like to answer your questions—"

Marjorie didn't realize just how frustrated the detective was. For nearly two months she had dodged police interviews. She'd been cagey and evasive when she did talk to them. Detective Barnes had been on the case for only three weeks, but the image of Jay Orbin's torso in the desert wasn't something he could get out of his mind. At this point in the interrogation, he was seated on a folding chair, leaning forward, facing Marjorie. Marjorie was seated near him, leaning forward. Between her knees, standing on the chair, was an open can of soda she had been drinking from periodically.

Detective Barnes reached into his portfolio, briskly swept out an item and held it in the air between them. "We'd like to know where the rest of Jay is."

Marjorie instantly swiveled her knees to her left, away from Barnes and his show-and-tell item. "Oh god! Oh no!" Her hands flew to her face; she bent her head down and continued her exclamations of distress.

"And I think you know," continued Barnes firmly.

What he was showing her was an 8 × 10 photo of the torso found in the blue tub on October 23.

"No, I don't," she insisted. She still faced away from him with her head down. He continued to hold the photo in the air. "I can't believe you just did that! I don't believe you just did that!" she said in a flood of distress. The picture had not been so upsetting, however, that she spilled the soda can she'd been holding between her knees. In the moment she first saw the 8 × 10 color photo of her husband without his head, arms or legs, Marjorie had deftly picked up the soda can from between her knees before pivoting away from the sight. As her left hand flew to her face, the right one balanced the open soda can neatly upright.

Detective Barnes had reached the limit of his patience. "You're going to jail tonight for credit card fraud, Marjorie."

"Why?!" Marjorie cried out with more perturbation than ever before. "This has all been a trick!"

The only response was the sound of the door slapping shut behind Detective Barnes. She was left in the room with the "good cop," Sergeant Lane.

"This has all been a trick! Oh my god!" Marjorie exclaimed over and over.

"There's no trick here," Lane asserted. "That photo's Jay Orbin."

"Oh my god!"

"I told you every piece of everything I know—"

"This has all been a trick!"

"Who tricked you with what?"

"May I just call my attorney, please?"

He showed her the phone in the room which she could have used at any time. She dialed and left several frantic messages. She kept getting voice mail instead of a live receptionist. In between leaving messages on the machine, she vented her unhappiness to Sergeant Lane and also simply talked to herself, as if thinking out loud. The desperation of being unable to reach her attorney, compounded with knowing that her eight-year-old son was in the other room, became unbearable.

"I don't know of anyone doing anything wrong. . . . I don't know of anything . . . If I can find out, I will, but I don't know right now. I don't know. They do this on purpose! At night, when you're afraid and you know they know your child's being taken from you is the worst thing that could happen—it's leverage. I didn't do anything!"

"You're looking at it wrong."

"Am I?"

"Sure."

"I don't know. I don't understand. I don't know what to do. I don't know anything. I don't know anything to say. I don't know anything to tell."

Marjorie reached into her bag and pulled out some small items. She set them down and began flipping lids and unscrewing tops.

"I just—when my lawyer comes to help . . . I don't mean to look like the scariest creature on the planet—" Marjorie was applying makeup to her face from the assortment in front of her. "I'm sorry. I'm vain or whatever, I don't know. Don't let them treat me like a dirtbag—"

Marjorie left one last message on the law firm's voice mail: ". . . I am down here at jail and they are arresting me and, ummm, I need help. I don't know what to do." She hung up and said to the air: "Somebody, somebody, anybody—come help me!"

Marjorie was prepped for arrest and jail. As she stood up and submitted to pat-downs and handcuffs, she asked whether she'd be able to see her son. Noah, she was told, had fallen asleep and been carried down to his grandparents.

Marjorie's cuffs were adjusted and the processing officer asked her a series of personal questions about where was she born, what her home phone number was, and so forth. Marjorie was cooperative and compliant. But when she was asked for her parents' phone number, she said, "I don't have any parents." But a moment later she softened up the statement. "I have . . . my mother is still living, but I'm not in communication with [her] . . ."

Marjorie characterized the police interview as brutal, saying that "they used threats, intimidation, wearing me down, cajoling and bullying and coercion. And they used my son." Her anger over it would last for years. But her stay in jail for credit card fraud was brief. She was back home by Sunday, within twenty-four hours.

The next week started with a fresh hell of their own for her karate school associates: David Rueckert and Jennifer Longdon were shot that Monday morning. By the following weekend, forty-three-year-old Marjorie had texted the man's distraught teenage son, "Wanna play?"

David Rueckert survived the attack, as did Jennifer Longdon, though she woke up to life in a wheelchair, and Rueckert, with a bullet lodged in his head, was blinded. His long hospitalization and lots of rehab meant that he was unable to run the karate school.

At age nineteen, his son Jessiah Rueckert took over the family business.

CHAPTER TWELVE

"A Most Amazing Human Being"

Poring over phone records, detectives had noticed multiple calls between Marjorie and a certain number in Las Vegas over the course of three days they were very interested in: September 7, September 8 and September 9. This number had the most traffic of any in Marjorie's phone history. They followed the trail and found the number belonged to a "Susan Dermott."* During the October search warrant, days after the discovery of poor Jay's corpse, an Arizona driver's license had been found among Marjorie's things. This driver's license belonged to a Susan Dermott.

On Monday, November 15, 2004, Detective Dave Barnes decided it was time for a little trip up to Las Vegas.

---

* Denotes pseudonym.

He had accessed a nationwide database and discovered a Nevada driver's license for a Susan Dermott. Accompanying him was Detective Michael Meislish. The two went to the Las Vegas address on the Nevada driver's license but ended up at a PO box in a strip mall.* It took more database searches to come up with another address to try. By 3 P.M. they were knocking on the door of an apartment on Quail Drive in Las Vegas, with nothing but a furiously barking dog answering them. The two Phoenix cops went to the office of the apartment manager, who confirmed that a Susan Dermott did currently live there.

The detectives returned to Quail Drive at 9 A.M. Tuesday. This time, Susan Dermott let them into the apartment herself. She was a tiny little thing, just five feet and 105 pounds. Other than that, she looked a lot like Marjorie, with platinum hair and a stunning figure. But whereas Marjorie Orbin was hawkeyed and sharp, Susan Dermott was dreamy and soft. She laughed as she showed the detectives her wristwatch, which was set to 6:00. It was now past 9:30. Her watch, she giggled, was displaying Kelly Standard time. Yes, Kelly. She didn't go by "Susan" anymore. They should call her Kelly now.

Dermott had been up all night working at the Spearmint Rhino Club. A twenty-thousand-square-foot extravaganza of adult entertainment, the club was broken up into many rooms, connected by open doorways. Naked girls were strewn throughout, and Dermott was one of

---

* A PO box is not accepted as an applicant's address at most DMVs. Therefore, the Nevada DMV most likely mistakenly took Dermott's PO box address for an apartment address.

them. In fact, it was just one of several clubs where she stripped.

First they asked her where her Arizona driver's license was. She said she had surrendered it to Nevada DMV when she got her new license here.

No, they told her, it was found in the possession of Marjorie Orbin of Phoenix. Did she know Marjorie?

Oh, yes, Dermott said warmly. She fairly "idolized"* Marjorie. She dreamily reminisced about the days when Marjorie was the choreographer for the Platinum Dolls. She wanted the detectives to understand that the Platinum Dolls was like a "Folies Bergère for strippers." Marjorie was with Michael J. Peter in those days, Dermott said, and she had taught Dermott everything she knew, taught her how to be a lady. She said Marjorie was "a most amazing human being" and it was Marjorie who "got me where I am today." She considered Marjorie more like a relative than just a friend. She'd known her first in California, in "certain circles." It was some years later they had noticed each other again at a gym in Scottsdale, Arizona. Then-twenty-five-year-old Dermott had at first not recognized Marjorie, who by that time would have been thirty-nine and struggling with weight from her pregnancy and long fertility treatments. But the two women had gotten close again immediately.†

Yes, Dermott had heard about Jay Orbin being missing. The younger and smaller woman said her friend sounded

---

* Quotes taken from Dave Barnes's official police report of the trip to Vegas.
† Dermott was not precise with the dates, but the reunion is believed to have taken place around the year 1999 or 2000.

frazzled these days. Marjorie had told Dermott that Jay was "out there" some place and he was just doing this to "mess with her." In other words, still alive and deliberately taunting his wife by seeming to disappear. On the other hand, no, Dermott had no knowledge of Jay ever doing anything like this anytime before. She had to admit she'd also heard that "part" of Jay had been found. But she was quick to repeat Marjorie's refrain that Jay never carried money in his pants pocket, always his shirt pocket, so maybe that "part" wasn't Jay after all.

As for her friend's relationship with her husband, Dermott never heard of any fights. The two had "a different kind of love" and their son Noah was the center of it. She had heard, though, that Jay was buying himself a house near their current home and Marjorie was considering leaving him. Did she know if Marjorie had a boyfriend? Not really. She'd heard about a guy named Gary or Larry, just someone Marjorie "goofs around with" at the gym.

Marjorie had advised Dermott of her "pendulum" theory. Any guy who was super "anything"—wealthy, handsome, charming or anything else positive—was sure to be just as awful in some other aspect as he was wonderful in the first. She told Dermott to look for guys who live at the bottom of the swing of the pendulum. In other words, right in the middle. They may not be super rich or super handsome, but neither were they going to be super awful either. Dermott thought it was good advice. She believed Marjorie had chosen Jay for that very reason; he was right in the middle.

Marjorie often talked about how good Jay was to her and how much he provided for his little family, including planning for their futures. But Kelly Dermott did not want to talk about the Orbins' "intimate" lives, which she found "gross," as if talking about her parents having sex.

Marjorie was a "super Mom" to Noah, in Dermott's eyes. But Marjorie's in-laws were "kooky" and "old."

The Phoenix detectives needed to make sure they were all talking about the same person. Did Kelly have any pictures of Marjorie? the detectives asked. Of course, was her cheerful answer.

Soon the detectives were looking at two framed photos of Kelly Dermott's "idol": Marjorie Orbin.

The detectives had sent a flurry of subpoenas into the private and professional lives of Jay and Marjorie Orbin. In late November, one of the most important ones came back.

Although she told varying stories to customers, possibly with the intent of avoiding harm to sales, Marjorie repeatedly told police that Jay was back on the road from September 9 through 17, when she last spoke to him. Sometimes it got hazy about where he was on September 8, but she had settled into the story that he may have come back into Phoenix on September 8, but she had never actually seen him. This was due to her and Noah having strep throat. She had warned Jay in the morning on the phone that it would be best for him if he didn't come near their germs. So as far as she knew, he had stayed at the warehouse that night, then he was back on the road on the 9th to recoup the sales in Florida lost due to Hurricane Frances. She did not know for sure because she had certainly never laid eyes on him on the 8th.

Detectives had tracked Jay's Citibank credit card and

knew that he'd used it in Tucson on September 7 and 8, and for gas purchases in Phoenix on the 8th. They even had surveillance video of the white truck getting gas with this card late that Wednesday afternoon (4:35) in the neighborhood of the 55th Street house. But the next day Marjorie had started using it, beginning with the purchase of several hundreds of dollars' worth of cleaning supplies. When confronted with this, Marjorie insisted she could not explain why the credit card was with Jay at the end of Wednesday near their house yet she was using it less than twenty-four hours later, if she had not seen him in Phoenix that day—or seen some third party who may have been with Jay on the 8th and then transferred the card to her.

They tried again to get her to say that Larry Weisberg had given the card to her, but Marjorie continued to defend Weisberg vigorously, though she started to leave open a little doubt that it was possible he might have gotten into her purse and, as the detectives proposed, "planted" it on her.

When some of the subpoenaed paperwork came back in late November, however, it cooled the detectives on the pursuit of Marjorie's bodybuilding lover. This stack of paper built quite a scaffold around Marjorie herself.

Jay's cell phone had never been found, although other items he'd had with him on that trip certainly had: his checkbook, his briefcase, even his contact lens solution. In late September, Marjorie had bought a new phone to replace the missing unit but kept Jay's number.

Subpoenaed phone records showed that Jay's original cell phone, like his credit card, had gone on his last known sales run. The phone was in San Antonio, Texas, on August 29, the day after Noah's birthday party at the bowling alley. The next day the phone was in Houston, Texas. On August 31 it was in New Orleans, Louisiana. On September 1 it reached Pensacola, Florida. Heading back west on the 3rd, the phone pinged in Birmingham, Alabama, then Jackson, Mississippi, then back in New Orleans. On the 5th, the phone was in Houston, then it passed through Albuquerque, New Mexico, on the 6th and by the 7th was in Tucson, Arizona. In Tucson, Jay—and his phone—would've been just two hours from home.

Before 9 A.M. on the 8th, calls from Jay's phone were pinging off towers in the Phoenix metro area. The last call to register from Jay's phone that day was at 4:31 P.M., near the gas station close to his own house.

On September 9, Jay's phone was still close to home, with calls pinging off a tower about six blocks from the Orbin home. Jay's cell phone actually called the 55th Street house land line.

Later in the day, while Marjorie was shopping for cleaning supplies, Jay's cell phone called hers.

Both phones pinged off the same tower.

Over the next three weeks, at least two dozen times when Jay's *missing* phone pinged off a tower, Marjorie's phone pinged off the same tower within a minute or seconds. As if this evidence weren't damning enough on its own,*

---

* The cell tower records proved the phone was either in Marjorie's possession or in the possession of someone very close to her, because its route followed her route. Because the calls from the two phones so closely matched each other in time, it seemed to police that the person holding Jay's phone must have been standing right next to Marjorie—or was Marjorie herself. Otherwise, it would be impossible to explain how the two phones made calls within moments of each other. The calls had to have been coordinated.

on September 20 several of Jay's associates had received calls from him. None had heard his voice, but some had heard the Rush Limbaugh show in the background. The subpoenaed cell site records showed that Jay's phone, the one that had traveled to Houston, New Orleans, Pensacola and back, on September 20 was pinging off towers in the northeast Phoenix metro area as it called his friends.

Marjorie's phone was pinging off the exact same towers—Bell Road, 32nd Street, and Scottsdale Road—at the exact same times.

Was Larry Weisberg involved in the disappearance of Jay Orbin? Investigators could not answer that question yet. But with the cell tower information, it now seemed impossible to believe that Marjorie herself was not.

On December 1, 2004, DNA confirmed that the sad person in the blue tub had been Jay Orbin. His brother and parents could begin planning a funeral. Some things were certain: Jay's credit card, cell phone and white truck had made it to Phoenix on September 8. After that date, his credit card and phone and Bronco truck had ended up with Marjorie.

And after September 8, Jay was missing. So was his gun.

On December 6, 2004, after a grand jury indictment, Marjorie Orbin was arrested at her home on the charge of first degree murder of Jay Orbin.

For months his family had tried hard to find him, their suspicions of Marjorie's behavior—so out of step with the behavior of everyone else in Jay's life, from his far-flung customers to his close friends and family—growing reluctantly. But the arrest still came as a swift and sudden shock. Jake Jr. remembered the emotional bombshell. "On December 6, I was coming into town [from San Diego] for my brother's funeral on the 11th, to prepare the eulogy and all that kind of stuff. And as I'm coming in I'm talking to [Detective] Dave Barnes and we're chatting on the phone about 'anything new?' He says no." Jake recalled this conversation taking place just as he was passing Gila Bend, a tiny cotton-growing town on the edge of the Tohono O'odham Indian Nation. In about ten more minutes he would enter the Phoenix metroplex. "I get to town. I eat dinner with my parents. About seven o'clock I'm getting another phone call from Barnes saying 'Jake, I need you to come downtown, we've just arrested Marjorie.'" Jake, in spite of the family's growing estrangement from his sister-in-law, could hardly believe his ears. "[I had] no prior knowledge, just 'I need you to pick up Noah.' And I'm like 'What?!!?!' It was just complete shock.

"So, I pick up Noah. We try to figure out where he's gonna spend the night. This is all unfolding overnight now and we're 'What are we going to do? How long is she going to be there?' They said they arrested her because she was a flight risk."

After he had been kept away from his Orbin relatives as much as possible over the previous three months, it would be the beginning of a very close relationship between Noah and his father's loved ones.

Jake remembered the conversation he'd had with his brother in May, the one that he had barely taken seriously. Here it was just six months later, and the scenario his brother had prepared for was "actually unfolding."

Both Jay and Marjorie were unable to care for the baby who had brought them together. Jake needed to step up and raise Noah.

The next day, as Jay's executor and now guardian of his only child, Jake went back to the 55th Street house for the first time in weeks. It was something he had wanted to do but had not been allowed to by Marjorie, except for the SWAT raid, when he had been there to briefly, once again, retrieve Noah from the chaos.

As he was going through the things in the house now that Marjorie was jailed and he was caring for his brother's child, Jake found something interesting. He called Detective Dave Barnes. It was a receipt, Jake said, for a storage unit, dated October 1, 2004.

Detectives Dave Barnes and Mike Meislish, who had traveled to Vegas together to interview Kelly/Susan Dermott, picked up the receipt and then headed straight to the storage place. They found the manager, Sol Bruno, who remembered the striking blonde quite well. She'd told the manager that she was running away from her husband and she was frightened and needed to hide some jewelry. That was her reason for renting the unit.

But the manager believed she had removed the jewelry from his property three days later.

She had signed the receipt "Marjorie Marqui." The manager looked her up and found the company's corresponding paperwork.

The detectives walked back to the locker with the manager in tow. Using a pair of bolt cutters, they opened the unit. It was empty.

But back in the office, Bruno had something else for the detectives. When a new client came in to rent a unit, the company took a photo. He pulled a Polaroid out of his files. It certainly was the lady they were interested in: Marjorie Orbin. They took the photo with them and left.

The day Marjorie was arrested she made a phone call and yet another mysterious man appeared at the house on 55th Street. This one began visiting Marjorie in jail. Their conversations, as all inmates knew, were monitored. Police became aware this new man was running errands for Marjorie, errands involving money, jewelry and computers. After a few weeks, detectives paid a visit to one Bryan Todd Christy—with a search warrant. After several knocks on the door went unanswered, the property manager let the officers in.

Inside, after they called out "Phoenix Police" several times, two men nervously emerged from the bedroom.

The men were Bryan Todd Christy, whom they recognized, and his lover, Oscar Moreno.

Christy explained that he had first met Marjorie when he noticed her in a store because she looked so much like his friend Susan Dermott. He had later learned that the two women knew each other; the fact that Dermott had "learned everything she knew" from her "idol" Marjorie may have had something to do with their looking so much alike. This was about the time Dermott and Marjorie ran into each other at the gym. Christy, Dermott and Marjorie became fast friends. The trio shared confidences in a way that Marjorie did not seem free to in any of her other friendships. Eventually Dermott moved back to Las Vegas. But the friendships held fast for quite a while.

But Christy had fallen out of touch with both women

around spring 2004 when, as he said, Dermott had gotten into some things that made him uncomfortable. But he still absolutely "adored the girl" and Marjorie he "loved like a sister."

In mid-November of 2004, Bryan Todd Christy had received a call from the 702 area code. Although he had avoided Dermott's calls for months, this time he picked up. Susan Dermott was very upset and asked Christy if he knew what was going on with Marjorie; it was all terrible and Marjorie needed her friends, so Christy had to help her—right away! Christy called Marjorie instantly. They picked up their closeness right where they had left off. He heard that her husband was missing, but he did not want to pry and so did not ask her questions about it. She said she was afraid at night, so he began spending the nights at her house. On Thanksgiving Day, he went with Noah and Marjorie to a movie. Oscar Moreno was out of town, so it was just the three of them.

Marjorie turned to Christy the day she was arrested. The five-ten, 180-pound native Iowan began taking things out of the house for her and ferrying them to places she directed him to. This included cash. The day the detectives came with the search warrant, they asked him to account for everything. The police seized heavy trunks in the apartment which Christy said belonged to Marjorie. They told Christy the items did not belong to Marjorie, they belonged to the estate of Jay Orbin.

Christy responded that he was glad to get rid of them, and with the items they had seized that day, the police now had everything except for $1300, which he had sent out of state. He said he was sorry about it all and would retrieve the money and surrender it to police, but due to a variety of circumstances, it would take about two weeks. The police felt he was a reasonable person who had not understood the implications of what his friend had been asking him to do. The detectives left feeling that Christy was simply a generous soul who was loyal to his friends, to a fault. They left the apartment thinking they would get the $1300 exactly when he'd promised it would come.

The money didn't come.

But Bryan Todd Christy returned to jail frequently and turned out to be Marjorie's most devoted visitor. Police listened in as Marjorie gave Christy more and more instructions and Christy, incredibly, agreed to follow them. He went to ATMs and took cash out of Marjorie's accounts; he was in frequent contact with Marjorie's old friend, nightclub impresario Michael J. Peter; he mailed packages for her. Something they later learned was that at Marjorie's request, he also forwarded mail between inmates, who were not allowed to write directly to one another. But with Todd acting as a mail drop, Marjorie and her friends on the inside could write letters to other inmates who had been transferred.

Police began to trust Christy less and watch him more.

Finally, cops had had enough of Bryan Todd Christy's shenanigans. On May 18, 2005, they arrested him. Christy seemed unable to grasp the seriousness of serving as the errand boy for a murder suspect in custody. In tape recorded conversations between him and Marjorie, she herself had even spelled it out. She asked Christy to perform various tasks, she told him, since she could not ask her lawyer to do them, "because lawyers have to follow the law."

When Christy was arrested and brought to downtown police headquarters, Detective Dave Barnes conducted a frustrating interview with him in which Christy often diverted the conversation or flat-out refused to answer. Eventually the detective warned him that he was doing himself no favors with his clever and sometimes juvenile attitude.

> **DB:*** So what's gonna happen is you're gonna go to jail tonight.
> **BTC:** 'Kay.
> **DB:** You're looking at four charges.
> **BTC:** 'Kay.
> **DB:** They're all felonies.
> **BTC:** 'Kay.
> **DB:** Burglary. Theft. Fraudulent Schemes. And Hindering Prosecution.
> **BTC:** You're really grabbing at straws, aren't you?
> **DB:** No, not really.

The interview came to a close. Christy took the news that he'd be jailed and charged with felonies calmly, even impudently. There was some administrative fuss as Detective Barnes came in and out of the room and then told his prisoner there would be more waiting. In response, Christy's personality expressed itself abundantly. "Might be several more minutes," Barnes had cautioned. "No problem," Christy replied, "I'll take a nap."

Before they got to this point, Christy had alternated

---

* Official transcript from Phoenix Police report.

between "I choose not to answer that," rapid and babbling diversions, and moments of confident and loquacious candor. During this steeplechase of a conversation, Detective Barnes heard all about Christy's closeness with the two blond strippers and the frantic call from Susan Dermott that had sent Christy running to Marjorie Orbin's side six months earlier, in November 2004. Christy told the detective the same thing that Barnes had heard so often before, that Marjorie and Jay had an unusual relationship. But Christy, speaking with a certain artlessness, added the twist that Marjorie had had lots of boyfriends during the course of her marriage to Jay. Larry Weisberg was simply the latest.

Bryan Todd Christy's characterization of the love affair between Marjorie Orbin and Larry Weisberg put another damper on the theory that that romance was so intense it would cause a man's death. Detective Barnes asked Christy whether Marjorie had ever seemed upset in November 2004, when he was spending a lot of time with her and Jay's fate was still unknown, that Jay was missing.

BTC: Like I said, there'd be times she would just cry. I mean we'd be sitting there watching TV and it wasn't, you know, it—wasn't like you see someone shot or something and they cry or whatever ... seriously, I ... I can't remember the movies we rented on pay per view ... you could probably check by the bill but, seriously, she was just ...

DB: Did she ever talk about how this strained her and Larry's relationship?

BTC: I don't . . . not to be mean, I don't know that her and Larry were all that, seriously, I think.

DB: You think she is in love with Larry?

BTC: I honestly don't, un-unh, I really don't.

DB: You think they were planning on getting their own house together?

BTC: NO, unh-uhn.

DB: Getting married?

BTC: No, I don't believe that.

DB: Did you know Marjorie had Noah—or attempted to have Noah—call Larry 'Dad, . . . Father'?

BTC: That would surprise me. That would surprise me cuz I . . . I mean that's just terrible for her.

Throughout the interview, Christy was adamant that Marjorie's relationship with Weisberg was no grand love affair. He vigorously objected to the characterization that Weisberg ever "lived with" Marjorie, even though the detective repeatedly said that he was doing so during the time that Jay was considered missing, in the fall of 2004. Christy said that if the neighbors were to worry about the impropriety of any man staying at Marjorie's house while her husband was a missing person, the man to worry about would have been himself:

BTC: . . . I think about what'd the neighbors think, you know. Here's her husband missing six weeks and this guy's staying there.

DB: Right.

BTC: So . . . but I thought, you know, hey, I got proof that I'm a fag, so it didn't bother me.

DB: Did Larry ever spend the night when you were there?

BTC: No, hu-unh . . . nope.

DB: Okay, were you ever worried that Jay was all of a sudden going to show up and find another man living in his house?

BTC: Not me. Lar—he knew I was a fag. So was Marge.*

From the monitored conversations between Marjorie in jail and Christy when he was free, the detective knew that there was one more laptop computer that Marjorie had failed to turn over to police. Barnes asked Christy for it. He refused.

DB: Where's that at?

BTC: (small smirk/chuckle)† . . . Oh, just that I have a laptop that Marjorie gave me.

DB: You realize that you're withholding evidence?

BTC: I . . . I don't feel that's . . . how is that evidence, though?

DB: Cuz I know about the laptop.

BTC: Okay.

DB: So, is it at your apartment?

BTC: I will not tell you that. I do have a laptop that Marjorie gave me. I'll tell you . . .

---

* Although this statement may have seemed relevant to the case because Marjorie's sexual feelings toward Jay were under close consideration as they related to motive, police did not follow up on it during this interview.

† From the official transcript.

DB: You know, you could just be digging yourself a deeper hole, Todd.

BTC: I'm telling you the truth, officer. I will not lie to you. I have too much respect for you.

DB: What's the big deal about the laptop?

BTC: Cuz I feel like I deserve the lap—Seriously, all the work, you don't understand the work I did. Seriously, I mean, that . . . seriously, Marjorie tried to pay me. There's a couple times she tried to hand me a couple hundred dollar bills—

DB: You know that's a stolen laptop?

BTC: Really? That laptop is? I had no idea. I don't know that. The laptop is stolen? Um, I don't believe that cuz she gave me a . . . the receipt to it, so, and it was cash, so I feel that's hard to believe.

DB: Well, it was bought with proceeds from the estate.

Marjorie's friend continued to debate the point with the detective. For a few minutes, all they pinned down was the fact that Christy received the laptop from Marjorie *after* Jay went missing. This made the detective want it all the more.

DB: Okay, are you going to tell me where the laptop is?

BTC: Umm, no. But if need be, I will turn over the laptop if—if you need the laptop. I will gladly turn over the laptop.

DB: Well, I do need it.

BTC: Okay.

DB: So . . .

BTC: Would I be . . . by chance get it back or would
it be your property?

By the end of the interview, Christy had still not
revealed the whereabouts of the laptop. It took a melo-
dramatic visit from Christy's FBI brother to get the laptop located. Barnes and others drove to Tucson to pick
up the brother who flew in from over a thousand miles
away. Together, they all drove out to a Tucson home
with a Ford Escort parked in the driveway, covered by a
tarp gathering dust.

When his brother agreed to act as mediator, Christy
had finally revealed that the laptop was hidden in the
trunk of an unused car parked at his boyfriend Oscar
Moreno's parents' home. The parents had no idea.
Christy was nearly hysterical with panic that they should
find themselves in trouble.

Christy's brother had coaxed the location of the car's
key out of Christy and retrieved it. Now they were all
standing there and, as Christy had hoped, Moreno's parents were not home and were therefore oblivious to the
drama in their driveway.

The lawmen inserted the key and opened the trunk.
Inside they saw a purple-colored trunk with a padlock
on it. Inside the purple trunk, they found the long-sought
laptop. And jewelry. Lots of jewelry. It was later valued,
with the help of Jay's close associate Marshall Roosin,
as worth $375,000 retail.

When examined, the laptop held no evidence of
value in the Jay Orbin murder case. The only secret it

gave up was a slight bit of evidence implicating Oscar Moreno—whom they had not suspected yet—in helping to hide the thing. The laptop had become an object of great desire and mystery only through Bryan Todd Christy's curious mixture of loyalty and a sense of entitlement.

Nearly two weeks after Christy had been arrested and had become a guest of the county, Scott Halvorson from Blockbuster Video called police. He was calling from the store where Christy would have been working, if he hadn't been in jail since the middle of May. He had something in his hands that he wanted to get rid of as soon as possible.

Halvorson's information would underscore just how much Christy had been playing cat and mouse with those investigating Jay Orbin's death.

The video store employee told police that a week after Christy's arrest, Oscar Moreno had showed up at the store on an errand for his jailed lover. Christy had left some expensive cologne at the store, he said, hidden inside an empty video box in the back room. Moreno needed to retrieve it.

But store personnel searched the back room and couldn't find it. Moreno left empty-handed. Two days later, he called the store still looking for the cologne. Halvorson went into the back room to help search. Still, nobody found anything. Being new at the store, Halvorson noticed that a drawer was locked. He asked his staff about it. They told him it had never been locked before and they all believed that Christy had the key. Scott Halvorson was unhappy to hear it.

He forced the drawer open.

He found the VHS box. It was too heavy to hold cologne. He opened the box and received an unpleasant surprise. Inside the box he found two pieces of turquoise-and-silver jewelry. The staff at Blockbuster Video may have had only the sketchiest understanding of the murder case that the gregarious Christy had gotten himself involved in, but they did know that the murder victim had been a dealer in Indian jewelry.

Halvorson called police immediately and soon a detective was on his way to retrieve the secreted evidence.

Bryan Todd Christy had been theatrical, confident and wily in his interview with Detective Dave Barnes. As the adventure of the hidden jewelry proved, he had also held his cards close to his vest, all while chattering like a magpie. But he had peppered the interview with some valuable tidbits of truth from his own personal observations from his privileged seat in the theater of Marjorie's life.

One of those had to do with his keen eye for the physical appearance of his friend. During the October 28 raid at Marjorie's house—the one without the battering ram and the Taser and all the drama of the first raid before Jay's body had been found—cocaine and meth had been discovered in the master suite. Barnes now had in custody someone who seemed to have a closer view of Marjorie's inner life than most of the people around her, such as her in-laws and neighbors. This was a valuable asset. The detective asked Christy if Marjorie used drugs.

Christy responded with one of his flashes of frankness. He didn't have any direct knowledge of drug use by Marjorie. It wasn't something he felt she would share with him, because he was known to disapprove of it. But he had his "suspicions." When he had first driven over to Marjorie's house that November day when Susan Dermott had sent him running to her aid, he nearly hadn't recognized Marjorie. She was very thin, he said. She was deeply tan, her hair was different, but most of all, she was so much thinner than when he'd last seen her. He had certain theories about that.

Bryan Todd Christy was not the only one to remark about a change in Marjorie's appearance in the last months of Jay's life.

Noah Orbin's appearance had also been changing. Within weeks of his mother's arrest, his relatives were startled to see a dark line appearing at the base of the child's hair. "Not just naturally turning darker as you get older, but literally the straight line," recalled Jake Jr. "We were shocked that he wasn't a little tow-headed kid." At trial, Christy testified that Marjorie had been using Sun-In to bleach the little boy's hair.

"Within two months of her arrest," Jake said, shaking his head, "Noah's got brown hair and we're just totally amazed that she would be dyeing his hair."

CHAPTER THIRTEEN

A Trip to Florida

Shortly after the turn of the new year, Dave Barnes paid a visit to Jake Sr. and Joann Orbin. Marjorie had been in jail since before Christmas. Noah was living with the Orbins at this time. It was the middle of the school year and the family had decided to "ease the transition because we didn't want to yank him out of school so we kept him here in Phoenix to finish the second grade." The plan was for the child to live with Grandma and Grandpa until the end of the school year, then Uncle Jake would take him to San Diego and permanently provide a home for him. The little boy's grandparents told the investigator that Noah was currently doing well and had adjusted nicely to living with them. They told him Noah didn't ask or talk much about his father.

The one thing the child did say to his grandparents

was that his mother had told him that Dad had been "shot."

The grandparents wanted the detective to see a letter that Marjorie had written to the second grader from jail. Part of it went like this:

> *You know in your heart that your mommy didn't do anything wrong. . . . I have some really good friends that are helping me. . . . It has been very hard because of the other people around that could be helping but choose not to. If you want to, you can ask anyone that says they love you why they are not helping you get your mommy back. I think daddy would be ashamed of them for not helping.*

The last time the child had seen his mother had been December 6, 2004. She'd been wearing a short blue housedress and white tennis shoes, standing in the foyer of their home, surrounded by policemen who were handcuffing her.

The last time he'd seen his father had been three months before that, at his own birthday party. His dad was smiling and carrying a big cake to him. The discovery of the torso at the edge of town had been big news, as it would be in any city. Whether Noah ever caught a glimpse of news footage of his dad was uncertain. At least at one moment, according to Bryan Todd Christy, he'd been in the same room when the torso story came on TV.

"I was actually there the night the broadcast came across the television set. It was sometime in November. I think it was like a week or so before Thanksgiving, but

I really don't recall. I just remember it was Channel 5. I was sitting in the big couch. She was on the love seat. Noah was at the table. We were literally eating dinner in the living room. And we seen it and I just—I was utterly shocked and she seemed a little stunned by it, and her and Noah went to the bedroom and I just respected their privacy."

Christy remembered Noah being very upset by what he'd seen on television and vowing to "get" whoever "did this" to his daddy.

Police were still very much interested in finding the rest of Jay Orbin's remains. His parents, brother and friends were, too. In February 2005, they caught a lead. Marjorie's cellmate, a woman named Sophia Johnson, had been secretly meeting with police when Marjorie thought she was being taken out for weekly legal visits.

Sophia Johnson was about ten or fifteen years younger than Marjorie, but she was also a blond Scottsdale housewife. She was a tall girl, even taller than Marjorie, and had a fresher and softer face. What had landed her in jail was a kidnapping charge brought by her ex-husband over their young children, of whom the father had custody.

Johnson had been instructed not to pump her cellmate for information but just to report on things that Marjorie said of her own accord.* Police also tried to

---

* Sophia's comments to police were made from memory, as she obviously could not take notes in front of Marjorie.

cultivate other snitches. One woman named Lisa Sherman told them she had overheard Marjorie talking about the kitchen island in the 55th Street home. Marjorie had talked about having to move the island and that there might be something buried underneath it. In Sherman's opinion, Marjorie "had a fascination with cutting" and could often be heard talking about "cutting things." Sherman felt that what was being alluded to as buried under the kitchen island was the rest of Jay's remains.

Jake Orbin Jr. had earlier told police that during his family visit to the 55th Street house in July 2004—before there was any hint of trouble—the kitchen island had been a two-piece affair. When he rushed back on September 24 after hearing Jay was missing, he noticed that the island had been fused together into one and had also changed position from one spot in the kitchen to another.

Taking this together with Lisa Sherman's bit of jail gossip, Barnes got a new search warrant for the house. He also picked up the phone and called a Colorado company called Necrosearch. As executor of his brother's will, Jake had already sold the house. The new owner was planning to move in that very weekend. When the buyer received word from the detective that they wanted to rip apart his kitchen floor first, he agreed. He knew about the murder before the house had even gone into escrow. Even so, the news that the floor would be pulled out could not have been cheery.

Necrosearch, a nonprofit that stated its mission was to "assist law enforcement" in the "search for clandestine gravesites," sent two team members to Arizona. Clark Davenport was a forensic geophysicist and Angie

Southcott was a geologist. The scientists worked on a volunteer basis.

Dr. Laura Fulginiti, a forensic anthropologist for Maricopa County, also attended the dig. If anything was found under that kitchen island, Dr. Fulginiti would be the one to say if it had to do with a human skeleton, be it toe, finger or jaw.

The equipment itself was pretty fancy. According to Necrosearch, "a clandestine grave represents an intrusion into the natural and/or ambient environment." Therefore, they could employ sophisticated noninvasive technologies to look for telltale geological aberrations. If forward looking infrared (FLR) and ground penetrating radar (GPR) imaging tests came up blank at Marjorie's former house, the team would have to reassess their next step.

But the imaging did not come up blank under Marjorie's former kitchen. The screens blipped with what the experts called an "anomaly." The members of the team must have felt mounting expectations. Would they all be present when Jay's last missing remains were found? Would they be the ones to present the grieving family the chance to give him his proper—and complete—final rest?

The jackhammers were fired up and soon Marjorie's immaculate kitchen was a blizzard of broken tile and flying dirt. The kitchen island slowly rocked out of its nest. They set to digging in soil.

They dug some more.

They got closer and closer to where the oscillating screens had outlined an anomaly. Would it be all the missing parts? or just one? Would it be a limb? or the part that had housed Jay's big smile and beaming blue eyes?

The shovels reached the anomaly.

They prodded. They found moisture.

And that's all they found. There was no part of Jay. The instruments were so sensitive that the aberration they had flagged was a small pooling of water from a leaky pipe.

The policemen with their files full of suffering victims and the experts with all their doctorates were left standing in a jumble of empty hands and rubble. At least they could say they'd left no stone unturned in Jay's behalf.

Jake Jr. had taken over the tragic task of going over his baby brother's things—that would be a house and garage full of stuff and a commercial warehouse full of stuff, not to mention several vehicles between the two properties. It would take a long time to sort through it. The most important thing was to see to Noah's upbringing and care. Although everyone said he adjusted well, there was the bald fact that Jake's nephew had lost both his parents under terrible circumstances. Everyone wanted him to feel safe, stable and loved.

Many of Jay's possessions Jake Jr. put into a storage unit that he rented. Some items he started using. For instance, there was a dolly in the garage that came in handy for moving Jay's boxes around. Handling his brother's estate was a sad duty and a physically taxing one, with all the inventory from a wholesale business.

In 2008, the white cargo van was finally released from custody. Jake drove it carefully down an access road that conveniently ran between the police impound lot and the Jayhawk International warehouse. He had been warned about the deterioration of any rubber component over the course of three years of sitting in the brutal Arizona sunshine and dry air. The vehicle had not had any maintenance—no hoses changed, no fluids replaced, nothing. As he slowly drove down the sheltered road, Jake could feel the truck's neglected condition as it wobbled slightly and creaked, but it did make it to the warehouse safely. He planned to get the maintenance caught up before he could assess what to do with the vehicle further. When he returned to the warehouse later in the week, he climbed into the truck and started to back out. But immediately he knew something was wrong. He could hear a whining sound and the front end alignment lurched. Jake looked out the cabin window and saw the right tire horribly displaced from the carriage—it had not moved as far from the original parking spot as the rest of the vehicle had. The whining sound he had heard was the tire dragging laterally across the polished concrete floor.

Jake carefully shifted into first gear and rolled the vehicle back in place, where it met up with its right front tire. He called Phoenix Police right away.

Detective Kenneth Porter of the Homicide detail took a look at the undercarriage of the van. On the right side "the adjusting sleeve of the tie rod had been cut and was about to separate into two pieces. If the sleeve were to break in two the wheels would no longer 'track' together and the van would not be able to steer."*

The team photographed the tie rod in place, then got a

---

* From Phoenix Police report.

new tie-rod assembly and put it in the van in order to con-
fiscate the damaged one. Porter considered the damage in
context. "The front section of the van's frame assembly
did not show any signs or evidence of having been in an
accident or being driven over any obstacles in a manner
that would damage or 'scrap' the frame or suspension
elements."

The tie-rod assembly was a critical component of controlling the car. Porter could find no reason why it would
have been damaged in a natural way. He was ready to
take it out. "While I was removing the right side tie-rod
assembly the adjusting sleeve completely severed in two.
If this had occurred while the vehicle was being driven
the van would no longer steer."

This was even worse than it sounded.

"If this had occurred while driving at higher speeds,
such as freeway speeds, the lack of control of the vehicle
would be greatly aggravated. The van would not only be
unsteerable, but the wheels would become oriented in
different directions.

"Not only would a collision with other vehicles be
highly probable, the possibility of the van becoming
involved in a single vehicle rollover accident would also
be probable."

He gave a detailed account of all the surrounding
components and how none of them showed signs of
having suffered damage from wear or impact that could
explain or cause the singular break in that right sleeve.

Furthermore, there was one more very telling item.
Looking closely at the cut, "it had the appearance of
having been cut with a pinching type tool, similar to
a tubing cutter. Both sides of the adjusting sleeve were

'beveled' as would be consistent with a tubing cutter type tool being rotated around the sleeve."

A later lab report confirmed Porter's findings. The tie rod had been deliberately cut through with a compression instrument such as a pipe cutter.

At the rate the incision was rusted over, forensic experts also determined that the sabotage had to have been done years earlier.

Comments that many of Marjorie Orbin's associates and friends had repeated to police took on a new sinister quality. Marjorie had said to many people that it was "amazing" how Jay had not perished on the highways because of his constant traveling. She often added that "statistically" he should have died "by now," or that it was a marvel he hadn't "driven over a cliff" somewhere. She said he was "lucky." Jay himself had been afraid of a highway accident. He'd echoed Marjorie's statement that "statistically" it should have happened by now.

Her loyal friend Bryan Todd Christy was one of those who had heard Marjorie make this statement repeatedly.

He had also heard of worse.

In one conversation with Arizona state prosecutor Noel Levy and Detective Dave Barnes, Christy mentioned that when Susan Dermott still lived in Phoenix and Marjorie and Jay still lived in their house on Cheryl Drive, Dermott would often stay at Marjorie's house for days on end while Jay was traveling. The two would be sharing "breakfast, lunch, dinner," "spending the night," and "making costumes together.*

---

* From Phoenix Police report transcripts.

"Susan would tell me things that Marjorie had said to her—about Jay taking a trip and there was comments made about voodoo, voodooism, arsenic poisoning, stuff like that."

Of course the prosecutor immediately wanted to hear more. He asked if Christy meant that Dermott was telling him that Marjorie wanted Jay dead one way or the other. Christy agreed that's what he meant. He elaborated that he had been hearing this kind of talk for years.

"Susan would make comments to me . . . about she doesn't know how the man was still alive that Marjorie had given him so much arsenic or something . . . Uh, there was comments about voodoo, the voodoo dolls that Marjorie had used, you know, in reference that they were Jay or something."

Detective Dave Barnes was also in the room during this interview. Because of Christy's fidgety way of talking, the detective wanted to make it clear. "Did Susan actually say that Marjorie poisoned Jay?" he asked.

"Yeah. She said something about arsenic, 'I'm surprised the guy is still alive with that amount of arsenic.' I said, 'what?!!?' And she'd go 'oh, nothing.' "

Later they revisited the topic of the alleged arsenic poisoning of Jay. Noel Levy asked Christy if he believed Dermott to be an active participant in getting Jay to consume arsenic. Christy had a hard time admitting that he did believe she'd helped.

"Those comments that she made that . . . something about, you know, 'oh, Marjorie and I drank a bottle of wine last night and we—we tried to think of this.' I mean like, the way I interpreted, yes, that maybe she had a hand in . . . in planning on poisoning him and this and that at times. Yes. I, I did feel that. I did interp— that was my interpretation at the time, yes."

Even after he had been in jail for months on her behalf, Christy's opinion of Marjorie Orbin's love affair with Larry Weisberg had not changed. "I don't feel that she had feelings for him. As she put it to me, you know, just as 'woman-to-woman' intimate details of their messing around. [She said] he was boring [in] bed, he was nice to look at, easy on the eyes, as she put it, for his age, he was easy on the eyes. He was in very good physical shape for his age and that was really about it."

Bryan Todd Christy had been so close to Marjorie that he hid cash for her, hid hundreds of thousands of dollars of jewelry for her, had been entrusted by her with the future care of Noah in a failed power of attorney, moved vehicles for her jail friends, visited her in jail, lied to police for her, lost a relationship* and went to jail for her, yet she never told him she was afraid of Larry Weisberg or beseeched him to protect Noah from him.

What Christy *had* seen was Marjorie moving heavy boxes at the downtown warehouse. But she stopped when it came time to tote one of the heaviest outside. "You should probably carry this outside in case there's any news crews out there," Christy reported her saying

---

* Christy's relationship with Oscar Moreno did not survive his jail term and all the troubles over Marjorie's case.

to him. "My attorney doesn't want me carrying anything heavy."

For the Orbins, it was a time of unimaginable sorrow and confusion. Detective Jan Butcher remembered arriving at their house to tell them what had happened to Jay. "My eyes just teared up," the soft-spoken natural blond said, embarrassed at exposing her delicacy. She felt, in the hard-bitten world of Homicide detectives, she should've been flintier. "But they are just the best people, the Orbins, just the best. I couldn't help it. It was terrible. They were beside themselves."

Later, at trial, Butcher was often seen to be indulging her urge to comfort: she'd show up in court with Tupperware containers of home-baked goods and hand them over to Jakes Jr. and Sr. and Jake Jr.'s girlfriend Shelly and Joann. There was always a variety inside, from cupcakes to different types of cookies: clearly, she had been thinking about them a lot.

Detective Jan Butcher had had to tell them a lot of shocking things. Of course, none could compare with the discovery of Jay's remains, but these other revelations came as repeating assaults to their hearts. For example, although they knew that Marjorie had been married before, they were flabbergasted to hear the total number of marriages had actually been seven, by the age of thirty-three. And then came the news that Marjorie had already divorced Jay and that it had happened years ago. They could not believe the pair had kept this secret from all of them for, apparently, Noah's entire life.

They were never very sure about Marjorie's own family. They thought she had a twin sister. Detectives started looking for the twin until such close confidants as Susan Dermott and Bryan Todd Christy told them there was no such person. Even as late as five years into the case, Detective Butcher was still curious about Marjorie's family. Only one of them was heard from, through a letter, at trial. Her half brothers were unknown to just about everyone. To everyone but her own defense team, Marjorie denied having any other sibling than Allison Kroh.

But everyone knew about her connection to the uber-wealthy Michael J. Peter. He was out of prison himself now and had even won some significant post-conviction legal battles in his case. When Marjorie had been in jail for six months, Dave Barnes and two other detectives flew out to Fort Lauderdale armed with a search warrant. Jail-monitored conversations between Bryan Todd Christy and Marjorie Orbin had led them there.

The Phoenix cops showed up at Peter's company offices at nine-thirty in the morning, but no one was there. A phone number for an office manager was posted on a card in the window at the lingerie store below. The office manager was contacted and soon arrived on scene to cooperate. Her name was Deenie. From Deenie's cell phone, Barnes ended up in a conversation with the boss himself. The conversation was not recorded. The detective had to summarize it for the files.

The trip to Florida and the dealings with Michael J. Peter were not without their cloak-and-dagger aspects. Before arriving, the three Arizona detectives arranged with Florida law enforcement for some support. Detective Thomas Anderson of the Broward County Sheriff's Office had personally dealt with Michael J. Peter in earlier years, during the mogul's own criminal case. When Deenie got the boss on the phone in the office above the lingerie shop, Barnes handed the cell over to Anderson. Over Deenie's phone, Michael J. Peter appeared to be agreeable and easily admitted to receiving packages from Christy.

The impresario then told Barnes something he had not yet heard. The skin biz magnate had called Marjorie in the summer of 2004 and asked her to come back to him. Since that was the summer that ended with Jay's death, the detective very much wanted to hear more. Marjorie had told him, Peter explained, that she was happy with Jay and had a good life. Later, at trial, he told it as Marjorie turning down his invitation by talking about Noah, saying "she would never take the father from the son or the son from the father."

Peter also had an interesting version of his original split with Marjorie. "He did say back in the 90s they lived together and were to get married. He kicked Marjorie out and told me that was the worst thing he could have done as Marjorie was the best thing he has ever had," Barnes noted. From a man who "had" every expensive object one could think of, from yachts to jets, and literally thousands of beautiful women from coast to coast and across the globe, it was high praise indeed.

Marjorie had been in jail only six months at the time of this conversation and yet Michael J. Peter told Barnes he had already spent $150,000 on Marjorie's defense with the lawyer he'd hand-selected, Tom

Connelly. He had promised Connelly to cover at least
$400,000 of fees.*

Peter did not deny that Christy had mailed him jewelry on Marjorie's behalf. He admitted the value of it was
"around twenty or thirty thousand dollars." He even said
he had no problem turning it over to the Arizona lawmen. But these detectives had heard this kind of promised cooperation before from Christy himself. Trusting
Christy had cost them three plane tickets to Florida.
They wanted to know where the jewelry was right *now*.

Now that, Peter wasn't sure of. It just wasn't top of
mind. He wasn't sure where he'd put it. It might be in a
safe deposit box in Orlando. Or maybe he'd already sent
it on to Tom Connelly, in his capacity as an officer of the
court. Peter assured Barnes, somewhat righteously, that
he had advised Todd Christy to turn over all jewelry
and cash to the lawyers himself because it belonged to
the estate.

But where was it all right this minute as they spoke?
It definitely was not at his own house, no. He'd have to
"make some calls" and get back to them. The conversation ended.

The coterie of agents searched through Peter's office
and seized a letter from Marjorie, written from jail, and
some letters between Tom Connelly and Peter. While
they looked, Deenie told them that her boss was currently in New York, taking care of his sick mother, and

---

* Four years later, for Marjorie's case did not go in front of a jury
until January of 2009, Tom Connelly was still a member of the
defense team. The amount spent by then was unknown. Marjorie
also had two other lawyers for her trial, at taxpayer expense.

had been there for months. He flew down to Fort Lauderdale about once a week, she said, to take care of business.

Late that afternoon, about five-thirty, Broward County's Detective Anderson called the Arizona contingent. Barnes recalled that "Michael [Peter] had arranged for the jewelry to be delivered from a location in Miami. Deenie was to pick up the jewelry from the airport and deliver it to Detective Anderson. Michael would not say who was holding the items, only saying it was a friend of his who he does not want to get involved. Det. Anderson met with Deenie and took possession of the items." The contents of the package were not what they expected, "the items appear to be personal items of Jay Orbin's. None of the Indian jewelry was recovered."

More details of Marjorie Orbin's life, and especially that critical second week of September, were explored. School records for Noah were subpoenaed. So were his pediatric records. The doctor's office procedure, it turned out, was pretty specific where strep throat was concerned. It was considered a serious infirmity and could send a child into dangerous high fevers. Parents had two options: they could call the office on the phone or they could request an appointment through the Web site. Either way, records would be kept, especially on something as serious as strep throat. Any time strep was suspected, the doctors demanded the child be brought in for attention that day. If for some reason that was not possible, they directed the parent to bring the child to the nearest emergency room.

For suspected strep throat, there was no such thing as "calling in a prescription." The pediatrician's office was adamant: a child with suspected strep must be seen and a record made.

Both Jake Orbin Sr. and Joann Orbin had talked to Jay on the morning of September 8, 2004. Since it was his birthday, there was no mistaking the date of these conversations. They had both been told by him that Marjorie had not prepared a celebration for him because both she and Noah had "strep throat." Furthermore, he planned to stay away from the house for most of the day for that very reason.

Late that evening, Phoenix Police computer experts had determined, Jay Orbin had stopped by the pediatrician's Web site. He had used search engines to learn more about "strep throat." By all accounts, even Marjorie's, he was a doting father. It would surprise no one that he'd be interested in what was going on with his little boy.

But was Jay's interest in strep throat more ominous than that? According to his parents, Marjorie had told him that she had it, too. Had he come home, found her hale and hearty, and become suspicious of what she was telling him? Had he asked if the sleeping child—for Noah, in all his interviews, did not remember seeing his father after his own birthday in August—had been given medications and received unsatisfactory answers from his wife?

When subpoenaed after Jay's disappearance, Noah's pediatrician's office had no record of any calls from the Orbin family for strep throat anytime in September.

Noah's last office visit had been months earlier, and he had no visits and no Web requests at all in September 2004. Marjorie never produced any records verifying the strep throat, from any doctor anywhere. The pediatrician's office believed she had been coming long enough that she should have known the procedure: strep throat could not be treated with "bed rest" or over-the-counter syrups or even with call-in advice. They believed she would have known he'd have to come in.

CHAPTER FOURTEEN

Battered Justice

By the fall of 2008, Marjorie Orbin had been sitting in jail for four years but had not yet come before a jury. She had not seen her son, Noah, since the day she was arrested. He had gone from a cuddly second grader to a gangly twelve-year-old. His uncle, Jake Orbin Jr., had married his girlfriend Shelly, and Noah had been living with the couple in San Diego, California, for the last three years. The newly constituted family had lived in a terrible limbo. They wanted Noah to have a stable life with normal school days and activities, but Jake also wanted to be present in court in Arizona to see justice done for his baby brother, Noah's father. Finally, it looked like the trial was going to go forward in January of 2009. Jake planned to uproot the boy and his new wife one last time, and made plans to arrange an early retirement from his dream job at the San Diego Parks

Department in order that by the turn of the new year he, Noah and Shelly could return to Phoenix and be settled in time for Marjorie's trial to start.

While the Orbins transferred from San Diego to Phoenix, Detective Dave Barnes was pursuing some personal goals. The last year had not gone well for him. While Marjorie's case was undergoing various legal maneuvers, Barnes had been working hard on other cases. In 2005 and 2006, some months after Marjorie's arrest, Phoenix had suffered a series of serial sexual murders attributed to a fiend dubbed the Baseline Rapist. Baseline Road was the southernmost thoroughfare for much of the city of Phoenix, with developed land on the northern edge and legally protected desert on the southern. The earliest attacks had occurred more or less along this street, so police had dubbed their perpetrator after it. The violent attacks spread out geographically as time went on, but the name stuck. Detective Barnes was working directly on the Baseline Rapist case while lawyers wrestled over points of law in Marjorie's case. Sometime after the Baseline Rapist was identified as linking several tragic cases, a second serial killer was deemed to be also active in the community. This one was called the Serial Shooter* and his victims were stacking up as well.

With two serial killers on the loose in the city, resources were strained. Tensions were high. After suspects in both those cases were arrested in 2006, Detective Barnes's relationships with various coworkers burst into

---

* For the full story of the Serial Shooter, see *A Sudden Shot: The Phoenix Serial Shooter* by Camille Kimball.

shreds. When the mayor gave out commendations to the Baseline investigative team, Barnes's name was left off. By many accounts,* Barnes was enraged by this exclusion. A series of accusations and counter-accusations flew around the police department in an administrative storm of epic proportions. When the dust settled, Barnes had been demoted from Homicide detective, an elite position with a high salary, to the newbie position of patrol officer. He later still attended Marjorie's trial as case agent and sat at the state's table with prosecutor Noel Levy, but when not in court, he was a uniformed cop in a marked vehicle making traffic stops and settling bar fights. He no longer had a desk in the elite Homicide unit. He no longer had a desk at all.

On Saturday, October 4, 2008†—as all the rest of the players in Marjorie's case were scrambling to make their last preparations for trial—Dave Barnes, patrol officer, entered the mostly empty Violent Crimes Bureau. It was 11 A.M. He was on duty but alone. At first he swiped his assigned security access card across the electronic reader, but his card was no longer valid and the door would not open.

But the device recorded his attempts.

Then Barnes asked for access from the sergeant on duty. Sergeant Bill Lindvall had Barnes write his signature on the sign-in sheet, then beeped him in by remote. Secretary Vicki Waddell noted Dave Barnes's arrival as well.

---

* Affidavit for a Search Warrant SW2009-003088 Detective Theron Quaas, affiant.
† Affidavit for a Search Warrant SW2009-003088 Detective Theron Quaas, affiant.

On Sunday, October 5, 2008, photos of the desk and work area of a female Phoenix Homicide detective, Celeste Martoni,* appeared on a blogger's Web site. The blog post was titled with the female detective's name "and Pictures of Her Cube." The photos showed her Phoenix PD–issued nameplate leading into her cubicle and several personal items in her work space, such as photos of her children and calendars noting her kid's soccer games and so forth.

Phoenix PD detective Theron Quaas had been watching that particular Web site. He saw the pictures go up on Sunday. Quaas found the photos not only alarming, but very relevant to his own work. He did not yet know about former detective Dave Barnes's Saturday visit to the Homicide Unit, where he no longer belonged.

That Monday, when all the detectives showed up for their regular workweek, the nameplates for Martoni and her husband, also a Homicide detective, were found to be missing. Soon more photos began to appear on the Web site that Quaas was monitoring, showcasing the two nameplates in a variety of locales, in a fashion similar to the familiar pop contrivance of a traveling garden gnome. In vitriolic posts on the blog, the married detectives were referred to as "Mr. and Mrs. Potatohead." The photos then began to feature two actual Potato Head dolls along with the nameplates. The photos were always underscored by insulting and sarcastic captions, often with demeaning sexual content.

Detective Quaas went to the grand jury and obtained

---

* Denotes pseudonym.

some subpoenas. He gathered a lot of evidence, including camera information and cell phone records leading to the person most likely to have not only swiped the nameplates out of the police station but also taken the photos of the detective's work area with her personal items.

Detective Martoni was increasingly upset by the way the Web site constantly attacked her. The clandestine invasion of her work space was bad enough, but the photos were becoming especially threatening. The Potato Head dolls with her nameplate and her husband's were photographed outlined in white corpse tape, with sharp instruments pointed at them. The detective took down all her personal items from her work area. She changed desks. She began to exhibit signs of depression, with fits of crying and hair-trigger nerves. Her husband was showing the strain, too. Both spent on-the-job time dealing with this situation and their frayed emotions.

The other Homicide detectives in the unit also found the situation to be disruptive. They had all received an e-mail a few weeks earlier that was allegedly from their female colleague. The e-mail address contained her full name, but none of them believed that the content could have come from her. Indeed, Martoni vehemently denied any connection to the message or to the e-mail account it came from.

The e-mail, dated July 17, 2008, at 1:49 P.M., contained a long diatribe against the department in general from graft, to rape, to child porn. It made frequent references to the two married detectives, referring to Celeste Martoni as "Blowjob Martoni" and claiming she regularly "gave blowjobs" to fellow cops at the end of their shifts at her previous precinct. The e-mail, allegedly from "Blowjob Martoni" herself, urged the other Homicide detectives to go to that Web site, the same one that had been upsetting her for months with its references to her, photos of her cubicle, and staged Potato Head scenes, for more such content attacking her and her husband primarily, as well as some other Phoenix cops.

Special Investigations detective Theron Quaas was assigned to the case. None of the half dozen Homicide detectives who received this e-mail believed that Celeste herself had sent it, despite her full name being part of the e-mail address, but most of the homicide detectives told Quaas they had a good guess who *had*. Many of them felt the attacks on the Martonis constituted criminal activity, and urged the detective to pursue the matter vigorously.

Quaas did so. He quietly went about conducting interviews, serving subpoenas and poring over forensic evaluations of computers, phones and cameras.

And pictures of "Mr. and Mrs. Potatohead."

On Thursday, January 29, 2009, Marjorie's trial, with her life at stake as the state sought the death penalty, finally commenced. Prosecutor Noel Levy took the rostrum and faced the jury. In the benches in the gallery sat Jay Orbin's mom and dad, his brother and sister-in-law, several other family members and loved ones, and both local and national reporters. At the prosecution table, Detective Jan Butcher was in her place as "third." She had started the Orbin case as a Missing Persons detective but since then had been promoted to Homicide. Next to her was Dave Barnes, currently a patrolman, but still considered lead detective on this case.

At the defense table, Marjorie wore the kind of conservative housewife fashions she had never worn when she was actually living as a wife and stay-at-home mother. Her hair had gone from platinum blonde to a honey brown, and fell simply around her shoulders. Glasses rested on her nose. She was surrounded by a team of three lawyers, two paid for by the people of Arizona, one paid for by Michael J. Peter. She sat ramrod straight. Since it was somewhat tucked away from view behind the table, jurors probably did not notice the bulky security belt under her clothes. But the deputies sitting near her could flick a switch and activate a strong electric current should she become a threat to anyone in the room.

Prosecutor Levy gave the jurors his overview of the case, painting Marjorie as ruthless, greedy and lascivious. But Marjorie's team had reserved their opening statement for later: they would not give any speeches until it was time to present their defense. Levy started calling witnesses, beginning with Officer Jay Krook, the officer who'd been the first one on scene when the 911 call came in on Saturday, October 23, 2004. A blue plastic tub with a lid on it, sitting in the desert, had been pointed out to Krook. He had lifted the lid. What he had seen inside was why everyone was in court that day.

Levy called more police officers to the stand. He called the medical examiner and the forensic anthropologist, and more gory details of the tub's contents came out. A fingerprint specialist identified Marjorie's prints on the can of Glade found in the Bronco.

Joann Orbin, Jay's mother, took the stand and described her last conversation with her son, wishing him a happy birthday and hearing of his plans to return to Phoenix shortly.

Joann had waited so long for this proceeding, where she might see her son's killer called to account. She, and all the Orbins, were relieved the trial had finally gotten under way. At two weeks in, she was hoping it wouldn't be long before there was some sense of closure brought into their lives, the agonizing limbo brought to an end, a formal condemnation by society of the one who had taken an innocent life.

Levy started calling people who knew Marjorie. Her former cellmate Sophia Johnson testified that Marjorie had confided to her during jail conversations that she had, in fact, killed Jay. She said Marjorie spoke of her former husband with contempt, especially in her assessment of his physical attributes and what she deemed his sexual inadequacy. One day, according to Johnson, Marjorie had said she was "dying inside" with Jay and needed to "find a way out." In the cell she shared with the younger Scottsdale housewife, Marjorie had also talked a lot about Michael J. Peter, and how allegedly during his own criminal troubles a few years earlier, "during the trial she lied for [him] during testimony."

Sophia Johnson said she had later become afraid of Marjorie. Apparently, when Johnson was transferred to state prison, after her stay in county jail, where she had met Marjorie, an inmate had attacked her and let her know the beating was "from Marjorie." Johnson also testified that Marjorie had said that when she learned "a hair was found on Jay . . . she immediately flushed all of her hair extensions down the toilet." Johnson understood them to be blond extensions. Although the timing was off, that offered an explanation for why at least one set of hair extensions had been found in the trash at the 55th Street house during the SWAT team raid. Johnson was also one of the many people to whom Marjorie had claimed that Noah was not Jay's biological child. Bryan Todd Christy was another. Many of Marjorie's associates inside the jail were told this. Several outside the jail, from her housewife days, had been told this as well.

Sophia Johnson said Marjorie had laughed and joked that Jay's body had been "chilled" and cut up "in alphabetical order," because she was "so organized." According to Johnson, Marjorie also said that both HBO and A&E were working with her to do a big special on how poorly the justice system was treating her. Marjorie had talked to Johnson about how her friend, Bryan Todd Christy, had told her that his brother in the FBI had judged the case against her to be "fucked up" and "they" would be checking into the detective "to tear him apart."

Marjorie's former best friend Sharon Franco, who'd once idolized Marjorie, testified that she, too, was now afraid of the woman. By the time she testified in 2009, her last name had become Rueckert—she and Jessiah Rueckert had gotten married. Franco said her former friend had often expressed disgust for Jay Orbin's physical presence as well as a desire to be rid of him. Marjorie had gone so far, Franco reported, as to say that one day she'd like to shoot Jay in the face, cut him up and leave him in the desert.

Jessiah Rueckert, now a married man of twenty-three, testified next. He admitted that he *had* had a sexual relationship with Marjorie when he was seventeen and she was forty-two. She had known him since he was in middle school.* Her flirtatious text to him after his father's shooting† had not been completely without context, but it had upset Rueckert because he was dealing with the trauma of what had just happened to his father. Also, he'd felt committed to Sharon Franco by then. Considering the animosity between the two women at that point, he felt Marjorie's sexual pursuit made him a pawn in an ugly game.

Jessiah Rueckert also described the discord at the karate studio and the general belief that Marjorie Orbin had been its epicenter.

Jan Beeso, the woman whom Marjorie had enlisted to babysit Noah overnight on September 16, 2004, was not allowed to testify about the out-of-character request. Though she wanted to appear, defense attorney Herman Alcantar argued to have her excluded and prosecutor Noel Levy did not oppose the motion. The jury would never hear Beeso's observations of Marjorie in a strange state of agitation, giving to a woman she hardly knew excuses—including saying that she'd been fighting with

---

* At seventeen, it would have been illegal for Marjorie to have the sexual relationship with Jessiah that he confirmed in court. But her interest in him may have even begun much earlier. In interviews, Marjorie described touching the boy intimately when she caught him during karate spotting and her hand slid in between his legs when he was just fourteen.

† As of 2010, the Rueckert/Longdon shooting remained unsolved.

Jay all night—as to why she had suddenly wanted her child out of the house.

A second jailhouse snitch who was brought to the stand, on February 11, 2009, after Joann Orbin's testimony at the two-week mark, turned the trial on its head. This woman, Charity Hill, had told prosecutors that when they were in custody together in jail, she had heard Marjorie make statements similar to the ones Sophia Johnson had heard. But now on the stand, in front of jurors, Hill recanted. A frustrated Noel Levy called a halt to her testimony. During the informal break, he muttered something about the "penalties for perjury." Not only did Hill hear him say it, but her attorney, Yvette Kelly, also heard him. Kelly was infuriated that the prosecutor would threaten her client, and Marjorie's defense team also felt the prosecutor was intimidating the witness.

Suddenly the proceeding that the Orbin family had waited for for so long was no longer about the man they loved and lost. As of February 11, 2009, it became all about Charity Hill, a young woman in jail awaiting trial on murder charges for allegedly holding down a fifteen-year-old boy's legs while her boyfriend strangled him with zip ties.

Noel Levy was officially accused of prosecutorial misconduct. In a convoluted morass of law, rules and regulations, Jay Orbin, the murder victim, seemed forgotten. Lawyer Yvette Kelly even took the stand to testify, not about what had happened to Jay, but about the "threat" to her client. Charity Hill testified again: not about Marjorie but about Noel Levy.

And then, on top of everything else, a juror was heard to make a remark about the incident. A whole new motion was filed, this one on juror misconduct.

Hearings were held behind closed doors, legally referred to as "in camera." This offended the sensibilities of *Arizona Republic* reporter Michael Kiefer, who got his newspaper to file motions to open up the proceedings.

The trial of Marjorie Orbin entered a state of suspended animation for ten long days.

Testimony resumed on February 23, 2009, but none of the serious misconduct-related issues had been resolved. The testimony being heard now could end up a great waste of time if a mistrial was granted, which was quite possible. A couple of days later, the defense raised a new issue: it objected to the Orbin family being seen to pass notes to the state's table.

The platform of justice was getting strained to the creaking point.

With all these issues unresolved, the jury heard from Marjorie Orbin's former boyfriend Larry Weisberg for several days, and then from his daughter and son-in-law. As the month of March began, Detective Jan Butcher took the stand, the first detective on the case, the one who'd started taking Jay's life apart when he was still a missing person, someone his family could still hope was alive.

Dave Barnes sat at the defense table and provided support to prosecutor Noel Levy as he introduced dozens of pieces of evidence through Butcher. None of the mistrial motions had yet been ruled on. The trial was lurching forward in front of the jury, but behind the scenes the ink and paper was stacking up at an alarming rate.

Also behind the scenes, Special Investigations detective Theron Quaas was still doing his work regarding the harassment case. On March 9, 2009, amid a squall of shocked phone calls, Judge Arthur Anderson, with the cooperation of both defense and state counsel, called another trial hiatus and sent the jury home.

The reason? He had just learned of the worst threat to the already wobbly trial: on March 9, Phoenix Police officers, on the strength of a search warrant put through by Detective Quaas, had raided the home of former detective Dave Barnes. Barnes, already having suffered the humiliating demotion back to patrol, was now being investigated by his own department for *criminal* activity.

On his search warrant affidavit, Detective Quaas had listed identity theft, computer tampering, theft and "harassment." After March 9, Barnes was removed from even patrol. He was placed on administrative leave pending a criminal investigation.

When Jake Orbin Jr. heard what had happened, he said, "I was 'you're kidding!'" He threw his hands up in the air to punctuate his sense of catastrophe. "I was ready to stop the trial myself. 'With so much going on now, let's just throw it in and start over.'"

But two excruciating weeks later, Judge Anderson had not ruled on any mistrial motions. He called jurors back anyway. Detective Jan Butcher took the stand again and testimony resumed. All the mistrial motions were still pending—for prosecutorial misconduct, for juror misconduct, for police misconduct—but prosecutor Noel Levy doggedly carried on, taking Detective Butcher through the hundreds of pieces of evidence that the investigation had turned up.

Just four trial days later, a colleague from the County Attorney's Office called in to the assembled courtroom team to inform them that Noel Levy had been hospitalized for a personal medical situation. Levy had no second attorney at the bench with him. There was no choice but to stop the trial a fourth time. Jurors were sent home yet again.

It was now April.

Judge Anderson did not want his trial to fall apart. He ordered Noel Levy to attend court in a wheelchair. Even though he was by then under criminal investigation, Anderson ordered Dave Barnes to return to court as well.

But Barnes had been shaken to the core by the experience of Phoenix Police officers showing up at his home and executing a search warrant. Worst of all, the warrant had been sealed, so he didn't even know yet what evidence had brought them to his house. Compelled to attend court, Barnes, the detective who had looked into the blue tub and the life of the man it contained, the detective who had decided that the blond woman sitting at the defense table ought to be brought before a jury of her peers, claimed his own Fifth Amendment rights.

Dave Barnes refused to answer any question but that of his own name.

CHAPTER FIFTEEN

Hanging by a Thread

Marjorie Orbin's trial had started in January 2009, during the gorgeous desert winter, the time when tourists flocked to Phoenix's golf courses and enjoyed the outdoor seating at bistros and eateries. With all the bizarre twists and turns repeatedly stopping the trial, it had now dragged past spring and into summer when the sidewalk scorched and tempers frayed.

Prosecutor Noel Levy had gamely left his hospital bed and arrived on the eleventh floor of the central court building in a wheelchair. But within a week or two, he had suffered another medical setback, unrelated to the first, and this time Judge Arthur Anderson gave way. Noel Levy was permanently excused from *The People vs. Marjorie Orbin*. The trial went into another hiatus while the County Attorney's Office was given a chance to select and prepare a new prosecutor.

Prosecutor Treena Kay burst into the case with the velocity of a fireball and the glamour of a movie star. Coming into the case cold, she immediately had news for the defense team: she had discovered that jail snitch Sophia Johnson had been provided hotel housing earlier in the year at county expense, through the intervention of Dave Barnes. The defense, incensed that it had never learned this from the ailing Noel Levy, now upped the ante. They begged the court to declare a mistrial based on outrageous and flagrant prosecutorial misconduct.

An arduous battle now began, involving both Noel Levy's and Dave Barnes's conduct in relation to Sophia Johnson. How could her testimony be trusted with so much "swag" on the table for her? And how could the *state* be trusted, since it had apparently deliberately deceived the defense about the extent of its involvement with her?

Prosecutor Kay also briskly informed the court that the tribulations of Dave Barnes were of no material interest to her since she would be proceeding without him. She had no intention of defending him, because she had no use for him.

But Dave Barnes had become very interesting to the defense. They wanted him, they told the judge, and would fight to compel him to testify. They believed what he had to say might end up *helping* their client, rather than convicting her.

Barnes, accustomed to sitting next to prosecutors during trials, now had a defense attorney of his own. At one point, Judge Anderson himself put questions to

Barnes under oath, but the disgraced detective continued to shield himself with the Fifth Amendment. Anderson said Barnes's decision to insert the Fifth Amendment into a proceeding that was part of his job, not part of his own criminal case, "was not well taken and the court denies him the privilege."

Barnes refused to budge. He would not risk saying anything at all in the Orbin murder trial.

The clash headed to a higher court.

Meanwhile, there were other parties also very interested in knowing just what the evidence was that had resulted in a search warrant on the Barnes home. In the summer of 2005, just before Phoenix's two serial killers were beginning to emerge, longtime *Phoenix New Times* reporter Paul Rubin had gotten into an imbroglio with Barnes.

Phoenix PD had launched an investigation into Rubin, due to Barnes's accusations. But although Barnes had complained he had directly witnessed the reporter misusing a police computer in a criminal manner, internal investigators found that the computer had never been misused at all and they could not validate Barnes's statements. The incident contributed to Barnes's deteriorating relationship with his department and their assessment of his reliability for judgment and truthfulness.

Paul Rubin was cleared. When Barnes himself turned up as the subject of an investigation four years later, Rubin's paper, the *New Times*, of course, was curious and fought to have the search warrant affidavit unsealed.

Although Barnes himself maintained public silence after his home was raided, his wife went on the radio show of former congressman J. D. Hayworth and breathlessly characterized the search warrant raid as a "home invasion," perpetrated because her husband was a "whistleblower." The owner of the Web site that had published the Potato Head photos was also raided, and he too publicly opined that it was a corrupt police force attack on freedom of speech. While he made no official statements on radio shows or in court, Barnes himself was believed to be talking to many reporters off the record.

But no one, certainly not radio host Hayworth or any of the reporters Barnes might have been entertaining off the record, had seen the case built by Detective Theron Quaas. It was still under seal. So no one really knew why the raids had taken place. The "cause" of the noble whistle-blower and his blogging mouthpiece was taken up by freedom of speech watchdogs on the Internet, who created a cyber dust storm of loud defenses of what they took to be a freedom of speech issue.

But Quaas's investigation, as recorded in his files and the sealed search warrant affidavit, had little to do with whistle-blowing or freedom of speech. The blogger was raided not for criticizing Phoenix PD or even for the malevolent personal depictions of the married Detectives Martoni. According to the affidavit, Quaas had a great deal of evidence, including text messages, e-mails, and electronic camera data, that indicated Dave Barnes, in his capacity as a detective, had committed illegal acts, even that Barnes may have had improper

dealings with the wife* of the Baseline Rapist suspect.
Quaas's evidence also showed the Web site owner to be
the alleged nexus between Barnes and the Baseline Rapist suspect's wife, who was fiercely loyal to her husband.
And it was having been left off the mayor's commenda-
tion for his work on that high-profile case that had so
enraged Barnes in the first place. Furthermore, most of
the blame for that omission, according to Quaas's investigation, was believed by Barnes to go to the male half of
"Mr. and Mrs. Potatohead."

Quaas had also alleged that Barnes had inserted
himself into the Web site owner's divorce, potentially
improperly bringing the force of the police department
to help the blogger dominate the proceedings against
his wife.† In November 2008, with the Orbin trial just
a holiday season away, Barnes had written up criminal
paperwork on the blogger's separated wife, involving
their children. Supposedly, the blogger had simply seen
a patrol officer at Home Depot and asked him for help.
The officer had gone to his home and taken the report.
But the patrolman, one Dave Barnes, never mentioned
in his write-up of the wife that he had had close personal contact with the complainant for months, contact

---

* Her husband by that time had been convicted of raping two sisters.
  They had survived to testify against him; therefore, that trial
  was held first. At the time of the investigation into Dave Barnes,
  the Baseline Rapist was serving time for those rapes as well as
  awaiting trials for several murders. His wife had launched a tireless
  public campaign in support of her husband and against the police.
† Affidavit for a Search Warrant SW2009-003088 Detective Theron
  Quaas, affiant.

that was detailed in the many electronic records, such as texts and e-mails, between the pair that Quaas had subpoenaed.

Barnes lost in higher courts his appeals to claim his Fifth Amendment rights in Marjorie Orbin's case. In high summer, the trial well over six months old by then, he took the stand as a defense witness. He answered questions about Sophia Johnson, admitting that he had arranged for the county to supply her with about two months' worth of rent at a hotel, some food baskets and rides to court. He also admitted that he had appeared on her behalf at her own sentencing and asked that court for leniency because of her cooperation in the Orbin case.

After so much drama, Barnes's testimony seemed anticlimactic. But it was the defense's opportunity to display that the state might not have been pure as the driven snow. After all, Barnes was already on the Brady list, a roster kept by prosecutors in every jurisdiction in the United States of detectives deemed discredited for trial. The Brady list was born out of a sixties-era U.S. Supreme Court decision holding that prosecutors have a duty to disclose officers who have a troubled history, because it may be "exculpatory."

The trial limped along. Three jurors were dismissed along the way. Jake Orbin Jr. sat in the back of the room every day. When court wrapped up for the evening, he went home and faced his young nephew, whom he was attempting to raise on his dead brother's behalf. A seventh grader now, Noah was kept away from the courtroom and the sight of his mother in custody and his father in hideous photos.

With all of the trial's miseries, from hospitals to

misconduct to police raids to the dwindling number of jurors, Jake worried that it would all go so wrong, justice crumbling away in a landslide of mishaps, that he would have to return his nephew to the woman he believed had committed unthinkably gruesome atrocities upon the boy's father.

CHAPTER SIXTEEN

Jigsaws and Freezers

Some of the most devastating evidence against Marjorie Orbin came from Lowe's surveillance video tape. Jurors' eyes followed footage of Marjorie, in her characteristic ponytail and black exercise pants, as she lifted two blue Rubbermaid tubs with gray lids out of her Lowe's shopping cart and helped the cashier find the UPC codes. Police had tracked down the history of the blue tub found so sadly in the desert and discovered it was specially produced for the Lowe's retail chain. At trial, Lowe's personnel testified about the purchase made on-screen: the tubs in Marjorie's cart matched the tub in the desert down to the very UPC code she was seen displaying to the cashier. The video of this September 10, 2004, purchase was played many times for the jury at different times in the trial.

The blue tub discovered on October 23, 2004, had

contained the incomplete remains of the smiling man with the gift of gab and the mania for showing off pictures of his little boy; a man beloved by family, friends and clients. But in court, every single grisly detail had to be exposed and argued over. The photos they saw and the details they heard were beyond tragic.

Investigators believed Jay Orbin had been murdered on his forty-fifth birthday, September 8, or possibly early on September 9, 2004. The blue tub was discovered seven weeks later. The state of decomposition was pronounced. Some tissues had liquefied. But Phoenix was still quite hot in September and on into October as well. With that kind of heat, decomposition should have been very rapid and complete within a very short amount of time. But in spite of the partial liquefaction, much of the partial corpse remained intact. Indeed, the tub's discoverer had told first responders he could tell it was human because he "could see the belly button."

If the corpse had been in the tightly sealed plastic container for weeks when the temperatures were still frequently over a hundred, forensic analysts would've expected it to be in much worse condition.

One of the first things the medical examiner suggested was that the corpse might have been frozen for at least some of the time between September 8 and October 23. Upon close analysis, state's experts had discovered what they said were signs of freezing and thawing at the cellular level.

The defense disputed this point.

If Jay's body had *not* been frozen, there were limited explanations as to why it was in such good condition nearly two months later. One of the best would be that he, in fact, *had* been alive for some of those weeks. At times, Marjorie had told various people that Jay *was* alive and even stalking her during the weeks after September 8.

Defense experts claimed that a deep red or purplish discoloration would be present if the body had been frozen, but that all that could be seen on this corpse was some slight pinking. The defense also pointed out that the discoloration of freezing could be expected to show an outline of the clothing on the corpse because the clothing, as it does on a living person, serves as insulation: the skin underneath it would freeze at a different rate. Defense expert Dr. Michael Iliescu, speaking in a soft Romanian accent, noted that in his opinion the only difference between the flesh under the victim's denim shorts and that outside them could be attributed to skin sloughing, also caused by the presence of the cotton fabric.

Neither could the prosecution produce a freezer. In the family garage, there was an upright freezer full of horizontal shelves. Police had tried to remove the shelves but determined they were not designed for removal and could find no trace that they had ever been forced out and replaced. It would be impossible to place a two-hundred-pound human torso in there.

One or two of Jay's associates later told police they had once seen a horizontal deep freezer either at the warehouse or in the family garage, or that they had heard Marjorie talk about a special purchase of about a thousand dollars' worth of meat she had frozen. Marjorie's friend Bryan Todd Christy also remembered a remark she'd made about a large quantity of frozen meat. To Christy, she had said that Jay was the one who'd bought it. But the information was ethereal, and no trace of such a freezer was ever found. No purchase or delivery record could be traced, no removal order. If Jay's torso had been frozen by Marjorie, a suitable appliance could not be firmly connected to her.

Perhaps someone else had frozen him? Perhaps he had *not* died seven weeks before the tub was discovered? Both of these theories would be in Marjorie's favor.

The medical examiner could offer more insight, albeit not a full explanation, for the delayed state of decay, an explanation that did not involve freezers: the torso had been scooped out and expertly eviscerated.

In typical pathology, the soft organ tissue would decompose at the most rapid rate. This internal decay, with its festering community of microorganisms, would then quickly consume the more durable muscle tissues. But in Jay's case, someone had expertly delayed the decomposition process on his corpse by removing his spleen, liver, pancreas, intestines and everything else normally found in a human abdomen.

It wasn't just a slapdash effort. No one had been in a rush when they did this to him. The spine had been severed at the vertebrae T12 on the upper side and L1 on the lower. This was the first possible place to make a cut that would leave the macabre butcher free of having to saw through human ribs. Before the sawing of the bone, however, the internal organs would have been removed. An amateur might make it through such things as the stomach and intestines: these organs would be easily visible once the skin and peritoneum had been sliced through. But the human kidneys were a bit trickier. They do sit below the ribs, just barely. So they would be associated with the portion of the torso that was found. But they were tucked away.

"They are 'retroperitoneal,'" said defense expert witness Patrick Hannon. "If you didn't know they were there, you would not see them." And yet they were not present in the blue tub: someone had known they'd be there and had gone to the trouble of removing them.

The gutting of this man's body also aided the criminal in completing the task of removing his arms, head and shoulders. By removing the internal organs, the way to the spine would now be clear. The bulky housing of a jigsaw, the boxy part that holds the motor, could be maneuvered in the cavity while the jigsaw's short blade could reach the vertebrae. With the internal organs still present, the short blade would never reach the backbone from the front.

Furthermore, the body had been drained of blood. "There was no marbling on the body which is related to probably extensive blood loss prior to the body being cut up."[*]

The defense's Dr. Michael Iliescu, a forensic pathologist who had left a general medical practice in Romania in 1991 to come to the United States, believed no jigsaw had been used. He gave extensive testimony that the vertebrae could not have been reached under the circumstances by a short jigsaw blade, even with the internal organs scooped out. Ghastly photos of the partial corpse were shown to the jury while Iliescu pointed out the small "wings" that stuck out from each human vertebra, formally called the "transverse process."

---

[*] May 20, 2005, #218 Additional Autopsy Supplement.

Jay's spine had been sawed in half, but the transverse process of the vertebra at the top of the torso had no damage. Dr. Iliescu said the short blade of the jigsaw could not have preserved the transverse process, which has a downward slope, and still reached the core bone. He said the instrument used must have had a longer blade with greater reach.

He proposed a Sawzall, a reciprocating saw shaped something like a swordfish. While jigsaws had been recovered from the Orbin home, however, no Sawzall was associated with Marjorie.

There were no arms in the blue tub, and no head. The corpse had been severed above the umbilicus and below the breast line. The cut was made at T12 and L1, with L1 remaining mostly on the torso and all but a small chunk of T12 missing and presumed still attached to the upper part of the body.

There were thighs, but no shins or feet. Each leg had been severed through the joint, just below the kneecap. Dr. Iliescu also did not like a jigsaw for the knee cuts. He thought there was too much flesh around the bones for a jigsaw to work properly. He said any time a jigsaw had to cut through anything with a diameter exceeding its own stroke depth, the greatest length the blade could reach when fully extended, the blade would break.

According to Dr. Iliescu, the corpse's bone surrounded by its flesh would have exceeded the stroke depth of a jigsaw by three or four centimeters. For a jigsaw to have been used on this man's knees, he said, the malefactor would have had to first cut away the flesh in order to expose the bone. If that had occurred, he said, they would surely have seen cut strokes going lengthwise down the femurs, but he could find no such stroke marks on the femurs from the blue tub. The inevitable conclusion, he said, was that anyone attempting to use a jigsaw to cut off these legs would have been frustrated in his or her attempts by a series of broken blades. The malefactor could never have completed his or her macabre task. Again, a Sawzall would be a much better tool, Dr. Iliescu said, something with a longer blade and motor housing that would not be jammed up against the body it was trying to cut.

There *was* a known Sawzall in the case, the defense said. But it did not belong to Marjorie Orbin. The Sawzall they had found, they said, belonged to Brad Fritz, who was Larry Weisberg's fond son-in-law.

The matter of whether or not the body had been frozen also figured into the discussion of cutting. Forensic anthropologist Dr. Laura Fulginiti, appearing for the state, said a frozen body would be much easier to cut. Unfrozen, she explained, the body "would be squishy, it moves around, it's hard to control." She was asked if she could recognize an intentional method in the things that had happened to the body. Certainly, she said. "If I were going to cut up a body, how would I do it? Exactly like this! Dispose of the soft tissue, freeze it, then cut the vertebrae."

Dr. Fulginiti had not performed the autopsy, but she had attended it. More large photos appeared on the screen. This time the view was Jay Orbin's knees. She pointed to vertical marks on the bones. "This is where the flesh was peeled back by a hand knife," she said, "to expose the bone for cutting." She herself had been able to repeat the effect in an experiment with a donated human bone.

"The jigsaw," she said, "cut through it like butter."

She did not like a Sawzall as the instrument. She said cut marks left by a Sawzall would be even and smooth, while the cuts found on Jay were "jagged, have grooves and were not as clean" as those a Sawzall would leave. She explained that a jigsaw was known to be a "little messy" and "chips the bone." This was exactly the condition she found on the bones of the torso. She said the short blade would need several maneuvers before it could cut all the way through. She held an actual jigsaw blade up to the photo of the bones. She maneuvered it in a quasi-radial fashion and it fit perfectly with the marks on the photo. A Sawzall would have needed no such maneuvers: the long blade would have lain straight across the limb, the flesh still on it, with room to spare on either side. In fact, the blade she was using on the stand had been seized from the JayHawk International warehouse. Police had found an opened package of jigsaw blades there and two were missing from that package.

And then there was the matter of the blade tip. Dr. Fulginiti pointed to an off-center wedge shape in the border of the cut on the L1 vertebra. She fit the slanted nose of the jigsaw blade into the wedge: another perfect match. The Sawzall blade was displayed. Its nose was straight up and down. Aligned with the cut's border, the Sawzall blade looked out of place. It would have been difficult to explain the jig in the border if that instrument had been used.

But there remained the question of the transverse process, or the winglike projections that jutted downward from the sides of the vertebra. How could the short blade of the jigsaw reach the core without hitting them? The housing of the motor itself would crush them as the perpetrator pushed close in to buzz through the part that surrounded the spinal cord.

Dr. Fulginiti, who had been barred from the courtroom during all other testimony, especially Dr. Iliescu's, found the question odd. She used a doctor's plastic model of an intact spine to make sure everyone could understand the three-dimensional configuration of the wings, the central spine and the saw. The saw, its housing and the hand holding it had entered in through the empty abdominal cavity. It had plenty of room to maneuver back and forth. The *blade* had entered the vertebra from the direct front at a moderate upward angle. The saw would have been about a thirty-degree angle from parallel with the spine. After some radial repositioning as it made several cuts, the blade had snapped through the rear of the vertebrae. The wings, or transverse process, sprang out from the back side of the vertebra. In order to damage the transverse process, a cut would have had to be made at a right angle, ninety degrees not thirty degrees, and cut all the way through or approached from the back. The most efficient thing to do was exactly what had been done, Dr. Fulginiti theorized: hold the saw parallel to the length of the spine and lower it into the previously gutted cavity, then tilt in under the ribs that, although attached to higher vertebrae, were built to descend as they curved around into the thorax, the area just above the abdomen. The result was an upward slanting cut that transacted the L1 vertebra core, never touched the transverse process and extended into the lower rear portion of the T12 vertebra. How the transverse process of the T12 vertebra, not the L1, had been affected was unknown since that portion of the body was missing.

The blue tub had weighed in at 206 pounds. Accounting for the weight of the tub itself and all of the tape and plastic and cardboard found inside, the defense calculated the torso itself weighed 185 pounds. Dr. Patrick Hannon, a compact man who had emeritus status in functional anatomy and a Ph.D. in education at Northern Arizona University, extrapolated from the weight of the torso that Jay himself had weighed around four hundred pounds. Testifying for the defense, he said that this presented a very real problem, because the laws of biomechanics simply would not permit a 130-pound, five-foot-seven woman to lift such a heavy body into a deep freezer, even had one been found. Hannon lectured the jury about "sliding friction" and "horizontal force" and gave formulas that he said governed biomechanics. Dr. Hannon said Marjorie would have had to turn the freezer on its side to have any hope of getting the full-sized, unmutilated corpse into it. Then she'd have had to lay him on the floor. Then she'd have had to get on the floor, too, and scoot him with her feet. Once she scooted him into the freezer, she'd have needed a fork-lift to get the freezer back upright. Inside the freezer, the full-sized male would have had to be contorted in order to get the lid closed for freezing. But it was likely a man of that size never would have fit inside in the first place.

But suppose she had got him successfully in and

out of a freezer? According to the defense's theories of biomechanics, it would still have been impossible for someone of her size to lift the 206-pound tub into the back of an SUV. Both sides believed an SUV had been used to transport the tub to the scrub desert at Tatum and Dynamite Road.

Dr. Hannon brought a blue tub, identical to the one that had held Jay's remains, to court with him. He also brought forty-pound bags of rock salt. He came down from the witness stand and in front of the jury filled the blue tub with rock salt until it weighed about two hundred pounds. Then he measured the height of the table where Marjorie was currently sitting, files and documents spread in front of her. The table was within a couple of inches of the height of the tailgate of the suspect SUV, the abandoned green Bronco, about thirty inches. Hannon asked one of Marjorie's defense attorneys, Herman Alcantar, to stand behind the table and brace it.

Then he proceeded to attempt to lift the two-hundred-pound tub filled with salt onto the table. He had already established that he himself was also 130 pounds and five-six. He said he'd be a good biomechanical stand-in for Marjorie as she had been at the time (four years later, she weighed more than at the time of the murder). He asserted that, calculating all the weights and heights involved, Marjorie simply could not have produced the horizontal force to get that tub up into the SUV: the tub would have slid down and the 130-pound woman would have slid back.

Marjorie rolled her chair backward out of the way. Attorney Alcantar made some jokes as he steadied the table and the blue tub knocked up against it with former gym teacher Hannon's efforts. The doctor, a competitive weight lifter in his youth, huffed and puffed, but time and time again, he slid backward on his feet just as the tub seemed on the verge of making it over the top. It thudded to the floor repeatedly. Dr. Hannon looked up smiling.

"A one-hundred-and-thirty-pound woman could not do it," he said definitely. "But it would not be a hard task for two large men," he added.

Prosecutor Treena Kay had watched the antics involving the shifting salt and the thudding tub with a poker face. When it was her turn, she popped up with her characteristic energetic step. "Would your experiments and calculations be irrelevant," she asked Dr. Hannon, back in the witness stand, "if a person had a ramp and a dolly available to them?"

Dr. Hannon lost his aplomb. "A ramp and a dolly?" he asked. "I was never told about a ramp and a dolly." He was silent for a moment. "Yes, I agree with you," he said, "they would be irrelevant."

Photos of the garage from the day it had been searched were put up on the screen for the jury's view. Standing near a wall in the garage, a wheeled dolly was clearly visible. But this dolly did have a very short base, Dr. Hannon pointed out, craning his neck toward the screen beside him. He said the dolly in the photo would have been very awkward and unreliable with the two-hundred-pound tub, which was much wider on every surface than the base plate of the dolly.

A folded metal ramp was also visible in the garage. The defense objected that it was a common enough item, found in many homes with SUVs, often used for loading motorbikes and ATVs into the back of the vehicle.

But the Orbins had no small recreational vehicles that fit in the back of the SUV.

And the ramp was a new purchase.

Kay brought in Linda Mills, the WalMart store manager who remembered selling it. Mills referred to the ramp as a "dog item" because it was the sort of thing that took a long time to sell. She thought it was easy to carry around because she herself remembered carrying it under one arm from the aisle to the cash register for the customer who wanted it, a blond lady with a ponytail and black exercise pants. This had been done the day it was purchased from Mills's store with an Orbin credit card.

That day was September 15, 2004, a week after Jay was last seen and a week before he was reported missing. Kay also pointed out to Dr. Hannon that on the day Marjorie had reported Jay as a missing person, she had listed him as a 260-pound man, not a 400-pound one.

Jake Orbin Jr. returned to the stand. He had sat anxiously through the testimony about the dolly with the narrow base plate and flimsy proportions. Now he talked about that dolly himself. In settling Jay's affairs, he had used it many times. It had some special features, Jake said. The photo of the dolly against the wall in the garage appeared on the screen again. He pointed to latches and joints, subtly embedded in the rods. Something happened when you released those latches, he said. A new photo was projected on to the screen. The dolly was now a cart with a base nearly as wide as the dolly was tall. It was cleverly designed to fold into itself in such a way that the cart base disappeared into the vertical rods. When it was fully extended as a cart, everyone could see, the blue tub would easily fit onto it and sit comfortably and stably.

But would it fit onto the ramp? Dr. Hannon emphasized that for the cart to roll up it would be much better off if it had one ramp for each side. In other words, a double track, one for each set of wheels, instead of the cart fitting narrowly onto the one track.

No second ramp was found.

Dr. Hannon also calculated that for the 130-pound woman to get the 200-pound blue tub up onto the thirty-inch tall tailgate, the ramp, whether it was single or double, would have to be about twenty feet long.

It was less than twelve feet long.

Whose experts were right?

The only thing the two sides weren't arguing about was the central premise that whoever had done this had to have been very, very cold-blooded. With all the detailed decisions of anatomy required, the lifting and maneuvering performed, the meticulous methodology applied, all done in intimate contact with a dead human being, an unseeing face to look at, for hours on end, any person with a shred of conscience or compassion would have fallen apart emotionally well before the grotesque deeds had been completed.

After five long years, including many months of trial with its cavalcade of medical and misconduct delays, would someone finally be held to account for doing this wretched thing? Would the brute who could icily dismember the father of an adoring child be removed from our streets? Was that person even on trial here?

* * *

By August 2009, the judge had ruled there was "an insufficient basis to dismiss this case for prosecutorial misconduct" based on the "separate instances" involving the trial's original prosecutor, Noel Levy. But the trial was running a new risk: only thirteen jurors remained. That left a very thin margin of just one alternate juror to fill in if personal emergencies or other situations continued to thin out the jury box. The trial could not continue without a full twelve.

Then prosecutor Treena Kay noticed something she didn't like. She didn't like it at all. She filed motions about it. Hearings were held. A juror was called in. Questions were put and arguments made. A decision was made, but Kay did not like how it turned out. She went to a higher court. And there she won.

After eight months of testimony, juror number eight was dismissed.

Treena Kay had seen the juror sleeping in court. She had clocked the naps. They were not momentary "eye rests." Juror number eight was missing chunks of testimony and showing a disregard for the process.

That was the last alternate. There were still several more weeks to go. This was a capital case. It could not proceed without twelve citizens to agree on the evidence. Without twelve of her peers, the state could not pass judgment on a human being's right to live. Was it possible that Jake Orbin had left his San Diego coastline home and uprooted the victim's child for a trial that would come to nothing? What were the chances that every single one of the remaining jurors could last for the rest of the case, without any family emergency, health crisis, financial hardship or mistake in conduct?

If they lost even one more juror, the whole trial—already missing its lead detective and the prosecutor who had started on the case five years ago—would go in the trash heap.

CHAPTER SEVENTEEN

Two Blondes, Two Torsos

On June 18, 2009, defense attorney Robyn Varcoe, a petite brunette dressed in a white pantsuit, took to the rostrum squarely facing the jury. Placed around her at various spots in the courtroom were the macabre props so indicative of this trial. Directly behind her, propped lengthwise against the judge's high bench, was a blue Rubbermaid tub. To her right, at the defense table and within easy reach of the woman accused of putting it to a horrible use, was a fully functioning jigsaw.

Varcoe could not dispute that something horrible had happened to the father of a little boy, the son of the elderly couple in the benches, the little brother of the blue-eyed man sitting near them. But it was not the child's mother who had done this terrible thing with the buzzing blade. "It was Larry Weisberg," announced Varcoe, "who caused the death of Jay Orbin."

She said the bodybuilder had inadvertently chanced upon his lover's husband in the garage at the 55th Street house. Jay had come home unexpectedly, and a confrontation took place between the two men colliding in the same house. In a fit of masculine rage, Larry Weisberg had shot and killed Jay Orbin. In the aftermath, Varcoe claimed, the bodybuilder had abandoned his passion for the man's wife. Instead of a lover, according to the theory she now placed before the jury, Weisberg had turned the woman into a scapegoat.

Based on Marjorie's similarities to a murder defendant in another recent Phoenix case, Weisberg had decided to frame her.

This was how Valerie Pape entered the Orbin case.

On January 27, 2000, a delivery man had been unloading a shipment of potato chips at a Bashas' grocery store, located in what's known to the Phoenix metro area as the "East Valley." Broadly speaking, Phoenix could be divided into Central Phoenix, from liberal and urbane to seedy and impoverished; the West Valley, rural, blue collar or industrial; north Phoenix and Scottsdale, monied, acquisitive, fine living; and the East Valley, conservative, yuppie, Mormon.

There was plenty of prosperity in the East Valley, but not so much that a Jaguar didn't stand out.

The delivery man noticed a petite blond woman driving a blue green Jaguar, acting furtively around the industrial back side of the Bashas'. She was quite pretty. He watched while she looked this way and that. Despite her efforts, though, she clearly failed to notice him. From the beautiful British automobile, he saw her awkwardly retrieve a full plastic garbage bag. It was clearly too heavy for her small frame. She struggled with it as she headed toward a Dumpster. With a great deal of effort, she swung it up over the metal frame of the container until it cleared the top edge and sank over the other side.

The potato chip man found the woman's behavior and her appearance and even the act of hauling a large bag of trash in the space-spare luxury Jaguar very odd. He took down the plate number of the Jag, but he couldn't decide what else to do. He later mentioned what he'd seen to a cabdriver in the neighborhood. His tale sparked the interest of the cabbie, who drove over to the Dumpster behind the Bashas'.

Equipping himself with a pocketknife, the cabbie climbed over the Dumpster's edge and easily found the bag his comrade had described. He reached forth with his knife and cut the bag open.

He did not see everything that was inside, but it was enough. He ran back to the potato chip man, and soon they were able to flag down a policeman. The officer followed their directions to the Bashas' Dumpster and opened the bag further.

Inside the officer found the awful specter of a human torso, an adult male.

Law enforcement followed the license plate registration to an address. It was a Scottsdale home, some forty miles from the site of the Mesa Dumpster.

The man who lived at the house had been reported missing four days earlier.

His name was Ira Pomerantz. Given his home and

that Jaguar, Ira Pomerantz clearly had money. Inside the house, police encountered the petite and very pretty blonde whom the potato chip man had described. She was Valerie Pape and she was Ira Pomerantz's wife. At first Pape feigned having no knowledge of her missing husband's whereabouts. But officers soon confronted her with the fact that she had been seen dumping a human torso into a Dumpster forty miles away. There could be no mistake. Her license plate had been recorded.

Pape admitted that the man in the Dumpster was Pomerantz. But she claimed she did not know how he died or how he had come to be cut up, only that she had done the dumping.

Pape told officers that she had come home one morning three days earlier to find Pomerantz dead, faceup in a pool of blood in the kitchen of their home. She had tried to hide his body, she said, because there was a history of domestic violence between the pair. She had feared his death would be wrongly attributed to her. In her panic, she had disposed of him and reported him missing.

Pomerantz's adult daughters and his first wife rushed forward to defend the dead man's character. In all their long marriage, the first wife had never known Pomerantz to be violent, and she could not believe it now. The girls agreed, and they had no fondness for their tiny "stepmother."

Officers did, however, find a recent restraining order against Ira Pomerantz. He had been a nightclub owner but had recently fallen into financial distress. The club, Rhythm and Cues, had filed for bankruptcy. Pape herself ran a hair salon at the toniest of addresses, Marshall Way in "Old Town" Scottsdale. This small district, bisected by Scottsdale Road, was home to art galleries, posh boutiques and fabled eateries. The tourist magnet district was extremely pedestrian-friendly, decorated with horse hitches and bronze statues.

But the police found that Pomerantz had bought the salon for his wife, and it did not necessarily turn a profit. With his cash business now bankrupt, the salon seemed destined to fail, too.

Unless, perhaps, life insurance policies could be cashed in.

The medical examiner had begun looking at the torso right away. Soon a bullet was found embedded in the flesh: Ira Pomerantz had been shot in the back. This wound was certainly fatal, the ME said. Within a day, law enforcement had found the murder weapon. It was hidden behind the seat in the blue green Jaguar that Pape was still driving.

The pretty blonde had been seen dumping the corpse like trash on Thursday, January 27, 2000. She was arrested the next day.

After her arrest, Valerie Pape admitted that "a gun had been fired" at Pomerantz and she had been the person to fire it. Pape used an odd and distancing way of referring to the act, as if all the facts did not add up to "I killed Ira with the gun," but instead as if detached actions had been loosely strung together and held only the faintest connection to her.

Lurking on the edge of the investigation was a man who had been living in the guesthouse at Pomerantz and Pape's Del Lago home. Michel Sauvage, a Frenchman, worked at the salon in Old Town with Pape, but his relationship to her was uncertain. His relationship with her husband was more clear: Pomerantz had wanted him out. But somehow, the man whose violence Valerie Pape claimed to fear was unable to oust the Frenchman from his own home. But Sauvage was never charged, arrested, or otherwise officially implicated in the crime. It was believed he returned to France, leaving the ugly headlines—and Pape—thousands of miles behind.

Valerie Pape herself was French. In court she began to request a French-English interpreter, and her lawyer tried to get her initial confession suppressed on the basis that no interpreter had been present. But Pape's English typically was flawless to all who dealt with her. The confession stood. Eventually, she pleaded guilty to second degree murder and there was no trial.

Pape passed through the Estrella jail, located on the cusp of Phoenix proper, but in late 2002 she entered the state prison system as #171086, a medium security inmate in the Santa Cruz unit at the Perryville prison complex, in open-air conditions, surrounded by farmland and desert. Like many of the county's inmates, she may have viewed the state prison facility as an upgrade. It must have been a relief to trade in the county jail black-and-white striped "pajamas" for the jeans and work shirts of the Santa Cruz unit. But for French-bred Pape, an American cell in the lonely desert was not satisfactory. By 2003 she was bound for France under an international prisoner exchange treaty. Under this treaty, she'd serve out her sentence courtesy of the French taxpayer, not the American.

Valerie Pape was loaded up by prison transport at Perryville and driven the thirty or so miles to Phoenix Sky Harbor airport. The U.S. Marshall's Office took custody of her and put her on the first leg of what would be a very long journey to her homeland and family.

But while she was in the air, something happened. The long trails of paper caught up with the people who had cared about Ira Pomerantz the most, his daughters. Over time, Pape had engaged in a prodigious series of scrimmages with her dead husband's daughters. There were lawsuits over what constituted Pape's own property and what should rightfully go to the man's heirs.

As soon as they learned that Valerie Pape was trading the frontier justice of Arizona for what they perceived as a cushy French pseudo-prison, the daughters raised a riot. Calls were made, letters written, and newspaper articles appeared. Pape must have been staring out the window above the clouds as some of this was going on. Whether the French prison would be cushy or not, she must have been eager to be closer to her mother and other loved ones from her childhood. But when Pape deplaned in Boston, a surprise was waiting for her. The maelstrom had climaxed and not in her favor. She was immediately marched back onto a plane headed west, not east across the Atlantic. She would not be going home to France. Ira Pomerantz's daughters had seen to it their father's murderer would stay in the same rough-and-tumble territory where she had committed her terrible crime.

Valerie Pape admitted to killing Ira Pomerantz by shooting him with the gun found in the Jaguar. But she steadily maintained that she had not cut up his corpse. She would never say who did. She said she cleaned up the blood on the kitchen floor from his shooting, but she was starkly silent when it came to explaining anything about the gruesome dismemberment job.

She never revealed the whereabouts of Ira Pomerantz's head or limbs.

The case of a desirable blonde dumping the dismembered
torso of her despised husband, complete with upscale
Scottsdale trappings and international intrigue, had certainly kept the newspapers and news stations in Phoenix
busy for years. It would be easy to believe that in 2004,
someone with a corpse on his hands and a convenient
blonde nearby would have seen the similarities to Valerie
Pape. The tale of Pape's dramatic international about-
face in Boston was only a few months old at the time Jay
Orbin went missing.

Robyn Varcoe, from Marjorie's defense team, wanted
the jury to believe that that was exactly what had happened. She told them in her opening argument that Jay
Orbin and Larry Weisberg had unexpectedly run into
each other in the garage at 55th Street. She said that in
that terrible moment, there were two guys who would not
back down. The husband, angry and territorial on September 8, had met a violent end at the hands of the lover,
trapped and jealous. She said the lover had then found
himself unprepared, with a body on his hands. Varcoe
reminded the jurors of Weisberg's crazy behavior the day
the SWAT team had rammed in Marjorie's door.

In his panic, Weisberg's passion had turned to self-
preservation. With the Valerie Pape news stories in mind,
according to Robyn Varcoe, Weisberg had rapidly cooked
up his plan and carried it out. He dismembered the body
and then planted it near Marjorie's neighborhood in order
to frame her à la Valerie Pape.

Varcoe showed the jurors the blue tub propped up behind her. There was no way, she said, that her client (a slim woman at the time of the murder, although admittedly more stout in figure now at the defense table) could have hefted a two-hundred-pound tub full of Jay's remains. It would have required "superhuman strength," she said.*

Varcoe said it had been Weisberg's idea to report Jay as a missing person. Marjorie, the attorney said, must have known what was in her garage and how the evidence would look. This put more pressure on her to acquiesce to Weisberg's plan.

Varcoe held up the jigsaw. A small woman herself, it seemed an awkward and unlikely instrument in her hand. She told the jury that Jay's dismemberment had been so finessed in its execution that it would have required a butcher, a hunter or a medical professional to carry out. And Marjorie, a dancer and mom, was certainly none of those.

But neither had Valerie Pape been.

After Robyn Varcoe's speech, and after the defense had presented its witnesses, the prosecution shot back with a rebuttal case and closing arguments were made.

On September 1, 2009, the case went to the jury.

---

* Nowhere in her statement did Robyn Varcoe call attention to the fact that Valerie Pape, a much smaller and less athletic woman than Marjorie Orbin, had been seen by witnesses to do exactly that, heft the torso remains of a much bigger adult male. Varcoe must have hoped that the jurors did not know the details of the Pape story well enough to recall this fact on their own.

CHAPTER EIGHTEEN

A Greed and a Need

On September 14, 2009, Marjorie Orbin was dressed in a fine black cardigan, gray slacks and a white shirt blouse with subtle black and gray pinstripes running through it. Her hair was specially groomed into soft curls. Reporters and television producers filled the space directly behind Marjorie. Two video cameras were trained on her.

Jay Orbin's family and friends filled the benches behind the prosecution table. Detective Jan Butcher, called in hastily, was in her detective daily wear, not dressed in her more formal court attire. The lawyer at her side, prosecutor Treena Kay, was in a café au lait–colored suit and a white top.

At 4:15 P.M. Jake Orbin Jr. hurried in. He seemed heated, and retreated back into the hallway. When he came through the doors again, he had taken off his jacket. He had walked six city blocks from his car to the courtroom. In another city that may not sound impressive, but this was Phoenix, where the concrete of downtown absorbed and radiated the heat. There was no breeze and the UV rays were intense. But the weather was probably not entirely responsible for his flush and agitation. He had been waiting five years for this day.

At 4:25 the Michael J. Peter–financed attorney Tom Connelly hurried in, frustrated by a long drive in that had had him worried about missing the verdict, and leaned down to Marjorie when he reached her end of the table, his hand sliding down her shoulder blades in a gesture of comfort and solidarity.

Twelve jurors filed in. Eight men and four women. They were dressed for the Phoenix summer, in polo shirts, jeans, and cotton blouses.

Juror number fifteen was announced as the foreperson. She was a fortyish woman with straight brown hair and thin shoulders. She handed the verdict form to the bailiff.

The bailiff crossed the room and handed the form to the judge who looked at it, then passed it on to his clerk, who stood and read:

"Count One, First Degree Murder—Guilty."

There were muffled sobs and gasps from one side of the courtroom. Jake's wife, Shelly Orbin, softly whispered "thank you" to the air.

But Marjorie Orbin did not react at all. She had no family members sitting behind her, no friends. She sat rigidly as the rest of the verdicts were read:

Count Two: Theft, Count Three: Fraud, Count Four: Theft, Count Five: Theft—all guilty.

The state of Arizona had three phases to a capital murder trial. The first phase was guilt or innocence. Marjorie had just completed that portion of the trial and failed. But there were weeks to go yet before the jurors would be excused and Marjorie's fate would be settled.

The second phase was called "aggravation." Jurors had to find if aggravating factors applied to the crime. If aggravating factors, which were strictly defined by law, were found to be present, the prisoner was eligible for the death penalty. When Marjorie next appeared in court, a week after she'd been adjudged guilty by a jury of her peers, prosecutor Treena Kay asked the jury to apply two of the state's qualifying aggravating factors. The first one was that the crime had been committed in consideration of pecuniary value. In other words, it was done for money, whether in the form of cash, securities, ownership of a business or even the mere expectation of such a gain. The second aggravating factor she asked them to apply was that the crime was committed in an especially heinous or depraved manner. The "needless mutilation of a body" was an example given under the law of "especially heinous or depraved."

Kay began her speech at 1:20 that afternoon. She told the jury that Jay Orbin had been outgoing, larger-than-life and that he had "loved with all his heart." She said, "Jay had it all. But that wasn't enough for the defendant—SHE wanted it all. . . . She killed Jay, and she TOOK it all." Kay led the jurors through the Orbins' finances and their odd divorced-but-still-acting-as-man-and-wife arrangements. As Jay's beneficiary, Marjorie would receive everything—as she herself had often mentioned to people, from her friends to her brother-in-law to even Detective Jan Butcher. But under the decree, if they went their separate ways she'd only have gotten $700 a month in child support. Her former lover Michael J. Peter had been willing to take her back, but she did not want that. She wanted to be independent. Marjorie had told jail informant Sophia Johnson and others that once her legal troubles were over, "she wouldn't need anyone to take care of her, she'd be set." Prosecutor Kay reminded the jurors of the recorded conversations Marjorie had made from jail with Bryan Todd Christy where she directed him to hold and hide money and assets for her, and not to "give it to the attorneys, they have to abide by the law."

Kay said that Marjorie "had a greed and she had a NEED to hold on to that money."

The prosecutor then turned her attention to the frightful condition in which Jay's body had been found. Kay made it clear that "there was no need to dismember Jay to kill him." She reminded the jury that Marjorie was "extremely handy" and that Jay's friends joked that his wife was "Tim Allen."* Marjorie knew how to do cutouts for countertops and sinks; she'd even built

---

* After the sitcom *Home Improvement*, where comic actor Tim Allen portrayed a professional handyman known as "Tim the Tool Man Taylor."

a kitchen island. She was "not the typical Scottsdale housewife who hires people to do these things." She was strong and had been known to lift heavy and unwieldy objects. Kay pointed out that it had taken two different instruments to do this terrible thing to Jay—the knife to cut the flesh and the jigsaw to cut the bone—and noted it had taken two rubber tubs, one for Jay's torso and another, whereabouts still unknown, for his head, upper body, shins and feet.

The prosecutor also repeated how other inmates had reported that Marjorie had joked that she was so organized, she'd even cut her former husband up in alphabetical order. At last, Kay connected the facts of the case to the specific point of law, that "to chop up the father of her child is 'shockingly evil, especially heinous or depraved.'"

By 2:00 it was the defense's turn. This time lead attorney Herman Alcantar took center stage. No more than five-foot-two, with a deceptively down-home style, Alcantar kept his opponents off-guard by seeming like a favorite uncle. But the one person who seemed less and less fond of him as the trial progressed was his own client, Marjorie Orbin. She was about to get the last dose of him she could stand.

Alcantar told the jury they had reached the most difficult phase of the trial because they were being asked to keep an open mind after they had already reached a very difficult and emotional decision. He told them the standard for aggravating factors was still "beyond a reasonable doubt."

"Emotions may get to you," he warned them in his softly beguiling style, "they may cloud your ability to judge facts objectively." Then he recalled for them a story from the annals of American jurisprudence, about founding father John Quincy Adams. Some redcoats had committed a terrible massacre in a North Carolina town. When the dust settled, several British soldiers had been arrested. John Quincy Adams was drafted to defend the soldiers, a very unpopular position to be in. "There was a lot of emotion in that trial," said Alcantar, "but the defense that Adams used was, 'can you prove that these are the RIGHT redcoats?' Every single one of the British soldiers [was] found not guilty. Those North Carolina jurors were able to put aside their emotions and look at the facts."

Alcantar loosely tied the story to his own leading suspect, Larry Weisberg. In a self-deprecating manner, utilizing his own small size to rhetorical advantage, Alcantar talked about how Weisberg was a "wannabe military type." Then he turned to Weisberg's son-in-law, Brad Fritz, a potential accomplice. Fritz, who had been applying for the Arizona police academy when the case was first under investigation in 2004, was "a real military type," said Alcantar.

The diminutive jurist then told another military story, this one from Vietnam, wherein a decorated South Vietnamese Ranger had been mistakenly killed by U.S. Marines because, he said, "the marines misinterpreted the circumstantial evidence before them." The lesson, said Alcantar to the jurors, was "you have to find SHE did the mutilation and no one else." He also made the distinction of what the purpose of the dismemberment might have been, "mutilation by itself is not enough, it must be 'the intent to disfigure.'"

He also talked about the issue of the freezing of the corpse. Where was the freezer? The only freezers found on Marjorie's property could not possibly hold a human corpse. Where was the freezer that had supposedly held Jay's body? That was the last question Alcantar left with the jury, before sitting down. It was 2:35 P.M.

Treena Kay, the energetic prosecutor, strode to the rostrum, her high heels tapping swiftly across the floor. "There are no redcoats," she said, "it was her." She pointed to the defendant.

Kay said Marjorie had never so much as paid the household bills before, but when she learned the insurance benefits could not be paid out until Jay's body was found and the policy was about to be canceled for lack of payment, "she hopped to it: she called Mr. Little [the insurance agent], she paid the premium. And she let him know the body was found. She doesn't have to play the wife anymore to get the money. No more Scottsdale housewife. No more pretending to like Jay. She was disgusted and done."

"Freezing isn't mutilation," Kay declared, "chopping up is. She needed someone to find the body so she could collect sooner rather than later. She took that tub to a busy intersection so it could be found."

Kay spoke for just ten minutes then made her final statement. "There is only one redcoat—the redcoats have all been identified." She swiveled to her right and took her place at the prosecution table.

The jury retired to deliberate. For many trials the aggravation phase went by quickly, as did the arguments themselves here, in less than two hours. This panel only had two aggravating factors to consider, so some observers lingered in the courtroom, thinking the verdict might come in before the day was through.

But it did not.

Tuesday wore on and still no verdict came in on the aggravating phase, the phase that would determine whether Marjorie was eligible for the death penalty. Late in the day, a question came in from the jury room. The question gave a glimpse into the group's deliberations. "Is dismembering a corpse considered an aggravating factor if the dismembering was done for convenience, not for spite?"

During the time that the jury was out struggling with this question, Marjorie was allowed to wait in the courtroom, because the panel was expected back at any moment. After five years in jail and nearly ten months in trial, her frustrations were peaking. With the jury out of the room and the question of innocence no longer an open one, she began to let loose. During those hours, she spoke in increasing volume to the guards near her. Tom Connelly and Robyn Varcoe came and went. Herman Alcantar was not present. He took the brunt of Marjorie's disdain. She couldn't stand the "redcoats" speech. What did redcoats have to do with anything? Couldn't he have done better? She rolled her eyes and made guttural noises of disgust. Alcantar was not up to her standards. It was a great wrong he had done her, leaving her life in the hands of such a ridiculous speech. The guards she was addressing maintained noncommittal expressions on their faces, occasionally giving her a mild half smile or nod.

The hours wore on as her diatribe grew. If an attorney was near her at the moment, Connelly or Varcoe, they'd make a comforting comment or lay a soothing hand on her back without joining her attack on their colleague.

As the hours wore on, Marjorie's harangue swept in the nimble prosecutor who had stepped in mid-trial and hadn't wavered for a moment since. Treena Kay was a liar, Marjorie said repeatedly. She turned to the guards and gave them instance after instance of what she characterized as Kay's lies. How could this jury condemn her to death, she asked, when Treena Kay had stood before them and lied?

There were also others who'd lied, according to Marjorie; she scattered their names and testimony into her day-long tirade. Some of her favorite targets beyond Alcantar and Kay were her former friend Sharon Franco Rueckert and her dead husband's brother, Jake Orbin Jr. Her ire was expansive now that it had been both stoked and emancipated by the five guilty verdicts. She tossed her long hair behind her shoulders and her sharp eyes frequently scanned the room. She kept her back ramrod straight. By the end of the day, there was still no verdict on the aggravation phase, and Marjorie disappeared behind the walls of the courtroom, to be returned to her cell west of downtown.

On Wednesday afternoon, September 23, 2009, the jurors finally returned. Marjorie was present to hear the decision, but none of the Orbin family had made it in. The jury found at least one aggravating factor and that was all that was necessary to invoke the death penalty. They decided she had committed the crime for pecuniary gain. The dismemberment, according to the question they had sent in during their deliberations, in their view may have been carried out in order to get the body to fit in containers, not as a way to express contempt and hate for the victim*.

Perhaps Alcantar's speech had hit its mark at least with some of the panel, after all.

The third phase, the penalty phase, was where the defense put on a special case for mercy, called mitigation. Victims were allowed to read victim impact statements. The defense in capital cases would often try to portray the condemned as a little child, as someone's loved one, as someone who did some good in life or who suffered travails that put the person's crime in a softer context. The goal was focused on one thing: to save the prisoner's life. The burden was now on the defense.

On Thursday, September 24, 2009, Robyn Varcoe made a brief opening statement. She wanted the jurors to think of one thing: should Noah Orbin be left an orphan?

Treena Kay jumped up less than five minutes later to urge the jurors to remember *why* Noah was in peril of becoming an orphan, because Marjorie had "killed the father of her 8-year-old son." Kay chastised the defense and said the defendant should not get "credit" for a murder by turning it into a mitigating factor. Furthermore, mindful of the people who had made sacrifices to raise him, she said, "Noah is not an orphan. He has family. He is loved."

---

* The jury's finding is a matter of record. Some of the jurors were later interviewed and gave their reasoning and thought process.

Prosecutor Treena Kay had one other person speak directly to the jury. As she told them, he was a man who had given up his dream job, sold his balmy San Diego home and come to the hot desert to take care of his young nephew. He had also taken over the role as family spokesman. It was Jake Orbin Jr.

Jake wore a Hawaiian-style shirt covered in palm trees in browns and greens as he ambled up the aisle and crossed into the court past the rail. He gave the jury his cheeriest face as he opened his remarks. He told the jury that he and Jay were six years and two days apart.

"He's my little brother. He made everyone around him smile. He was a bright light in my heart," Jake said. "Everyone who knew him has suffered. Words cannot express our pain. We could not sleep at night when he went missing; we felt we weren't doing enough. Then we had to hear that he had been dismembered—it was more than we could take.

"My parents have aged a decade. Dad is angry all the time. Mom is crying all the time. There is no light to guide our family. We struggle at Christmas, on [Jay's] birthday, on the anniversary of his death. There are no more late night emails. Instead we live in the past, reminiscing about the kind of person Jay was—happy, smiling. Gone forever. Our family is broken.

"He wanted to be able to see his son more often—" Jake, the genial big brother, always trying to be the stalwart plank in his shattered family, suddenly suffered a complete breakdown. His face crashed into a tight grimace of pain. His words stopped. His stifled sobs took their place. He gathered his breath, and then forged ahead. "—and not be on the road all the time. Well, he's not on the road anymore, not because he's retired. He's just gone. Murdered."

Jake held up a photo of four male Orbins. He called it the "guys photo," which showed "Jay and Jake, Dad and Noah."

"Every day Aunt Shelly and I send Noah to school. Noah relies on us. It is especially hard for Noah. I try to be there for him. But I know in my heart Noah wishes it was Jay.

"Every year on September 8 we celebrate Jay's birthday at one of his favorite places. We have a cake and we tell stories. Noah writes a note to his father and none of us adults look at it. We have a little ceremony and Noah leaves it behind and we bury it so Jay can read it in heaven. We let one balloon go and as it sails off, Noah says 'I miss you, Dad.'"

Jake finished his statement by saying he could never be as great a brother as Jay had been to him.

What Jake had not told the jury was how the family hoped they would decide the issue of life or death. Nor had he directly addressed Marjorie or told her what the family thought of her. There was a good reason he did not say these things. Arizona law forbade it.

When the jurors began their deliberations, they could not know exactly how Noah's current guardians felt about the death penalty for his mother. They would have to decide on their own, for a little boy they had never met.

Mitigation specialist Alan Ellis, a member of the defense team whose job it was to interview the defendant's family members and other loved ones, had taken the stand earlier. He showed a black-and-white photo of two tiny blond girls. The older one was Allison Kroh, and the baby propped up against her was her little sister Marjorie. A letter from Allison was then read to the jury. In the letter Allison told the jury that a painful surgery had prevented her from coming to the trial in person, but she wanted them to know that she believed in her sister and that Marjorie was a good person. She told them that as children, Marjorie had been "my little shadow." As an adult, Marjorie's "main purpose was to be a mom." Allison said Marjorie had "risked her life" for fertility treatments, and when they were successful, Marjorie was the "happiest" she'd been in her entire life.

At the defense table, Marjorie sniffled while her sister's letter was read.

The other letter was from Porter Freeman, the man whom Marjorie had worked for at Church Street Station some twenty-five years before. His letter told the court Marjorie had been a good worker, and although he hadn't seen her in a quarter of a century, he would still be happy to hire her back. He wrote that when she'd managed employees at his restaurant, she'd imbued them with "so much energy and zest, you could tell who she trained."

Alan Ellis displayed for the jury more photographs from Marjorie's youth, showing her as a majorette at Lake Brantley High. Photos of her as a showgirl and stripper were then mostly skipped over, and the courtroom caught up with Marjorie again as a proud new mother with Noah as a newborn in the hospital. Then Noah's nursery in the Orbin home became the backdrop for a photo of mother and child and Ellis pointed out to the jury that Marjorie had built the nursery herself. Another photo showed Marjorie at the retail store temporarily operated by Jayhawk International. Ellis pointed out the cabinets—she'd built those. Multiple shots of her posing with Noah as he grew up filled the screen, many showing her happily kissing her child. Few, if any, of the photos had Jay in them.

The photos of Marjorie ended when her son reached the age of eight.

The entire presentation of Marjorie's life—from childhood through the age of forty-three, when she was arrested, including the two letters written by her sister and her former boss—took less than twenty minutes.

At 2:05 P.M. on September 24, 2009, the jury saw for the first time something they had been waiting for nine long months to see.

Marjorie Kroh Marqui Tweed Woods Cannizzaro Mottram Radesits Orbin stood up to speak.

She wore a brown cardigan over a sherbet top and brown dress slacks. Around her waist, underneath the knit tops, an electric security belt spoiled the effect of what would otherwise have been graceful lines and made her seem bulkier than she really was.

When Marjorie crossed the courtroom to take the rostrum that hot September afternoon, she was ready to tell the jurors what was on her mind—but only a fraction of it. For the last two days, the lawyers in chambers with Judge Anderson had been heavily editing Marjorie's speech. She had written into it many of the vituperative sentiments she had expressed loudly to a mostly empty courtroom while waiting for the jury to deliberate in the previous phase. During that dressing-down, she had exclaimed that "they hold my life in their hands—I want them to hear what I have to say." She wanted to tell the jury how much everyone else had lied, especially Treena Kay and Sharon Franco Rueckert and Jake Orbin. And she wanted to tell them quite clearly that they had gotten it wrong, that she was innocent.

She would not be allowed to say any of that. The judge heavily excised her speech, and it was left to Robyn Varcoe to explain to her client that she would not be allowed to call anyone else a liar, attack others in any way, argue the points of the trial or proclaim her innocence.

Her first statement, carefully edited by Judge Anderson, was "I still maintain my belief in my innocence. I made a lot of poor choices. I was 42* when I was arrested, I am 48† now. It was humiliating and frightening. I had never been in trouble in my entire life before.

"When Jay died, I lost my spouse and my best friend and my extended family." Her voice was wobbly and high-pitched with nerves and emotion.

Then it dropped an octave, with a note of resignation laced with intimacy when she talked next about her relationship with the dead man. "Jay knew me very well. And he loved me anyway. All of me. People said we were opposites because I was such a glamourpuss and Jay was so down-to-earth. But in every important thing, Jay and I were just alike."

---

* She had actually turned forty-three more than a month earlier.
† She was still forty-seven. She would turn forty-eight in five weeks.

She underscored the deepest connection between them when she said, "I used to give Jay a Mother's Day card on Mother's Day because of all he went through with me during the fertility treatments."

Marjorie's next statement made the Orbin family sitting about twenty feet away from her visibly wince, reach for one another and shake their heads:

"I can't imagine being in Joann's position, something having happened to my son." Marjorie herself was tearful and sniffling. Her voice had soared up again into a high register.

She apologized to the jury for her personal demeanor during the trial. She had been admonished not to react emotionally to the testimony, but she didn't want them to think that she was emotionless:

"It took every ounce of my being to keep still. I nearly cracked a tooth trying to keep still."

She told them it was a tough thing they were being asked to do and it was tough for her, too, because "I don't know you at all and you don't know me. I can be bitchy, bossy, critical and negative. But I can be funny and sensitive. I have a strong faith. I have spent a lot of time on my knees asking for forgiveness and guidance these five years."

She looked up from the paper she was clutching in her hand and directly at the jury. "Please be merciful— do not give me the death penalty. Neither choice is a winning situation. Life in prison is pretty serious. And only God has the right to take a life."

She gathered up her handwritten speech (done in pencil, the only instrument allowed her) and returned to her place between Tom Connelly and Robyn Varcoe.

Herman Alcantar sat on the other side of Varcoe, slightly insulated from his client's smoldering ire.

From his high bench, Judge Arthur Anderson instructed the jury not to revisit the question of guilt or innocence, no matter what Marjorie had just said to them.

The lawyers made three more speeches. Herman Alcantar told the jury the question of life or death was the most important part of the trial. He told them Marjorie may have irritated them during the trial, but they should remember the trying circumstances she was up against and that they were not to judge her for her likability. He said her statement of innocence could be used by them to judge her demeanor. In other words, he left unspoken the question, how was an innocent person to act when she'd been jailed for five years and her child was being raised by someone else? Anyone might be frustrated, tense and anxious. He reminded them that if they voted to have Marjorie executed, her son Noah would be left an orphan.

Prosecutor Treena Kay by now seemed almost as irritated as Marjorie had revealed herself to be when the jury was not present. She popped out of her chair, marched to the exhibits, picked up a blowup photo and faced the jury. "She [Marjorie] stood before you and said she was a team with Jay and Jay was her best friend." The prosecutor lifted the edge of the stiff cardboard and revealed to the jury the poster it held. It was the horrifying photo of Jay's headless, armless, legless remains. "This is her 'best friend.'" After flashing the photo, Kay rapidly tilted it facedown again and returned it to the exhibit table. "It was her greed, her sense of absolute entitlement that brought us all here, that made Noah an orphan. I ask you to impose the death penalty."

On this important question of life or death, with the burden of proof of mitigation on the defendant, it was the defense who got the last word.

Robyn Varcoe stood up. She said Sophia Johnson, once Marjorie's cellmate, had access to all of Marjorie's files and could have cooked up her own testimony to match the facts of the case, including the statements of such people as Sharon Franco Rueckert. After Jay went missing, Marjorie was simply "paying bills," not transferring cash to her own personal account. She had not signed powers of attorney over Noah's guardianship to "strangers" but to people who knew Noah, such as Todd Christy. Or to Michael J. Peter, who had the wealth to provide for Noah lavishly. All those people who said Marjorie had claimed Noah was not even Jay's son? That was just their confusion over the in vitro process. Had Noah called Larry Weisberg "Dad"? It had been an accident of a confused child missing his father, not something Marjorie put him up to.

Varcoe said if they spared Marjorie's life, the jury would be preserving the chance for some kind of a mother/son relationship. There was no indication, she said, that Noah did not want a relationship with his mother. In the gallery, Noah's uncle Jake and grandmother Joann Orbin shook their heads in disagreement.

But Robyn Varcoe plunged ahead. "The state should not take away the mother/son relationship. It should not say that Marjorie has no value at all. We ask for life."

CHAPTER NINETEEN

Life or Death

The jury discussed life and death for six days. Very late in the day, at ten to 5 P.M. on September 30, 2009, all gathered in the courtroom to hear their decision. It was just moments away from another night of agony for Marjorie, wondering whether her life was to be ended with a syringe filled with poison; another night of stress for the Orbins, waiting for the case to be officially over.

For downtown Phoenix, a concrete oven, the late afternoon rays of sunshine entered the grove of tall buildings like a barbecue lighter. The air was bone-dry, with humidity less than 10 percent. At street level, on the courthouse steps, real estate speculators gathered to hear foreclosure notices read out, the brand-new commuter train chugged into its ninety-degree turn toward the East Valley and protestors against the county sheriff were gathering up their signs and water bottles, getting ready to head home for the day.

Up on the eleventh floor, just a stroke before 5 P.M., the clerk read out the verdict from the slip.

Marjorie's life was to be spared.

The jury was dismissed after nearly a year of service. At the defense table, Marjorie hugged Robyn Varcoe, both women tearful with relief. Marjorie had another weepy hug for mitigation specialist Alan Ellis. There was no hug for Herman Alcantar. He gracefully stayed at his end of the table and said, to no one in particular, "It's kind of a fifty percent victory." His point was well made. Marjorie had been on trial for her life and her life she still had. There should be no undervaluing that payoff.

Three of the jurors appeared on the hot courthouse steps to meet the media. The other nine had been escorted out a back entrance. The three revealed their reasoning. "A lot of us felt for Noah. We felt that if she were still alive, he could have the opportunity at the age of eighteen to ask him herself why she had done this to his father. If we had her executed, he would never have that chance," they said.

What about the question of an accomplice? Had Larry Weisberg wrongfully escaped the reach of justice?

"She was a very capable woman who could do anything she wanted to—by herself," the three jurors said emphatically. "We believe she had no help. We thought a lot about that. She did it by herself. Her defense team was strong, but they didn't have any facts."

Perhaps she had been coerced or manipulated by Weisberg? The answer was strongly negative. "She's outright guilty," they stated. "Larry Weisberg was a guy who spoke from the heart. He didn't have anything to do with it.

"We know Jay and Marjorie were in that house together on September 8. There is no evidence that he ever emerged."

Also appearing on the courthouse steps were Jake Jr. and Shelly Orbin. The couple, who would go home in a few minutes to Jay's young son, said they were elated that it was over. The jury had reached the right decision on both questions. Yes, Marjorie was guilty. But no, they had not wanted the death penalty. It was despicable what she had done to Jay, but when all was said and done, they had not wanted Noah's mother killed.

Also on the courthouse steps that day was a crew from the television program *48 Hours Mystery*. Throughout the ten long months of trial, they had kept a camera mounted near the ceiling, pointed right at Marjorie, and on key days, they'd brought in another camera on a tripod on the first gallery bench behind the prosecutor. *48 Hours* producer Cindy Cesare had attended the trial frequently, flying in from out of town, and other producers also showed up from time to time. The on-air correspondent for the *48 Hours* piece would be tall, sandy-haired Peter Van Sant, a former resident of Phoenix himself.

There was a sign posted on the courtroom doors advising spectators that they were not allowed to communicate in any way with defendants in custody, so no words or looks or gestures were exchanged between Marjorie and the *48 Hours* people, but she was keenly aware that these representatives from CBS were present. Outside the courtroom, the crew worked the story vigorously and kept in close contact with Marjorie's lawyers and even with the jail.

Marjorie's former in-laws were also on very friendly terms with the television people. They spent hours being interviewed on camera, sharing their memories of Jay Orbin, hoping that the piece the national crew wrote up would serve as a memorial for their son and brother. They offered up home videos from Jay's life, Christmas and family gatherings, including the last video of Jay, at Noah's eighth birthday. In the halls at court, under no such restriction as Marjorie was, the Orbins often chatted with Peter Van Sant or Cindy Cesare. The Orbins were eager to share Jay with a national audience. They could never have him back, but somehow the thought of viewers across the land getting to know what a great guy he was was comforting.

On November 21, 2009, the Saturday heading into Thanksgiving week, the hour-long episode aired. The Orbins had notified all of Jay's friends of the air date, and they planned to be together as a family to watch the piece. But the show held a surprise for everyone, save Marjorie and her defense team. CBS, it turned out, had managed to convince the Maricopa County Jail to allow Marjorie to use one of their own video cameras in her cell. For six months, she had spoken directly to the camera and aired her thoughts. They called this unprecedented maneuver "Diaries of a Showgirl."

The show that aired on November 21, 2009, was a polished and compelling piece of television. Toward the end, Peter Van Sant confronted Marjorie with statements of hers he called "unbelievable." Prosecutor Treena Kay appeared on camera calling Marjorie a "liar." Detective

Dave Barnes appeared on camera calling her a "cold-blooded killer."

But it was the video diary that jumped out of the screen at the Orbins. They were deeply hurt by what they felt was a "platform for the 'Marjorie Show.'" They called off all cooperation with media from that point. They said they were embarrassed to have invited Jay's friends to watch it. They let CBS know they were furious. They felt the show had barely touched on Jay and was faintly negative about him, in contrast to being the memorial they had hoped for.

Marjorie's defense attorneys raised some fury of their own over the CBS piece. They demanded a new trial based on the existence of the home videotapes that Jake Jr. had turned over to *48 Hours*. They argued that if they could have played the tapes for the jury, the panel would have come to different opinions about the size differential between Jay and Marjorie at the time of his death. They would have decided she could not have lifted him because of how much smaller she looked in the video than she'd been at the defense table. They also believed it would show the jurors that Marjorie did not hate Jay, that she was affectionate and loving to him in the family gatherings captured on celluloid.

And if the defense was angry about the videotapes, they were absolutely incensed by the statements that former Detective Dave Barnes had made during his national TV interview. He had told Peter Van Sant on camera that the Phoenix Crime Lab had failed to test some of the hairs found in the blue tub. He made it sound like Larry Weisberg very well might still be implicated if the lab would just test those hairs.

What the CBS show did not have time to air was that Barnes was also suing the city of Phoenix at that time and claiming whistle-blower status based on his complaints about the crime lab. But his lawsuit did not acknowledge the long and twisting pile of evidence against him for alleged computer fraud, harassment and misconduct at the police station. Hearings were held on the eleventh floor after the *48 Hours* piece aired. Dave Barnes's claiming of his Fifth Amendment rights was attacked. On the *48 Hours* show it was clearly stated that he felt he had lost his position in Homicide because of his complaints regarding the crime lab "in *this* and other cases." Judge Arthur Anderson said he had allowed a certain amount of Fifth Amendment rights protection when Barnes finally appeared on the stand in Marjorie's case in late summer. He had allowed it, he said, specifically because he thought he had been assured that the policeman's departmental troubles, especially the raid on his house, had nothing to do with Marjorie's case. Now he was hearing that they did arise from this case. The judge felt hoodwinked. He stated clearly that Barnes's rights could not compete with Marjorie's. Protecting the man in his own unrelated case was one thing, but stacking his rights against Marjorie's in the same case was something entirely different. Marjorie had been on trial for her *life*. Nothing could trump that.

Furthermore, Judge Anderson told the court that he questioned if *any* Fifth Amendment privilege could be preserved when the person went on national television to talk about things he refused to talk about in the witness box.

On that national television show, Barnes had talked

about hairs found in the blue tub that had not been tested by the crime lab even though he had requested it. His accusations left in the viewer an ominous stinger of doubt about the case, although Barnes also stated on camera that he believed Marjorie was the true culprit. The defense team, as anyone might expect, came to that post-show hearing passionately in pursuit of the "untested hairs." They threw insults at the prosecution for withholding such colossal evidence. Defense attorney Tom Connelly reserved his greatest contempt for the missing prosecutor Noel Levy, who, like his lead detective, had disappeared from the trial halfway through, trailing whiffs of mistrust and ill will behind him. But Connelly thundered that Treena Kay had to answer for the case she inherited nonetheless, and it was nothing short of an outrage that the existence of untested hairs had been kept from the defense team.

Prosecutor Treena Kay jumped up in a torrent of exasperation. She had no idea what Dave Barnes had been talking about. She grabbed a fistful of papers and went through every mention of hairs there was. She accounted for each hair. Each had been tested, and those results had been made available to the defense. If Detective Barnes had some hairs that *she* did not know about, she would surely want to hear more herself. But it was her belief there were none. If such hairs existed, where in the stacks and stacks of paper she had was there a record of them? Who had found them, where were they stored, what was the tracking number Barnes must have used in paperwork if he had turned them over to the lab for testing, even if the request turned out to be futile? As for Barnes's Fifth Amendment rights, she cared little.

She had put on her case without him. His testimony was of no significance to her. She had won the case without him and, if necessary, would do so again.

The defense's wrath at what it thought was the prosecutor's sleight of hand deflated considerably. Connelly was more pacified as he stated what had now become obvious to all: "What we need is to get Barnes in here and find out what he's talking about."

Considering the former detective's recalcitrance, that was an issue for Judge Anderson. He also had the matter of the home videos that had aired on *48 Hours*. Anderson's parting comment on that issue was that the one person who knew best that those tapes existed and what use they might be put to was the defendant herself. It was a little late in the day, he implied, to claim that the state had somehow withheld them from her. With his black robes swaying, Judge Anderson disappeared into the back chambers and the hearing ended for now.

Marjorie herself was in attendance at court that day. Now that she had been convicted and the jury was gone, she had to appear in her jail stripes. She was still in the county jail, rather than the Arizona state prison system. She had fought for the right to stay in the county facility until the issue of a new trial had been decided. With the wobbly track of justice this trial had taken, it might seem there would be plenty of grounds for a new one. But when it came time to argue for it, it was the television show that took center stage. Marjorie would wait at Estrella Jail until she learned if the trial would be overturned. She was also awaiting final sentencing. The jury had given her life in prison, but the details were left to the judge. It would be Judge Anderson who would decide if Marjorie would get "natural life," meaning she would never leave prison until she died, or if she would get "twenty-five to life," meaning she could earn parole and early release if she worked at it.

Marjorie was not optimistic about her chances of winning a new trial. She felt she would have to get past Judge Anderson before there was any hope a new trial might be ordered. She thought if it came, it would come from an appeals court, not from the very same judge who had presided over the original bedraggled affair.

Life in jail was a far cry from the Florida yachts, Las Vegas clubs and Scottsdale gyms where Marjorie had spent so much of her adult life. But what was the same was the personality that Marjorie brought with her. Footage of her cell showed it to be as meticulously organized as her home had been. She was allowed some personal items as well as legal files, and they were all neat as a pin.

In her TV appearance on *48 Hours*, many viewers noticed that she seemed to have no shortage of makeup. Those who had seen her in person in court or in jail visits already knew that. She explained that some of her "makeup" was actually permanent; her eyebrows, for example, were tattooed on. Other makeup could be purchased through the jail commissary. Marjorie never appeared in court, in visits, or on camera without lipstick, which she griped was only available in jail in one garish color, though she said she frequently muted it via an old glamour trick of applying powder.

Marjorie's hair color had reverted to a warm honey brown. Her hair was long and thick, but it definitely betrayed her sunless life. None of the natural highlights that people living in freedom naturally acquired could be found in her otherwise sumptuous mane. In court, she sometimes complained to the judge about her hair products. What shampoo she did have was sometimes taken away from her in administrative vagaries.

What seemed to be the worst affliction of jail life for Marjorie was her weight gain. For a woman whose entire life and career had been based on physical appearance, this was a sore tribulation. Inmates in the Maricopa County Jail were fed their first meal of the day at a very early hour, around 6 A.M., and did not see another meal tray until 8 P.M. Eating only twice a day, many nutritionists have pointed out, can be hard on blood sugar levels, which have such an impact on weight maintenance. Marjorie described being "hungry all the time." If inmates wanted to eat in between meals, they could purchase a candy bar or a limited list of other treats from the commissary if they had money. If they were on a work assignment, however, they were nowhere near the commissary during the day anyway and would not be allowed to carry a candy bar to their work area.

The meals provided to the inmates on their twice-a-day trays were often starch-heavy, though Marjorie's diet was slightly different from the other inmates'. She had declared herself Jewish and received the kosher menu. Only the jail's Jewish chaplain could approve a kosher diet request for an inmate, and Marjorie enjoyed a close relationship with cantor Howard Tabaknek. She spent many hours in conference with him and looked forward eagerly to his visits. "He believes in me," she declared. "I just love Howard."

The home videos clearly showed Christmas celebrations, however, and Kirk Rogers, Marjorie's high school boyfriend, remembered Christmas trees in her home as they grew up. He had never heard that her family might be Jewish. Other high school classmates of Marjorie's were also surprised to hear that she was Jewish. They wondered if maybe she had converted to Judaism for one of her husbands. But Marjorie said in jailhouse interviews that she was Jewish by birth. Though her family had not been very observant while she was growing up, she said that "if you come from a Jewish womb then you are Jewish, and that I did." She thought her grandmother on her mother's side might be the source of the Jewish line.

When Marjorie's sister Allison Kroh was contacted, she gave a short gasp and said, "I do not want to disagree with anything Marjorie says or cause her trouble in anyway. But I am not Jewish. That's all I can say is I am not Jewish." Indeed, Allison stated that she herself was "Christian."

When asked, Marjorie said the Orbins were Catholic. But she said she had chosen her son's name, Noah, because it was from the Torah. She also remembered ongoing tension with her mother-in-law over breaking the tradition of "J" names in the Orbin family.

Marjorie did her best to keep some semblance of her dancer's figure. For a time, she may have been receiving help from her favorite diet aid—drugs. Oscar Moreno, the lover of Marjorie's loyal friend Bryan Todd Christy, had stated to police that she had recommended crystal meth and cocaine as slimming agents. In jail, there was a write-up about Marjorie's friend Susan Dermott sending her meth, adhered to the back of postage stamps on letters. Marjorie, it was alleged, would receive the letter then peel the stamp off the envelope and lick its back, sucking off the meth.*

When this practice was discovered to be common, the jail revamped its mailing policies. As of 2009, inmates were only allowed to receive postcards with the postage fee embedded. This made correspondence an even more forlorn experience for the inmates. They could write letters out, but could only receive paltry postcards in return. Their comfort and link with the outside world and those relationships they tried to hold onto at home were reduced to a few lines. And those lines had to be suitable for public consumption, as the postcard passed through the many hands of the U.S. postal system and then the internal jail system.†

Marjorie also tried to maintain her figure by religiously performing her workout routines. One jail guard testified that Marjorie was a "fanatic" about her martial arts practice.

The jail environment seemed uniquely suited to Marjorie's personality. In interviews she talked about actually "needing" to befriend younger women whom she could "mother." Marjorie always knew a clever

---

* Phoenix Police report.
† Maricopa County Jail policy as of 2010.

way to make a costume a little spiffier or could share a shrewd way to cut costs. In the stripping industry, she remembered keeping a brood of less experienced dancers lapping up her advice and tips. She often referred to them as "my girls" and always shared with them the same "pendulum" theory she'd told Susan Dermott about, that all men with too much of a good thing had corresponding bad traits, so it was best to look for those who were right in the middle: "They may not be that great, but they aren't going to be that bad, either."

In jail, Marjorie immediately started collecting a new brood of chicks. Within days, she had taken her cellmate Sophia Johnson under her wing. Johnson, jail guard Kathleen Mitchell testified, was young and frightened. Marjorie took it upon herself to show her the ropes. They were fairly inseparable for a time, but then there was the sudden removal of Johnson to protective custody. Johnson ended up a witness for the prosecution.

Although most of them did not end up as witnesses, guard Mitchell testified this was a pattern with Marjorie. She would be in the constant company of another inmate, usually a younger one, but then one day the two would have to be separated. The list of "keep aways"* on Marjorie was long.

In the early days of Marjorie Orbin's confinement, when Bryan Todd Christy was still a free man performing errands for her on the outside, one of the tasks Marjorie had him perform was putting money into the

---

* The jail's lingo for a continuing administrative order that one inmate be kept away from another in housing and other assignments.

commissary accounts of other inmates. Whether this was a way to hide Marjorie's own assets, a selfless act of generosity or an attempt to influence a network of incarcerated women was best known only to Marjorie herself. Some inmates told police she paid other inmates to commit assaults for her.

On the *48 Hours* show, a dark screen appeared with the words that Marjorie was now "in solitary confinement." It was true that after the first year, she no longer shared a cell with anyone and was kept away from the general population. But the jail called it "protective custody" and Marjorie said it was done at her own request. After one too many of these friendships and romances became a source of betrayal to her, Marjorie decided the best policy was to stay away from as many of her fellow inmates as she could manage. She claimed that Sophia Johnson had rifled through her files when Marjorie was not in the cell, and denied that she had ever confided incriminating statements to her. Going into protective custody gave Marjorie her own cell and cut off the supply of women who could turn snitch. If she never even knew them and could prove so by her so-called "solitary confinement," no jail snitch could ever be taken seriously again.

Sophia Johnson told police, and this was backed up with other documentation, that many of Marjorie's close friendships in jail involved intense romantic attachments. Bryan Todd Christy had alluded to this in interviews with Dave Barnes, by saying Marjorie was a "fag,"* but no one at that time seemed to have followed up on the comment (despite the many aspects of Marjorie's sex life that *were* explored in uncomfortable detail throughout that proceeding, especially her alleged sexual disgust for Jay).

One of the young women whom Marjorie was linked to was a slightly built former exotic dancer named Brandi Hungerford. Hungerford had been a South Korean orphan, a tiny child, adopted by an American couple. Her black hair, streaked with harsh blond highlights, fell down almost to her back at the time of her arrest, though later photos of her posted at the Arizona State Prison Web site showed a much more subdued appearance, heavier and with her hair cut into a demure pageboy.

Brandi Hungerford had been in the Maricopa County Jail for two years by the time that Marjorie arrived there. Brandi's own background was so similar to Marjorie's that it was chilling. Brandi was in jail for allegedly having leveraged her stripper life into an opportunity to murder a man—a jewelry dealer. The man was certainly dead, and Brandi Hungerford confessed as soon as she was caught. The corroborating evidence against her was prodigious, including dramatically incriminating security video and phone records. When her testimony against her accomplice in that murder was complete, Hungerford was moved to state prison and her intimate relationship with Marjorie necessarily came to a close. But by then, Brandi was afraid of Marjorie anyway.

---

* Phoenix PD interview with Bryan Todd Christy, May 30, 2005.

When investigators in the Orbin case, constantly sniffing for potential jail snitches, caught up with Hungerford in the other facility, however, she gave up no information useful to the case against Marjorie. She insisted Marjorie had never confided anything to her relevant to the case, although Detective Barnes wrote down that he had his doubts about that. Hungerford did confirm* that her relationship with Marjorie had once been romantic, using the often repeated jail explanation that "things happen in jail." She did reluctantly tell Dave Barnes how and why inmates became afraid of Marjorie. She said she was aware Marjorie had a long list of "keep aways" and that Marjorie liked to show the list to other inmates as a means of "intimidating others and controlling others." The detective wrote down that Hungerford told him she felt Marjorie had turned other inmates "against her" by showing them her name in her own legal file. "She described how Marjorie would go around telling people she was testifying against her . . ." But Hungerford and the detective both knew they had never met one another before and there were no plans to call Hungerford to the stand in Marjorie's case. The only way Hungerford's name had appeared in the file had been because other inmates had mentioned their romance. Until now, she had not even been interviewed by police. But someone who did testify against her, according to Hungerford, experienced similar tactics from Marjorie. She said it was Charity Hill, the same witness who had recanted her testimony and become

---

* Phoenix Police Report #2004 42022713.

the basis of allegations of prosecutorial misconduct against Noel Levy.

Reading through the stack of interviews with Marjorie's fellow prisoners, a picture emerged corroborating the characterization of Marjorie's pattern of close association with a particular fellow female inmate, only to have it turn sour suddenly. Many of these close relationships seemed to be romances, and Marjorie, it appeared, had a "type." The inmates' physical statistics were usually included in the interview, and many of Marjorie's closest relationships were with women who shared builds similar to Brandi Hungerford's, though she also had other relationships, which seemed mere flirtations by comparison, with much larger women.

By February of 2007, Marjorie had been in the Estrella Jail for two years. Dave Barnes traveled to a federal prison in Dublin, California, to interview an inmate named Christina Lambert. Lambert's height was listed at five-foot-nine and her weight at 245 pounds. She was a self-described "big girl" who liked to eat. She would accept commissary items from other inmates who shared with her, often in exchange for favors such as hair braiding.

Lambert remembered the first time she met Marjorie at the jail.* "Um, nobody liked her. Everybody hated her. Like . . . she was like 'the pod's most hated.' Like everybody thought that, like, maybe she was better than them or she was . . . And she exercised all the time, so, I kinda, I kinda admired her personality, you know? I

---

* Transcript from February 8, 2007.

kinda, I'm kinda like, you know, I see somebody that everybody hates and you know I'm like, 'well, she doesn't seem that bad to me,' you know what I mean?"

When asked who Marjorie's friends were, Lambert offered up that she knew Marjorie to have "little flings."

But she's bashful about this topic at first.

"Like, well, she had little relationships, like she'd mess around, like, you know, homosexual relationships or whatever. Not like—like they're gonna get married or nothing, but they'd just mess around. It's . . . I don't know why, but prison and jail does this to women. We just . . . We need to have comfort. That's what I think. My personal opinion," Lambert said. Barnes asked her if she had witnessed any sexual activity by Marjorie. Lambert was fervid in her denials. "No! No! I've never seen!"

But approximately an hour later, Lambert was more forthright about this.

"Were you close to Marjorie? Did you have any sort of relationship?" Dave Barnes asked her.

Lambert hedged. "Towards the end, uh, me and her were cool." Barnes wanted clarification, though, about whether Marjorie and Christina Lambert had ever had a sexual relationship.

LAMBERT: We started to kick it like that, but, I was ready to go, so . . .

BARNES: Okay.

LAMBERT: I was gonna leave any day and so I didn't really wanna get too close to her, you know what I mean? And I tried to make no type of connections like that, you know?

BARNES: Did it ever cross the line?

LAMBERT: Uhm, yeah, it did cross the line a little bit.

BARNES: Okay.

LAMBERT: But we had to nip that in the bud.

BARNES: I don't, I don't mean to get personal or—

LAMBERT: No! no! it's—

BARNES:—or salacious.

LAMBERT:—cool, it's okay. No. I understand.

BARNES: How-how did it cross the line?

LAMBERT: Uh . . . we kissed . . .

BARNES: Okay.

LAMBERT: . . . you know, I mean but . . .

BARNES: Did she come on to you?

LAMBERT: Uhm, I would say a little bit. Yeah, she came on to me. Yeah, a little, a little, a little bit.

BARNES: Did you like Marjorie?

LAMBERT: I thought she was very—very pretty, you know. And I admired her. Her strength, you know, because emotionally . . . physically, I feel like I'm a strong person, but emotionally, I'm pretty weak. Emotionally, I—I was a wreck, you know? I was always stressed out. I was crying. I was going through it with my—my family. Uh, my family got evicted and I couldn't call my mom and, oh, I didn't wanna start cuz I'm gonna cry.

Christina Lambert went on to tell Barnes that she'd admired Marjorie because Jay Orbin had been such a good father to Noah. She said her own children hadn't had a father. From Lambert's perspective, Marjorie had nothing but good things to say about Jay, including his size. She revealed that she herself is even bigger than the prison listed her, so Marjorie's admiration for size was important to her.

> **LAMBERT:** She said that he was a big man. That he was a really big man. That he was bigger than me, like in size, you know. And I weigh like 280 now* so I can only imagine how big this guy had to have been. He had to have been, you know and she said that she liked—she was attracted to, you know, big people, I guess.
>
> **BARNES:** She said that?
>
> **LAMBERT:** No! Like, you know, that, um, like, you know, 'cuz, well, she was trying to talk to me like in a romantic type of way I guess, you know? and so that's why she was saying, 'yeah, he's big like you,' you know?

If Barnes had been startled to hear of Marjorie describing herself as attracted to "big people" and using Jay as an example of her amorous ideal, just a few moments later it was Lambert's turn to be startled:

> **BARNES:** Okay, did she ever talk about her boyfriend on the outside?
>
> **LAMBERT:** Oh, she had a boyfriend on the outside?! No, I didn't—
>
> **BARNES:** Okay.
>
> **LAMBERT:** I ain't heard nothing about that!!!

---

* The prison paperwork listed her at 245.

> **BARNES:** Okay, she never mentioned anything about—
> **LAMBERT:** No.
> **BARNES:**—a boyfriend she might have had?
> **LAMBERT:** No.

No one but Lambert ever seemed to have heard Marjorie talk about Jay as an object of desire and his large size as a pleasing asset. Marjorie's frequent and ongoing expressions of disgust for Jay's size didn't square with Lambert's tales of sweet talk from Marjorie about larger sizes. Christina Lambert might have been even more shaken up if she had seen that the boyfriend Barnes was referring to, Larry Weisberg, probably had nearly zero percent body fat and that one of Marjorie's previous lovers had been a teenage professional karate instructor.

Perhaps Marjorie's romances with the smaller women were more spontaneous, while the ones with ladies such as Lambert could be seen as seductions designed for protection and networking.

Her old friend Lambert offered a bald and unceremonious depiction of the conditions at the Maricopa County Jail. She had been staying at the federal prison in Alameda County, on the east side of San Francisco Bay, inland from Oakland, when the Phoenix officials came to interview her. When Barnes suggested she might be asked to testify in Marjorie's Arizona trial, Lambert panicked:

"That County jail was the . . . that was the worst experience of my life! Of my life! I'm talking about, I've been raped. I've been beat. I've been jumped. You know what I'm saying? Uhm, that was the worst experience of my life. That was—it was terrible. There was mice and they would get in bed with you—and to—to be next to your body heat, they would jump in the bed with you. Wake up and there'd be mice all over you! I'm talking about—there's no way to keep the mice out! Because they would slide underneath the door. They would slide through the cracks and they would be in your home and it just was . . . it was just terrible.

"The food was horrible. The people were crazy. I was . . . it was . . . it was for me, to be as big as I am, I—I was . . . because all I kept thinking was I don't wanna get into any trouble. I don't wanna fight anybody! I don't wanna have to hurt anybody. And—and they were bothered in there, like within the first two weeks that I was in there, this one chick grabbed this other chick and bashed her head in to the little steel bolts that was on the floor! Her whole face was purple and black.

"I told 'em [Marjorie's lawyers] I didn't want to [testify]. I didn't wanna go back. I did not wanna go back and they said, 'okay, well, we can make it where you don't have to go back and, umm, or if—if you have . . . if we have to bring you in, then we'll make it within a, you know, short period of time, so we can get you there and bring you back.' But I know how it goes! Man! Oh, my god, my stomach hurts just thinking about it!"

In the *48 Hours* broadcast, viewers were shown that Larry Weisberg was at some point granted a form of immunity in exchange for his testimony. This immunity was granted two years deep into the investigation. By that time, detectives, try as they might, had found no evidence leading to the bodybuilder anyway.

Every piece of potentially suspicious evidence seized from his house, such as electrical cord or plastic sheeting, had been forensically excluded from the crime scene.

No matter what Dave Barnes would later say, no hairs were found to belong to Weisberg anywhere near the torso. And by two years into the case, investigators had had a pretty good taste of Marjorie's personality and capabilities—they no longer felt that she would have needed Weisberg. They had tried hard to go in that direction, but the trails of evidence always doubled back to Marjorie alone. Weisberg was even a bad fit as an accomplice, no matter how promising his hostile behavior during the SWAT raid had been. He appeared to be a man with an overlay of machismo, but far more bark than bite. He did not seem to have much of a grand passion for Marjorie, either, weakening the theory he would kill on her behalf. But police did wish they could get him to talk more freely.

On May 31, 2007, Weisberg was granted "use" immunity. Essentially what that meant was that while the man testified, no deputies could grab him and charge him with anything. If police *later* developed information that incriminated him, they were free to swoop in with as many handcuffs and Tasers as necessary. From the prosecution standpoint, it was a virtually risk-free offer. They thought the chances they'd ever want to charge Weisberg were remote. But the opportunity to have him appear before a jury and let them see for themselves whether he was credible was highly desirable. Prosecutors felt the jury would judge him to be as blameless as they had. Indeed, at trial, Weisberg came off as a frightened man who had inadvertently stepped on a hornet's nest.

Larry Weisberg explained that he had chased undercover surveillance officer Victor Roman that day because Marjorie had convinced him she was being stalked by someone or at least harassed by private investigators. He testified that shortly before her arrest, Marjorie had asked him to come over urgently. When he complied, she had said, "I'm frightened, I want to run away. And I want you to come with me." His response? "What?! Are you crazy?" Weisberg had been interviewed by police the day after Marjorie was arrested. He told them he wanted "to get as far away from her as possible." He said that for the most part he had believed in her innocence during that chaotic time from early September through early December 2004, but once or twice she had said evasive things that surprised him and made him wonder. His daughter, Jodi, had never trusted her from Day One. Both Weisbergs were upset that the little boy ended up calling Larry "Dad" while his father was missing.

Because Marjorie had told so many people that Noah was not Jay's natural child, Phoenix PD had the child's DNA tested. They were able to confirm that he really was his father's son and was now being raised by his real family who loved him.

If there was anyone whose relationship to the crime had possibly not been fully explored, it might be Susan Dermott. Records showed that phone lines between Las

Vegas and 55th Street were fairly buzzing with the constant traffic on September 8, 9 and 10, 2004. Through Bryan Todd Christy, police were able to determine that Marjorie was probably holding onto valuables for Dermott in an insurance scheme. This was why Dermott's driver's license had been found in Marjorie's possession. According to Christy, one of Dermott's first concerns when she called him that November day was these items that Marjorie was holding. When he drove over there, he said, Marjorie had immediately presented him with a fur coat, Mercedes paperwork and a few other items she said belonged to Dermott. It was Christy's understanding that Dermott had reported these items stolen and had collected insurance payouts on them.

Christy also made curious statements about Susan Dermott's "involvement." He didn't know if this was merely the insurance entanglement or something worse. He had a belief that Dermott was in Phoenix in early September. He did not have exact dates. He was basing this belief on a comment he remembered Dermott making. Something to the effect that she was sorry she hadn't had time to see him when she'd been in town, it was just that "Marjorie had some big stuff going on right now."

Christy also stated that he felt Marjorie and Susan Dermott were lovers. True or not, it was clear that the two women shared a high level of trust and intimacy. Unlike some of Marjorie's other protégées, Dermott never did testify against her. By July of 2005, Bryan Todd Christy had been in jail for weeks and had thought about the two women a lot. But his loyalty to Marjorie

was also far and above what most people would consider extraordinary.

"Would Susan be, uh, more likely to simply know
things or would she be a participant or both?" prosecutor Noel Levy asked him.

"I honestly don't know," Christy replied. "I mean—
not to be mean—I see Susan and Marjorie as the same.
I, I hate to be disrespectful, you know as . . . as I . . . as
I really analyze Marjorie a lot, the last couple months in
jail, if . . . if Marjorie has done this or knows about it, I,
I honestly can't say I could put something like that past
Susan. They're, they're two peas in the same pod. They
really are. I hate to say that, you know."

Police were beginning to test him out as a possible
informant, maybe put him in a position to get Dermott
talking. But Christy was not optimistic about success.

"Honestly, I think it's gonna take pulling teeth," he
said, adding that Detective Barnes had asked him if
Christy thought Marjorie was capable of murder, and
he'd hemmed and hawed as he replied, "That's what I
told the detective. . . . I think anyone's capable of anything depending on the circumstances. Uh, I think it
would take an act of God to get it out of Susan, but do
I think Susan knows what happened to Jay if Marjorie
knows? Absolutely! I believe that!"*

Christy also felt that Dermott was Marjorie's drug
supplier. It had been Dermott who was accused of lacing
her postage with meth in letters to jail, although Christy
was unaware of that situation. "I don't think [Marjorie]

---

* Police interview, July 15, 2005.

paid for 'em," Christy said. "My . . . my opinion per
Marjorie was Susan always took care of it. [Marjorie]
was worried about 'tweaking her weight,' as she put it,
because of her age and after the birth of the child and
I don't know what all—in her mid-40s or early 40s—
and, uh, that was really it."

As Detective Dave Barnes kept tabs on Marjorie Orbin's
jail cronies and confidantes, he heard changing stories of
what Marjorie talked about inside jail walls in regards to
the events of September 2004. Some of this might have
been due to the different levels of trust Marjorie had with
different people. At one point, for example, Sophia Johnson reported that when a certain third party was around,
Marjorie loudly proclaimed her innocence, even fearing
the area was bugged. At other times, tales of Marjorie
stating to a new inmate that she'd chopped up her husband "and you're next" floated up, but they could have
been attributed to prison culture and posturing.

But one story that began leaking beyond jail walls
with steadiness and frequency was that Marjorie was
telling many of her companions that she knew who killed
Jay and that she could not come forward because this person would kill her little son if she did. Sometimes when
the story reached the detective's ears, the person who had
heard it from Marjorie also could name a specific person,
"her boyfriend," "someone who was teaching her and
was with her a lot," "someone she was in bed with" and
sometimes even "Larry."

Marjorie had been incarcerated for the better part of
two years in the mouse-riddled jail so vividly described by

Christina Lambert, when that particular story came to Detective Barnes and prosecutor Noel Levy through official channels in April 2006. Barnes recorded in official documents that defense counsel (which at that time consisted of a different set of public defenders but still with Tom Connelly as third) told Barnes and Levy in a meeting at the County Attorney's Office that Larry Weisberg was the one who killed Jay. According to Barnes's report, the defense attorneys said that "Jay came home and interrupted Weisberg and Marjorie, which led to a fight and led to Jay's murder:[*sic*] Weisberg threatened Marjorie using Noah in the threat for Marjorie to assist him in disposing of Jay Orbin:[*sic*] Weisberg said that Noah would be in danger if Marjorie ever told what happened:[*sic*] the confrontation took place in the garage and Jay was murdered in the garage; Weisberg cut up Jay and made Marjorie assist him in the process and disposal of the body parts. It was inferred [that] the remaining parts are in the landfill.

"After we were told this," Barnes wrote, "I requested proof other than hearsay and a full statement/interview with Marjorie. I was told this would not happen and I should take them on their word this is what took place and I should work to prove this theory. Canby and Tallon [public defenders who were replaced by Alcantar and Varcoe later] got mad and left.

"Tom Connelly stayed back and told me that Marjorie is afraid to come forward which would put Noah in danger and further said: Marjorie does not want to cooperate or testify fearing Weisberg would carry out his threat to harm Noah.

"I responded [that] without a 'free talk' [talking

directly to Marjorie under circumstances that would protect her legal position] to prove her theory there is no support in the evidence. Connelly said he would talk with Marjorie about a free talk."

Barnes never received an offer of a free talk with Marjorie.

In the *48 Hours* piece, Marjorie repeated this story, claiming Larry Weisberg killed Jay and then threatened Noah. Barnes was shown in a later sound bite saying, "This is the first I've heard of it." Since the official record was full of notations Barnes himself made of information received through both snitches and official channels about this same accusation, it was unclear what Barnes was referring to in the sound bite.

On January 14, 2010, a grand jury handed down a true bill of indictment against Dave Barnes. The charges, including perjury, related to his dealings with the owner of the "Potatohead" Web site, who was also indicted, and the Potato Head photos themselves and the missing nameplates, not to Marjorie's case, although the dates of the alleged perjury show that the conduct in question was occurring in a different courtroom of the same building while Marjorie's trial was ongoing. Soon, the Phoenix Police Department terminated Barnes entirely. Several months after the indictment, however, the Arizona Attorney General's Office dropped the charges against him, "in the interest of judicial economy." But Barnes's troubles were far from over. The charges had been dismissed "without prejudice," meaning they could be refiled at any time, and speculation soared, even from his own attorney, that they would, indeed, be refiled at some point.

*   *   *

So far Noah Orbin has gone completely unharmed. No one has kidnapped him or injured him, even though his mother had begun telling the story of who the "real killer" was and how her son would be attacked if she did so. Noah did not write to his mother in jail. He had never been taken for a visit. According to his guardians, he read the letters she sent him, then rolled his eyes and passed them on to his caretakers. Larry Weisberg sold the house in Central Phoenix and moved to one far out in the West Valley. He testified at trial under the use immunity agreement—wherein he agreed to speak but could still be charged if evidence against him was developed—but otherwise made good on his statement of December 12, 2004, when he said he wanted to "stay as far away" as possible. He never visited Marjorie or wrote to her in jail.

Some weeks after the brouhaha stirred up by the *48 Hours* show, Marjorie decided she had had enough of Estrella Jail and of Judge Anderson. Even then, her case was still roiling from all sides. The day after Dave Barnes was indicted, Marjorie took the podium herself. It was January 15, 2010. Her hair was nicely curled; it must have taken great creativity and effort to get that done inside the jail. But she was wearing the black-and-white striped pajama-style suit of an inmate. Her days of "dressing out" for court were over now that she'd been judged guilty and the jury box was empty. Marjorie's pride and personality, so anchored in her desire to keep a smart physical appearance, even in dire circumstances, seemed to roll silently across her shoulders in the careful honey brown curls.

When it was her turn and the court allowed her to speak, her anger came through her restrained voice as she spoke to the man in the black robes. "A group of people have been convinced of something that isn't true," she said.

Several of those people, jurors now released from the trial and all its restrictions, had gathered in the gallery as spectators. They had officially labeled Marjorie Orbin a murderer, but they had also spared her life. As Marjorie's defense attorney Herman Alcantar had said that day, it had been "a fifty percent victory." By coming to court when they did not have to, the jurors showed they had become emotionally invested in the woman who now spoke.

Marjorie and Judge Anderson looked at each other straight on. For the first time, no cadre of lawyers buffered their face-off. The ironhanded silence that fell in the courtroom seemed to choke out the presence of all observers: Anderson from his high bench looked down, and Marjorie, her body tense, glared back. They seemed alone together.

Up until January 15, Marjorie had been requesting a delay on her formal sentencing so that the many issues raised by the troubles of Dave Barnes, Noel Levy and by the *48 Hours* episode could be resolved, in the hope that this trial would be vacated and she could aim for a new fate, one that took her out of jail altogether. But now she reversed that position. "I just ask that you go on so I can proceed to the appeals court who will see the facts do not support this case,"* she said.

---

* Marjorie's statement in court for which the author was present.

Judge Anderson started by complimenting her. No one who knew Marjorie could ever deny that she was a person of talent and drive, and Judge Anderson had not failed to notice that. He said she was quite an organizer and he had thought about her skills and abilities a lot. He also agreed with what everyone said, that Marjorie loved her son, Noah.

However, nothing could get around the "outrageous nature of the murder that was performed here." The judge paused. The distressing photos he'd seen in his courtroom must have been on his mind: a once cheerful man with no flashing smile, no blue-eyed happiness, no arms to hug his little boy, no legs to carry him to bed. Anderson took a breath and continued.

"I think the fact that you care so much about your boy cuts both ways," he said. A little edge crept into his voice as he said more rapidly, "It wasn't much of a concern to you when this murder happened. It wasn't much of a concern to you for the weeks that followed when the police were scurrying around trying to figure out what happened and you never reported a thing. And you continued to avoid, you continued to in some ways obstruct the investigation. And you say it with a straight face when you tell us how much you cared about Jay Orbin and how much you cared about your boy."

By now anyone with a TV set had heard Marjorie's explanation that Larry Weisberg had killed Jay and she had then gone along with a cover-up in order to protect her son. Weisberg, she had told the TV cameras, told her that he would "snap [Noah's] scrawny neck" if she didn't. Judge Anderson let her know he had been paying attention to her account of her behavior.

"Why didn't you seek help if any of the arguments you make are even remotely true? Why didn't you seek help? And you dismissed this, frankly, as 'bad choices.'

"These aren't 'bad choices,' ma'am. Your position is absurd and I don't believe one bit of it, frankly. Because if you cared at all about Jay Orbin, if you cared at all about your *boy*, with this business of Weisberg being responsible for this, you would have told the police. Because you had ample opportunities. You were alone with them in interviews. You had ample opportunities to get your boy into a safe haven. And you did none of it."

Marjorie did not move a muscle. She continued to glare at the judge, silently.

"What this seems to be is a revelation of your very darkest side, ma'am." Anderson had thought about the comfortable and otherwise quiet life Marjorie Orbin had lived as a Scottsdale housewife, picking up her child from school, baking birthday cakes, keeping her beautiful home in perfect order. "I think you were a good mom," he said. "I think for a period of time you cared about Jay Orbin."

He spelled out his vision of her descent from such a sheltered life. "It seems that cracks began to show. The testimony was you were becoming unhappy with this marriage. You sought others for your personal gratification: a teenaged boy to a man in his sixties. You did that for your own selfish reasons. As you pursued your selfish reasons—and also your desire to obtain [Jay's] funds escalated—the dark side started to come out. Until that day that you killed him. That's the jury's finding."

If he had occasionally looked at his desk while

gathering his thoughts, Judge Arthur Anderson made sure he was looking directly into Marjorie's face now.

"Ma'am, you are a murderer."

He had little use for her portrayal of herself. He said she "postured" herself as a victim and "I don't believe it for one moment. So while I understand your position, I don't give it much credibility."

The judge's thoughts returned to the one person who had never made an appearance in his courtroom. "We didn't hear much about Noah here, but he is such a monumental loser in this case. That poor kid has got to think about this. He has to respond to questions from his friends and classmates, people that read the paper. 'Where's your mom, where's your dad?' They used to be here. Where are they now?"

The judge shook his head slightly.

"I'm sure he misses you. You destroyed this family. He lost it all in a blink of an eye."

Judge Anderson struggled with the fact that the same woman who could sacrifice so much for love of a baby could do unspeakable things to the same child's father. "What you did to him is hard to imagine anyone doing to another human being," he said. There was no escaping the gruesome details he was thinking of. He invoked another Arizona case, but it wasn't the one the defense had tried to use. The grotesque annals of dismemberment in Arizona, incredibly, went back much further. "We have some prior history of that here in the Winnie Ruth Judd case back in 1932. A gal about twenty-six years old got into a dispute with two other women and killed them both. Shot them. Stuffed one into a trunk. Chopped the other one up and stuffed her into a trunk. Took them to a train station not very far from [this courtroom] and tried to go to California. But she was apprehended. That jury imposed the death penalty on her. But the facts are eerily similar here."

The jurors, some of whom were sitting now in the hard benches of the spectator gallery, had taken the death penalty option away, but Anderson chose the next harshest option.

"I don't know how anything is appropriate but 'natural life' for you. You can't be trusted in our society because when that dark side of yours is unleashed," he rubbed his chin somberly, "it's about as dark as it gets."

AFTERWORD

In writing this book, I thought constantly of Noah. Even as a second grader, this innocent child was aware of the most painful features of the case. As he grows, undoubtedly, more of the facts will be understood by him and cause him more pain. There is just no erasing what happened. I tried to concentrate most of the worst elements into one chapter, so anyone can easily skip it. However, as the Orbins and I both know too well, they themselves have already seen these sad details many, many times. It must be a pain too great to measure, too profound to describe.

Sitting in court for hours, week after week, near the Orbin family, I often wondered how they could go on. Sometimes I tried to picture what it would be like to be in their shoes. The mere thought made my stomach hurt and I would have to refocus my attention immediately.

I was deeply touched by the nurturing and protection that Noah's family gave him and the way they honored his father's memory and helped him to cope. Many people don't have first parents who care so well and so gracefully, let alone a second set.

People sometimes ask me how victims' families can stand to have the crime brought back to their attention through a true crime book. The question is a fair one, but in my experience, the answer is that these families know what happened, they are still living it, and they didn't happen to forget about it until a book came out and spoiled some blissful amnesia.

But what the victims' families are also living with is an intense loneliness, the loss of their loved one coupled with the feeling that no one else cares.

But other people do care, and do sympathize.

I hope that this book serves as a useful overview and tool for the people who were affected most. Sometimes it's easier not to tell the story yourself, but to let someone else tell it for you.

I hope this book brings Jay's big smile and loving heart to the attention of a community that will care and, by their very interest, let his family know they are not as alone as they thought.

I have written carefully, knowing that one day Noah's eyes may look on these pages. Some of it is very ugly. None of us can change that, and no one knows it better than the little boy who was in that house on September 8, 2004.

Sometime in the future, Noah may wish to know more. Then, perhaps, this book can help him understand the process that led to where everyone is today. And, perhaps, it can cushion that history by showing him that although this is a hurting world with incomprehensible things in it, he came into it through the power of love. It is the story of a father who spent all eight years of their time together making lists and pursuing details to insure that his precious child would continue to be loved and secure no matter what the world threw at him.

That's a love the whole world will admire forever.

ACKNOWLEDGMENTS

The first thanks go to the readers who have given me a few hours of their time. There is no one more important than the person who sits down and enters the world created in these pages. Sometimes these stories create ongoing curiosity and concern. All are welcome to stop by www .camillekimball.com where they will find extra photos, updates, links and more. I would love to see you there.

There are many people who come together in big ways and in small to make a book out of a jumble of circumstances.

I would like to thank Michael Kiefer from the *Arizona Republic*, Peter Van Sant from CBS *48 Hours Mystery*, Cindy Cesare from CBS *48 Hours Mystery*, Mike Kellogg from *48 Hours Mystery* (and from way back) and all the other producers, photographers and reporters who shared tidbits and insights inside that courtroom.

On the other side of the rail, I would like to thank Alan Ellis, Robyn Varcoe and Herman Alcantar; Treena Kay and Detective Jan Butcher; court reporters Mike Benitez and Lisa Edgar. Special appreciation goes to all the MCSO guards who sit through hours and hours of testimony so the rest of us can feel safe. A word of thanks to Prosecutor Vince Imbordino, who was not working this trial, but who appears in *A Sudden Shot: The Phoenix Serial Shooter* and before that worked on the Valerie Pape case. He was very gracious in helping out.

More thanks go to Stacy Stotts at the Maricopa County Jail, and to Richard D'Uriarte at the County. Lots of gratitude to Liz Hill, the genie with the magic power over logjams.

Much enthusiastic thanks to Patrick Millikin, Lorri Amsden, Lea, Ari, Wes, Patrick King, and Barb Peters and everyone else at her store, the incomparable Poisoned Pen, for some amazing attention and support that took a lot of work.

Thanks to Chevalier's Books, a charming place if ever there was one, in Hollywood and to Norman Dixon of Chevalier's and to Ron Kilgore of KNX Radio in Los Angeles and to PIs Bill Rhetts and Paul Huebl.

Another nod of the head goes to Lesa Holstine of the Velma Teague Library, to Kirsten Zollinger and Rachel Monroe at Borders, Donna Powers and everyone at Barnes and Noble, and a special shoutout to Angela's Café in Gallup.

To Danny Porat of WIBN Classic Gold who brought me into the 21st century and to so many friends, new and old, in the media, Melissa Sharpe of KYOT, Darin, Jean-Guy, Rusty, Joanne and Christopher from Wicked Attraction-Investigation Discovery, Scott Davis of Paranormal Matrix, Heather Dunn, Austin Hill, Jay Lawrence, Tara Hitchcock, Mike Watkiss, Scott Pasmore, Scott Light, Rick D'Amico, Andrea Robinson and so many more.

Deep under cover, behind the spotlight, a great deal of thanks go to: To George K. for being a one man army, unstoppable and without equal. To Cathy and Gary, great fondness and deep appreciation, as always. To Patricia, my right arm, and to Maggie, my left. To Kristy Kiernan, my fairy godmother. To Patty Gray for ongoing support and enthusiasm.

To Kim H., who deserves much better friends than me. And to Christa, a beautiful bride, precious, beloved, gifted. Christa, I am happily looking forward to the day we have to make room on the shelves for yours.

To other true crimers down in the trenches, always willing to share thoughts and techniques, Ron Franscell and Kerrie Droban.

To Robin Barratt, my British editor on the *Mammoth Book of the World's Hardest*, for always having a well-timed, encouraging word to send from halfway across the globe.

To my secret weapon, Dave Hocking, a bushel of thanks. I think of you as a superhero, complete with cape and mask, Editor Incognito!

Chief amongst those directly responsible for getting a story from my hands and into yours are my publisher and my agents:

To Shannon, Susan, Danielle and everyone else at Berkley, thank you. The work is hard and involves lots of eyeball-killing chores. And I only go through it with one book at a time; I can't believe you all do it every day, all year long! The art department did an especially wonderful job on this cover and I am very grateful.

To my film agent, Marianne, for shepherding good things into even better places. And to Dan Hayes and Patricia Mayer for standing guard.

And, most of all, to my dogged literary agent, Amy, who has leaped tall buildings and dashed into burning ones on my behalf.

Special thanks to Phoenix Homicide detective Cliff Jewell from whom I have learned so much and who continues to inspire me as well as guard me from harm. To Paul

Patrick, who knows how much I adore him. To Sherry, Bill and Mark and Jason, there is no place I would rather be than with you.

To Ted and Hrayr, I marvel every day at how you gave me back this life, one very much worth fighting for. As you both know, I owe you everything.

To Jake Orbin Jr., who always treated me like a dear sister even though he could not know how this would turn out. I hope I have not let him down.